Born the same year as the Bay of Pigs invasion of Cuba, *Newsnight* reporter Stephen Smith has been fascinated by the island since he first heard the hijackers' slogan 'Fly me to Havana!' He is a regular contributor to the *London Review of Books* and other newspapers. He lives in London.

Also by Stephen Smith

COCAINE TRAIN: TRACING MY BLOODLINE THROUGH COLOMBIA
UNDERGROUND LONDON: TRAVELS BELOW THE CITY STREETS

Cuba

The Land of Miracles

STEPHEN SMITH

For Ray and Rosemary Smith

An *Abacus* Book

First published in Great Britain by
Little, Brown and Company 1997
First published by Abacus 1998
Reprinted 1998, 1999, 2001, 2002
This edition published by Time Warner Books in 2005

A CIP catalogue record for this book is available from the
British Library.

ISBN 0 349 11967 8

Printed and bound in Great Britain by Clays Ltd, St Ives plc

Abacus
An imprint of
Time Warner Book Group UK
Brettenham House
Lancaster Place
London WC2E 7EN

www.twbg.co.uk

Contents

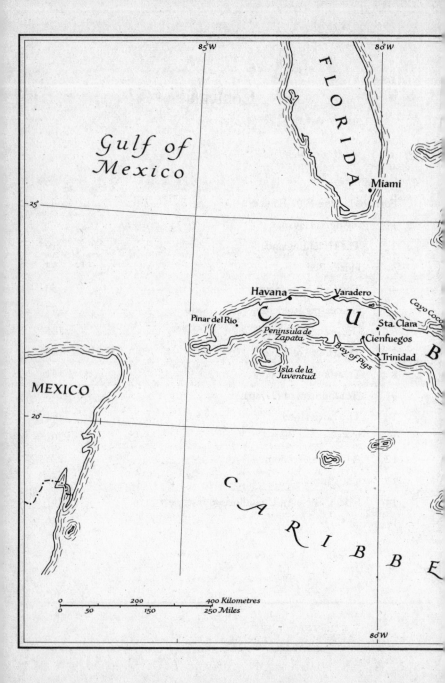

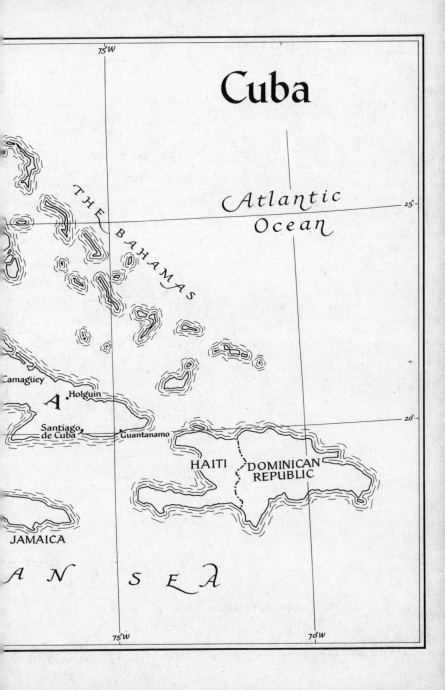

Two countries just
here lay side by side

Graham Greene

Foreword

IF YOU HAVEN'T BEEN to Cuba yet – what have you been doing? – or if, like me, you haven't been in Havana for some time, the good news is that things are getting better. The bad news is that things are getting worse. How to explain this seeming piece of Caribbean casuistry? Let's begin by saying that such a conundrum is perfectly typical of Cuba. When I was writing this book a decade ago, I hoped to suggest the contrariness of the island with my title, *The Land of Miracles*, which was borrowed from a nickname that the Cubans had given their home, a place where *habaneros* watched power cuts snuffing out the lights in one part of their city after another and observed with irony, 'Our town is like a flashing Christmas tree!' I'm glad to report that the indigenous sense of humour, which has been mysteriously overlooked in the vogue for all things Cuban in the past ten years or so, remains in excellent working order. Like the country's matchless rum, which is brought to market according to its age so that the toper knows if he is sipping a fresh, two-year-old mash or revisiting an old favourite distilled many moons ago, a new batch of wisecracks always seems to be coming into circulation at just the right time. A new one I heard concerns the latest crackdown by 'them' – the ubiquitous, unnameable powers that be – on the irresistible Cuban sirens who are in the habit of parting foreign men from their money, and indeed their trousers. The *jiniteras* tend to frequent certain bars, so the authorities put two and two together and decided to close down the premises concerned. In the *barrios*, the *cubanos* turned this into the 'sofa solution'. 'It's like the cuckolded husband who comes home to find his wife making love to his best friend on the sofa. So he throws the sofa out.' A people who can laugh at the sofa solution, a regime which can impose it: this is the sort of place where things can get better at the same time as they get worse. The Cuban novelist Pedro Juan Gutierrez observes in *The Insatiable Spiderman* (published in English in 2005), 'We get up. I shave, brush my teeth, make coffee and have a shit. I look out of the window. Everything is worse than yesterday, but traditionally, to save trouble, we don't say that. The correct thing to say would be: "I look out of the window. All's well."'

Ten years ago, the visitor could hardly fail to spot the difference between the Cuba that he was fortunate enough to enjoy as a tourist and the much less comfortable domicile of the Cuban citizen. These were 'the two territories which had been united as *la pais de los milagros*'. The unmarked but unmistakeable frontier which divides the two Cubas has not become more permeable; if anything, the disparity is now even more pronounced between 'the bureaucratic, exasperating country familiar to the Cuban in the bus queue, and the magical island, shaped like a crocodile, which the foreigner recognised as Columbus's paradise'.

Returning to Cuba after a little while away is a revelation. For one of the world's great destinations, it used to have some of the worst catering known to travellers. Now it's almost worth going for the hotels alone. There's the Armadores de Santander overlooking Havana bay, the offices of a nineteenth-century shipbuilders splendidly restored and converted, complete with its original marble staircase. The Hotel Raquel, named for its connections with the old Jewish quarter of the city, brilliantly fulfils its improbable brief of an Old Testament theme, down to a Garden of Eden restaurant serving kosher dishes. A parade of refurbished hotels such as these is the elegant centrepiece of an unprecedented restoration scheme. When I first visited Havana, the faded and tottering architecture was all part of the charm, of course, but it sometimes took an act of fortitude to look the other way as a tenement calved a landslip into the street right in front of you. The deterioration of this world heritage site has grown so advanced that it's positively dangerous. In the heart of the capital, there's a rockfall of masonry roughly every three days, as yet another building succumbs to the combined effects of time, neglect and the tropical elements. At the sight of wooden scaffolding propping up a trembling casa, wily *habaneros* instinctively cross to the other side of the street. But now an experiment called 'Fenix' (Phoenix) is beginning to bring the city back from the dead. And foreigners who might feel guilty about enjoying themselves in the impoverished surroundings of Cuba can rest easier, knowing that it's the money they spend in the hotels and bars of Havana that is paying for it all. Not only that, but the scheme also supports amenities including children's clinics and old people's homes. As in the case of the international smash film and album from Cuba, *Buena Vista Social Club*, masterly veterans have been coaxed out of retirement to make Fenix work – in this case, elderly artisans adept in working with limestone and wrought iron, the materials of the old town.

The project works like this: almost all of the hotels and restaurants in the centre of Havana are now owned by a state-run enterprise called Habaguanex. On Fidel Castro's communist island, profit is no longer the dirty word it once was, judging by the unsentimental decision to plough all of Habaguanex's takings into the restoration work. And with the same directness that a command economy like Cuba's is sometimes capable of, the authorities have taken the bold stroke of transferring the deeds of all the buildings of central Havana to one man, an architect who knows the city so well that its familiar sights are like the features of an old friend to him. 'It is like the expressive face of the social body,' according to Eusebio Leal. Appointed the city's official historian in 1967, Leal has been the curator of his hometown for almost as long as Castro has been running the country, taking up his post only eight years after the Cuban revolution. One of the people I wanted to see on my return to Havana was Leal, the man who was recreating the city out of its own ashes.

I was told that Señor Leal walks the streets of Havana constantly, brooding on his task. Cuban friends said that I would be wasting my time if I went looking for him at his office, close to the city's sumptuously moth-eaten cathedral. My best hope of finding him was to bump into him around town. Look for a man dressed from head to toe in grey – Leal favours grey exclusively – and wearing a distracted expression, they said. This seemed a hopeless task, like expecting to come across one of Britain's leading historians by wandering aimlessly through central London. But sure enough, after a fruitless trip to Leal's office, I rounded a corner and came face to face with a short, preoccupied man in grey fatigues. Eusebio Leal is an unassuming man, but not where his ambitions for Project Fenix are concerned. 'To recreate the city, not just to contemplate it, but also to live it; that is the challenge,' he says.

A preservation order was effectively slapped on Havana as long ago as 1982, with the award of world heritage status from UNESCO. But with the end of the Soviet Union, and with it Cuba's line of credit from the Kremlin, the odds on preserving the architecture of the city dramatically lengthened. 'The idea that it was impossible to restore monuments in countries like ours was fairly generalised,' admits Leal dryly. But Cuba is also a country where fifty-year-old Chevrolets somehow remain on the road. Trust the ingenious Cubans to come up with an answer to their conservation problem. They set up a real estate company, also called Fenix, and began converting foreigners' dollars into bricks and mortar. Their canny if politically sensitive insight was that tourism was a golden goose: accordingly, they began fattening it up. Splendid hotels like the Raquel and the Armadores de Santander now exert a centrifugal force on the redevelopment of old Havana, spinning out cash which in turn produces more growth. Fenix Project returns 45 per cent of what it makes directly to the tourism sector, to create more hotel rooms in old Havana: 500 and counting. These boutique hotels have in turn attracted boutiques: Benetton, Le Shark, a perfume shop, a perhaps unlikely museum devoted to the history of chocolate. Leal and his team have painstakingly surveyed more than 3,000 buildings in the historical centre, assigning each one a grade of aesthetic importance, a likely end use and a costed restoration schedule.

But this has brought muttering in the street that the pace of change is too tardy. In the *barrios* of old Havana, more than 70,000 people share 22,500 'units', many of which consist of jerry-built conversions subdividing already overcrowded *edificios*. Fenix is accused of hurrying slowly: making the city better for tourists, no better for *habaneros*, ignoring long-suffering locals in favour of a tourist-friendly 'golden kilometre' which links old Havana's photogenic plazas.

One night in the old town, I turned off this gilded strand and had a drink at the Bar Bilbao on Calle O'Reilly, a street named after a Spaniard with Irish ancestry who had once governed the island. Bar Bilbao didn't look the sort of place where tourists go, though it was only yards from the main drag. The bar, like the street itself, was all but deserted. A black man, Norbert, was effectively MC for this ancient dive, while an old, rake-thin white man in a suit prepared the inexpensive and yet potent mojitos which were the house speciality. Both men operated behind what may have been the original counter (from the thirties? Twenties?). The bar was decorated with the colours of the Bilbao football team, including a photo of the ladies XI, but what caught the eye were the antique fixtures, such as a huge brown till which looked like the radiator of an old Buick. A drunk was sitting at a table, the only other customer in the place. He told me (several times) that although he was black and I was white, we were brothers. Perhaps he knew this would soften me up for the moment when Norbert enquired if I wanted to stand my 'brother' a mojito. I said that I would. Norbert, with his talk of Chelsea and Michael Owen, persuaded me to accept another. The thing with mojitos is that you have to calibrate your consumption of them. One isn't enough, I find, while on the other hand, *three* isn't enough either.

Enter, at this point, the inevitable *mujer*: not a teenage *jinitera* but a working girl, a full-figured woman not afraid to write her age for me with her finger in the wetness on the bar: 39. I had the sense at first that she had just popped in – for cigarettes? One for the road? – after a hard day at the office. She explained that she used a typewriter – not a computer, mind you, a typewriter. But it seemed as though she was in no hurry to get away. At Norbert's gentle, almost courtly, prompting, I stood the woman a mojito, too. A musical duo materialised – an old boy on maracas, a younger man in a straw hat on guitar – and launched into '*Besame Mucho*'. This turned into a vocal number when my new companion began to serenade me. It was time to make my excuses and leave. The band cut up a bit rough: after two or three tunes, they were looking for a gratuity of five pesos (about £2.50), the straw-hat man explained tersely, so that they could eat, which was a fair point. I gave the band their fiver. Outside on the street, I was propositioned by a young woman, probably still in her teens, who wanted 25 pesos – all right, 20. When I demurred, she was affronted: what was wrong with her?

I recounted my impressions of O' Reilly, or some of them, at least, to Patricia Rodriguez, an architect who has the tall task of implementing Señor Leal's masterplan for Havana. Why were neighbouring streets booming while O'Reilly was overlooked? 'Some places have not been developed as much as others. We would love to spread the restoration all over the city but that's not always possible,' Rodriguez admitted. 'For example, we know that local homes are the biggest problem but they cost more.' Rodriguez insisted that there were spin-offs for everyone from the 'dynamic focus' of Fenix. About a third of its profits are spent tackling social problems, of which the most pressing is the chronic housing shortage.

It's ten years since the scheme was first mooted and a third of the old city has been restored. The master craftsmen who have been brought out of retirement to rebuild the city are in turn training young apprentices, aged from 17 to 21, passing the old skills on to them. And just as in the long-ago days of the former Spanish colony, artists are being brought over from Europe to work on the caryatids and fountains and courtyards of Havana. I asked Rodriguez if her task was not a little like painting the Forth Bridge. After this Caledonian analogy had been explained to her, she said, 'Yes, we do have something similar here. But like we say in Cuba, it's not a record but a good average.' UNESCO is now studying Fenix, to see if its principles can be applied to other cities in need of reclamation. Leal and Rodriguez have set themselves the ambitious target of completing their work by 2020, when Havana will celebrate the five-hundredth anniversary of its founding. Theirs is a very Cuban solution to the problem of redevelopment, Castro's communist state harnessing the spending power of Western tourists to pay for urgently needed welfare measures, and in the process reversing the picturesque decline of their capital city.

The natural inclination, when contemplating this (in many ways) idyllic Caribbean island, is to suppose that its shores are lapped – *kissed* –

by the most benign and torpid of seas. Looking at the waters off Havana from where I was staying, on the tenth floor of a Vedado *edificio*, you could be forgiven for thinking that they were indeed of a docile and forgiving disposition. But this is by no means the whole picture. Cuba may be in the Caribbean but its northern seaboard lies on the Atlantic. The sea is a deep, dark and roiling body of water, shading from a relatively friendly aquamarine to a fathomless blue, with shades of inky indigo. I walked along the sweeping promenade of El Malecon, enjoying one of my favourite views anywhere, even after the hot tropical wind and a briny *salsa* off the sea had combined to smear my sunglasses to a glutinous opacity. Taking the Malecon is like taking a steam bath; fittingly, the buildings are as pitted as bars of soap. For all Señor Leal's efforts elsewhere in the city, these old mansions continue to endure their long, stately erosion. It astonishes, all over again, to see families living in their gouged-out hollows.

At first sight, the Malecon is unchanged – remarkably unchanged, you might say of anywhere else but Cuba. But at intervals along the strip, there are now bars – counters, tables under canopies. The Hotel Deauville has had a lick of paint. I noticed a plutocrat living in a condo carved out of the carbolic wall of the Malecon. His place was all high windows and recessed lighting. The presumed millionaire slid open a glass door, stepped onto his decking and fell into a wicker chair, resting a careless espadrille on the railing of his balcony. On the seaward side of the promenade, a crowd was watching a man on the rocks below as he attempted to lure a pelican into his grasp. The bird evaded his outstretched fingers but appeared to be in no hurry to fly off. Even after the man had given up trying to catch it, the bird swam in one of the pools scooped out by the waves in the old sea defences. Perhaps this man had an exemplary charm, the sort of gift that the resourceful Cubans manifest to cope with their difficult lives, the charm of seducing seabirds.

As always, people were gazing out to sea. One young woman was clutching a sizeable piece of luggage, as if awaiting a ship which was about to steam over the horizon. It's difficult to describe the look on the faces of these people. It was the same look you glimpsed through the rusting courting grilles in the rotten old colonial buildings in the ghettos of *Habana Vieja*, on the faces of the women – old, young: it was hard to tell – sitting on rocking chairs in singlets and curlers, oblivious to a booming TV or cassette player. A look of wistfulness? No, that's much too fey for the circumstances. Resignation? It was beyond even that; it was like the look of a face carved from stone, the closest human features could come to reflecting the petrification of their surroundings.

In a 2001 epilogue to his magisterial *Cuba*, the historian Hugh Thomas writes, 'By chance, if not design, Cuba's isolation is a fulfillment at last of what the first advocates of independence desired.' The implacable water, the far skyline seldom broken by the silhouette of a cargo vessel putting into port – this all tended to reinforce an impression that Cuba was alone, cut off, cast adrift from the rest of the world, a failed experiment, a penal colony. Notoriously, it has become the latter, of course. Guantanamo had been an unremarked corner of the island at the time when I visited the base, in the unlikely guise of an arms dealer, and few knew of its incongruous niche as an outpost of the United States in Fidel's backyard. But since then the Americans have been using it to warehouse terrorist suspects, mainly detained in Afghanistan. I wondered how much most Cubans knew about what had been going on in Gitmo? They were certainly left in no doubt about the other notorious prison indelibly associated with the administration of George W. Bush, Abu Ghraib jail in Baghdad. Outside the US Interests Section on the Malecon, hoardings put up by the Cuban government reproached the Americans over their human rights record. They featured blow-ups of lurid images from the prison, accompanied by swastikas and straplines such as '*Fascistas. Made in USA*'. The billboards went up after cheery Christmas decorations appeared at the Interests Section, a square-shouldered grain silo of a building, including the number '75' picked out in winking lights. This was taken to be a reference to 75 Cubans who had been incarcerated on political grounds. The full handle of *El Commandante* is Dr Fidel Castro Ruz, and both critics and admirers like to say that the customary latin honorific is really a tribute to his pioneering work as the original spin doctor. While the world was preoccupied with the conflict in Iraq, Castro had exploited the fog of war which had been obligingly created in the White House to spirit the dissidents to prison.

On a stretch of the Malecon, the shouting match which has been going on between Havana and Washington for forty years now has its own amphitheatre, its own showground. Directly in front of the US Interests Section, the Cubans have built an outdoor stage which they call the Anti-Imperialist Plaza. Groups including the legendary Los Van Van play gigs there at cochlea-jangling volume, though the concerts are usually held on weekends, when the American expats can be expected to be enjoying the peace and quiet of their residences in far Miramar. This part of town is also notable for a new statue of Jose Marti. The sculptor's vision of the Cuban patriot depicts him clutching a young boy. The work was unveiled following the Elian crisis, a tug-of-war between Cuba and Miami over eight-year-old Elian Gonzalez, who was found clinging to an inner tube in the Straits of Florida on Thanksgiving Day, 1999. Other members of the boy's family, including his mother, had drowned in an attempt to flee Cuba for the United States. Amid much hoopla, Elian was eventually returned to relatives in Cuba at the end of a seven-month custody battle. 'Although officially designated as Marti's son, the sculpted boy's visage has an undeniable resemblance to Elian Gonzalez,' notes Ann Louise Bardach in *Cuba Confidential*. 'Marti's free arm is pointing accusingly straight ahead at the US Interests Section, and anti-American epigrams from Simon Bolivar and Marti are engraved in the base of the statue. But *la bolla en la calle* – the buzz on the streets – had another interpretation of Marti's gesture: '*Las visas estan alli*', 'Your visas are that way'! Walking past the statue to the Interests Section, I looked at the neon sleigh ascending a fortified wall, at the frosty homunculi of a snowman, at the pulsing '75', and thought that these were probably the only truly reliable illuminations in the entire city.

My friend Julietta had been the first to introduce me to the ironic nickname which Cubans gave their country; the memory of it came back to us in the lobby of the Hotel Presidente, when the lights abruptly guttered and went out. The hotel's guests must have wondered at our giggling. The first time I'd met Julietta, it had also been in the lobby of a hotel, the Inglaterra in the old town. She was 22-years-old then, about to graduate from university.

As the lights were flickering back on, I thought that Julietta was as striking as I remembered her. Her black hair was tied back, her pregnant belly was beachball-tight – but she was older now, a woman. She had been a girl when I first knew her, it seemed to me now. Julietta's second child was due in two months' time. 'It's a girl, I'm sure of it. I'm going to call her Mariana.' Julietta and her husband Ulises already had a four-year-old boy, Omar Antonio. They lived in Playa, with Julietta's trying mother-in-law ('the wicked witch') occupying a granny flat.

When power cuts were still a comparative novelty in Havana, in the 1990s, the government announced the 'special period in time of peace', an interlude of short rations, apparently without respite, which followed the demise of the USSR. I asked Julietta if there was a new name for the time that the Cubans were living through, an official title for the period of the sofa solution. 'I think it's called the Battle of Ideas,' she said. People were mobilised to take part in events – semi-spontaneous rallies, not wholly impromptu marches – in order to trumpet the virtues of *la Revolucion*. Every weekend, it was the turn of one provincial city or another to host one of these fiestas. 'Do you ever go to them?' I asked. She glared at me.

To the dismay of her father, Roberto, a loyal party man, Julietta had always been a spitfire, never one to hold back. But I was surprised at how unconstrained she was about discussing the difficulties of life in Cuba in the lobby of the Presidente. She said, 'There is a lot of tension now, after what has been happening with the money.' I had vivid memories of a day when all the dollars disappeared from Havana, when the banks mysteriously ran out of foreign currency, but that had proved to be nothing more than a temporary cash flow problem, a snafu of the special period. The dollar bill had been a defining signifier of that time, in retrospect, representing the private sector which was then tolerated by the Cuban government, albeit with poor grace. It was in this sector that families converted their front parlours into *paladares*, private restaurants;

women like Hilda, my old landlady, eked out their pensions by taking in paying guests; and a surgeon like the Doc made more money from driving his Dodge Colonel than he could in the operating theatre. Hilda had since gone up in the world. She and her son Nico had moved to a new apartment. They were still in the same building where I had stayed, but they were now on a higher floor. Hilda's new address meant that she was closer to the rooms where the young Fidel had once slept, dreaming of revolution. Number 603 remained a museum devoted to the strivings of the future *commandante*, and a sampler of the upholstery of Fidel's three-piece suite was still preserved like an apostle's relic. But Hilda's relocation owed little to the nearness of this beatified penthouse. She had wanted to remove herself as far as possible from the stink and the noise of the street. She craved the cooling breezes that blew in from the sea, over the buildings of the Malecon and into the fortunate sitting rooms of those whose homes had clear sight of the water. Like any proprietress of a boarding house in a popular resort, Hilda wished to offer her patrons a sea view. But she had put the 'No Vacancy' sign on her front door for good, because she'd had a visit from a man who warned her that she would be liable to pay tax whether her back room was occupied or not. The Doc had sold the Dodge and taken his family to Florida, joining the Cuban diaspora – as had Kiki, the *babalao*, the priest who had initiated me into the arcane rites of *Santeria*: his daughter had married a wealthy Italian and Kiki was last heard of practising his occult profession in Venice. And now, Julietta reminded me, the government had taken the extraordinary step of banning the dollar, replacing it with the convertible Cuban peso. 'These changes are really hitting people,' she said. 'They've been saving dollars, hoarding them, but they're no longer accepted in Cuba. Not legally, anyhow.' It might have had something to do with a court case, Julietta thought, an action involving Swiss banks which had interests in Cuba but also in the United States. Indeed, it was nothing other than that old familiar bugbear, the American embargo. The Washington of George W. Bush had ratcheted it up a few more notches, imposing new penalties on companies which dared to treat with Castro. The United States had also reduced the number of trips that Cuban-Americans were allowed to take to visit relatives in the land of their origins. And at the US Interests Section, officials had begun charging would-be migrants $100 just for an interview. (At least there was one use left for the greenback in Cuba.) In the crisis of the vanishing dollar bill, it was tempting to discern Castro's hand, too. Was he afraid of all that hard-won booty slipping through his fingers? I thought about an image I'd once had of him, Castro the robber king, Castro the pirate, his familiar bearded figure up to his boot-tops in doubloons spilling from sacks.

El Jefe had recently appeared on the world's television bulletins after taking a spectacular tumble as he finished a speech. He had been speaking in the city of Santa Clara in honour of his late comrade-in-arms Che Guevara, whose remains had been recovered in Bolivia and returned to the city where he had once pulled off a famous victory during the revolution. Leaving the lectern, the Maximum Leader had missed his footing. He had travelled on his stomach across the buffed stage before making a mosh-pit dive into the arms of anxious security men, while his ministers, including Castro's younger brother Raul, looked on aghast. What had happened that day in Santa Clara told you a lot about how things were in Cuba, about fear and paranoia at the heart of the regime, and about the ever-more crabbed and circumscribed endgame of the Castro years. Fidel wasn't mortally hurt but he was left with a broken arm and knee. He was rushed to his physicians, who were several hours' drive away in Havana. On the way there, he waved away a soothing shot of painkiller. Instead, according to official sources, he placed a telephone call from the ambulance to his colleagues, asserting both his complete consciousness, and the fact that he remained fully in charge of events at all times.

The one place where Castro's indignity was not shown in full was Cuba. The closest the official media came to covering the accident was with a couple of stills – before and after pictures – showing him at the dais and then sitting down again in another location, apparently none the worse for his experience. But many Cubans had watched the unedited footage on the Internet, and in any case, the full story had been circulated by street-corner gossip, otherwise known as *Radio Bemba*, literally 'Radio Big

Mouth'. In spite of what the novelist Gutierrez says in *The Insatiable Spiderman* about the Cuban everyman biting his lip, my impression was that people seemed more outspoken than used to be the case a few years ago. (Gutierrez's novel supports the point, in fact, since he not only published his observations in many foreign editions of his book, but publication did not prevent him from pursuing his writing career in Havana.) This lack of inhibition is partly because the waning of the ageing leader is all too evident. Cubans borrow from topical talk of weapons of mass destruction to say that they are awaiting 'the biological solution'. There's also an awareness that the cash-strapped regime is simply not capable of the massive effort required to keep tabs on all of its citizens. A Cuban friend has a put-down which he keeps ready for anyone who still needs to be convinced: 'Look, there are only three stupid people in the country,' he says. 'There's –' and here my friend strokes his chin, miming the grooming of a substantial beard – 'there's his brother, and then there's you.'

I had an insight into Cuban security, and how mortifyingly small-time it could be, on the street where I was staying. Guards were posted at night outside a house or museum dedicated to Haydee Santamaria. She had once cooked and washed for Fidel at Number 603 in Hilda's *edificio* a few blocks away, and had thus become a kind of Mary Magadalene of the Revolution. There were also uniformed men keeping watch over a library built in the art deco style, with deep blue stained-glass windows the colour of the sea off the Malecon. At first, the sight of this crepuscular muscle surprised – even alarmed – me. Were 'they' really afraid of a coup, in which these glorious premises of the people might fall? Then I was contemptuous – what could the *gusanos*, the 'worms' of Cuban Miami, or indeed the *malo elemento* within the resident population, come to that, possibly want with Haydee Santamaria's house? Then the prosaic truth dawned. The properties were protected because the least thing (to Western eyes) might be worth scavenging: electrics, light bulbs, old furniture, even sheets of toilet paper. (Hotels and restaurants still retained matrons who sat outside the cloakrooms with sheets of bog roll, a dish of tips and a forbearing expression.) But the people were not about to storm Haydee Santamaria's house. They couldn't be bothered, it just wasn't worth it. This was Cuba in the time of the sofa solution, but the country was also characterised by an utterly contrasting spirit, a ridiculous, even reckless sense that all would be well, that the good life was just one lucky break away, and this would from time to time rouse Cubans from their lethargy and despair. It was best expressed in a joke that Cubans liked to tell. It was a joke at their own expense, like everything else. One day a man hears a voice telling him to go to Las Vegas. He persuades his wife that they must leave for Nevada immediately. When they arrive at their hotel, the voice tells the Cuban to go to the roulette wheel at Caesar's Palace. He drags his wife to the casino. As they stand in front of the wheel, the man hears the voice saying, 'Number 22.'

'How much?' says the man.

'Everything!' insists the voice.

The Cuban puts everything on 22 – and loses. 'What now?' he cries aloud to the voice.

And the answer comes back, 'We're fucked!'

I wanted to visit the Che mausoleum at Santa Clara. If the figure of Castro had grown more isolated and ambiguous in the time since I was last in Cuba, the fortunes of Che had continued to enjoy their extraordinary posthumous revival. *The Motorcycle Diaries*, a film inspired by his youthful adventures in South America, had introduced the eternal revolutionary to a new generation. On the back of its success there was a new slew of T-shirts and posters and biographies: it seemed as though every word Guevara himself had written was also in print. Che had never been bigger. Even in Cuba, where decades of trowelled-on hagiography had inevitably taken their toll, he was still comfortably more popular than his one-time *companero* and his shrine was a draw, though the Cuban jokesmiths were saying that this was due to the large numbers of people wanting to touch the spot where Castro had taken a pratfall.

Ulises said that he would take me to see the Che memorial. The idea came up when I was visiting Julietta and Ulises at their house. It would be a busman's holiday for him. Like his wife Ulises was working as a tour guide, but he had a couple of days off and he said that fewer foreigners than one might imagine asked to make the journey to Santa Clara. I'd seen Ulises a few nights earlier, when he was clean-shaven and smartly dressed, having just left a party of elderly American tourists whom he had been chaperoning. Today, as he made us cocktails of rum and orange squash, he had two or three days' growth of beard and I thought how gaunt he looked. He had lost none of the seriousness that I had first seen in him, though he also had a sense of humour which I had failed to detect before. He wanted to talk politics, the future of his country, and was quite outspoken about it. I didn't know how worried Julietta was about him (she said she wasn't). He told me, 'I stopped being paranoid a long time ago.' He said that he answered the questions of holidaymakers as candidly as he could and Americans often wondered if he wasn't afraid that their tour bus was bugged. 'I say, "Yes, of course it is bugged, there are microphones all over the place. The thing is, the batteries don't work."' A typical Cuban sally (and not so far from the truth, one supposes).

Ulises and I took the *autopista* out of Havana to Santa Clara. It was empty, a long flat highway patrolled by turkey vultures. There was nothing to see on the road apart from the occasional truck, and no other sign of life apart from infrequent lines of people at the roadside, supervised by men in canary-yellow fatigues. 'Ah yes, the yellow. We call them the yellow,' said Ulises. It was the job of these custard-coloured figures to flag down the trucks and fill them from their petitioning queues of footsore hitch-hikers. 'People say, "I caught the yellow to work" or "I came by yellow".' Ulises himself had once been destined for much greater things than marshalling travellers, or even guiding tourists. The army had put him through university and he had been in line for an overseas posting, a trusted emissary of *la Revolucion*. 'If I'd played by the rules, I would be in London by now,' he said.

His privileged education, made possible by the Cuban state, had ironically exposed him to a world beyond the comforting certainties of the Cuban state, with disastrous consequences for his glittering prospects. A budding army officer and prospective diplomat, Ulises had had sight of *El Pais*, the *Washington Post*, the *New York Times*.

'Newspapers that the ordinary Cuban wouldn't see?' I said.

'Wouldn't have *heard* of.'

Ulises began to have his questions, his uncertainties. By his own admission, he was a stirrer, an awkward bugger. (It was not a trait which he had entirely lost. He was a serious person, he took himself seriously – he would perhaps regard that as a compliment – and he didn't have much time for any light-heartedness. The only time that I felt I really had his attention was when I was addressing his unexpected questions about cricket.) As an enlisted man, he had been called up by the army to take part in the Cuban adventure in Angola in the 1980s, fighting on the side of the MPLA against Jonas Savimbi's UNITA. Ulises said he was proudly looking forward to 'doing my humanitarian service' in Africa. On the eve of his departure, however, his father, himself a veteran, had asked to see him, and the older man had introduced Ulises in no uncertain terms to the facts of war for which his training had not prepared him. Ulises had survived and served three years in the Angolan conflict only to return to Cuba to find that his countrymen had absolutely no use for his patriotic sacrifice. 'I was demobbed and left to find my own way home from the barracks to my parents' house. A truck driver gave me a lift, just like these guys –' Ulises gestured at another line of long-suffering Cubans at the roadside – 'and when I told him what I'd been doing, he looked at me as though I was an idiot.'

The topography of Santa Clara is dominated by a statue of Che, a carbine in his mighty hand, a water bottle and a grenade at his hip. He overlooks a kind of coach park, where well-turned-out revolutionaries are periodically bussed to listen to speeches. Beneath his towering bronze, mortal remains which were said to be his were laid to rest in a sepulchre of blond wood in 1997. In an adjacent room, a museum devoted to Che has recently been opened. Here admirers of the dashing Argentinian can study back-issues of the rugger magazine he had edited as a medical student, or take a 360-degree tour around an inhaler which he had taken into the Sierra Maestre mountains before the revolution triumphed. A remarkable photograph shows Castro apparently checking the passport of

Peter Sellers who was wardrobed as Dr Strangelove: in fact, the stocky, balding man was none other than Che himself, the master of disguise, about to enter Bolivia illegally on what had proved to be his last hurrah.

As if a darkness has descended over their country, Cubans have compensated for the gloom by developing different faculties. Their defining genius is a kind of balancing act, between the African and Spanish aspects of their birthright, between Fidel and whoever happens to be occupying the White House, but also between poverty and survival. The famous Cuban dancer Carlos Acosta is a dazzling incarnation of this national poise. In his self-penned work, *Tocororo*, a deceptively homespun story of a country boy adapting to the wiles of city life, Acosta could almost be offering a metaphor for his island's struggle. Though the effigy of Che at Santa Clara is admirable in every detail, the Cubans' sense of direction tells them that he is facing the wrong way. He has his back turned on the city, which he liberated from the forces of Batista's hated regime in 1959. Instead, he gazes upon the granite steps where Fidel fell, the bleachers where the party cardholders come to pay homage to him. He looks down at a sanctified car park, at the drive-in of the revolution.

Stephen Smith
Havana, 2005

Foreword to the 1997 Edition

THE LAND OF MIRACLES is based on time I have spent in Cuba –
'the most beautiful land that eyes have ever seen,' Columbus called it –
during 'the special period in time of peace', the phase of rationing and
swingeing cutbacks, apparently without end, which has accompanied the
drying-up of aid from the former Soviet bloc and the tightening of a
United States embargo. I first visited Cuba in July 1990, after the
tumultuous collapse of Communism in Eastern Europe but before the
USSR was dissolved. I went back again in 1994, I lived in Cuba during the
summer of 1995, and returned during the winter of 1995–96.

For the opportunity of living in, and writing about, Cuba – and getting
paid for doing it – I am grateful to my publishers Little, Brown. In particular,
I am indebted to Richard Beswick for commissioning the book, and to him
and Andrew Wille for their shrewd guidance and encouragement in the
writing of it. My thanks are also due to Antonia Hodgson and Sara Todd.
This is a welcome chance to express my appreciation of a superb agent, Cat
Ledger. I would also like to thank my editors at ITN/Channel 4 News –
Stewart Purvis, Richard Tait, Sara Nathan and Sue Inglish – for their
understanding and support. I am obliged to Mary-Kay Wilmers of the
London Review of Books for permission to reproduce articles which originally
appeared in its pages. Thank you to Rosemary Smith for correcting my
Spanish, and planting the idea in the first place. For miscellaneous services
of information, advice and companionship, thanks to Julietta, Roberto, Hilda,
Nico, Nestor, Doc, Ivan, Purita and Ruswel, and to Lynn Wilson, Bill
Dunlop and Stephen Rankin.

Stephen Smith

1

Flying to Havana

BY THE TIME YOU READ THIS, Cuba will have taken her first faltering steps to becoming a liberal democracy, her links with the United States restored after a trade embargo lasting more than 35 years, and her revolutionary leader, the late Fidel Castro, no more than a fading— or perhaps not. Try again: it was on a breathlessly humid summer's night that a crack brigade of Cuban exiles waded ashore on the swampy Zapata peninsula; the second Bay of Pigs invasion was underway, but this time, with rioting breaking out in the cities, Castro's fate was sealed.

Well, maybe. Emphatic predictions of what would become of Castro have been popular in modern Cuban studies since the discipline was first thought of – say around 1959, the year of the Revolution. As far away from the centre of the study as the University of London Library, browsers are buttonholed by impatiently prescient titles, long out of print, along the lines of *The Last Gasp: Why Cigar Socialism Had to Fail* and *Reaping the Whirlwind: How The Stalin of Sugar Met His End*. (I paraphrase but the reader gets the picture, I hope.) Going about your research among the library shelves, you would catch sight of these would-be tide-catchers, left high and dry by the apparent inexorability of Castro and his adventure, and shudderingly avert your eyes. These books came to bury Castro but he had survived them all.

The conflicting but equally emphatic message I heard from a Cuban I knew in London was 'anything can happen in Cuba'. My friend was teaching me Spanish, a preparation for writing this book which I was undertaking in tandem with fossicking among the university stacks (that is, until my friend went missing from home, and my library notes were perhaps surprisingly snatched from a car during riots in Bradford). I came to put greater store by my teacher's words than those of the Castro deathwatch patrol: anything *can* happen in Cuba. Time will eventually give hawkish Cuba-watchers a vindication of sorts, of course – perhaps it already has: tell me, what's the latest from Havana? But I almost believed the Cuban writer, Antón Arrufat, who told me in old Havana that Castro (b.1926) was immortal. 'Fidel's death?' said Arrufat, referring to *El Comandante* by his first name as Cubans of all opinions do. 'It's one of those things that will never happen. The Japanese donated some trees, to be planted near Havana. Fidel went there with a watering can and he said on television that in the year 2050 he would be back to give them more water.'

Anything can happen in Cuba, the land of miracles. The title of this book is – God help me – an ironic one. At least, it is in part. It comes from a saying I heard regularly during the so-called 'special period in time of peace', which coincided with the writing of this book. The Cubans' answer to their problems was often a caustic joke. As power cuts plunged one neighbourhood of Havana after another into temporary darkness, *habaneros* would say with mock awe that their shabby city had been transformed into a flashing Christmas tree: it was a miracle! So little electricity to be had, and yet the lights in the hotels of tourists blazed steadfastly through the night: the land of miracles. In response to the indignity of stiflingly overcrowded public transport, the people of Havana would remark acidly, 'Nobody knows how many Cubans can fit on a bus.' It was a matter beyond manufacturer's specifications, indeed, beyond science: it was more like the bussing of the five thousand.

But if the land of miracles was what Cubans called their country when they were being sarcastic, it seemed to me that it fitted the bill in a wholly unsarcastic way, too. Columbus, the first European to set foot on the island, described it as Paradise, 'the most beautiful land that human eyes have ever seen'. Cuba had everything going for it, a tropical climate and scenery to match: mountain ranges, limpid seas and teeming agricultural basins. It had fauna which was exotic without being life-threatening. The Cubans had eradicated the threat of malaria and there were no poisonous species on the island, according to an official pamphlet I read, which more or less credited the lack of toxicity of the wildlife to the Revolution. Castro's Cuba went one better than the Garden of Eden before the Fall, it seemed.

The sting might have been drawn from Nature, but Columbus's paradise was not without its life-enhancing excitements. History had acted as a brutal Cupid between the races – the Europeans who colonised Cuba and the African slaves imported to work the fields – and the country was a delicatessen of coffee-based skin types, from decaff French breakfast to insomniac mocha. It was, in the words of the novelist Gabriel García Márquez, who had visited often, 'the most dance-oriented society on earth'. Cubans claimed the patent on every Latin American step you could name, not only acknowledged exports like the hoola-hooping salsa but even, audaciously, the tango, which others in the southern hemisphere naively believed they themselves had devised. Glossy fashion spreads jolted you with images of toothsome *mulatas* seen against Havana's bleached walls, its pale and interesting architecture. In the capital, and in provincial cities like Trinidad and Santiago de Cuba, there were stunning man-made creations to set beside God's. Both exhibitions weathered the Caribbean elements as best they could. The same was true of a unique collection of vintage American automobiles, as stately as family vaults. The cars were unchanged – never traded-in, never upgraded – since the United States imposed its embargo in 1960. Appreciative visitors saw the houses and the cars and found them remarkable. They wondered at the fact that the Cubans had somehow kept such exhibits in working order. More than that, they wondered at the fact that they had kept them at all. Elsewhere, the world had long grown out of a taste for such grandiose lines. For those who had a fancy for such things, the land of miracles even had miracles: the mother who healed sickly infants from beyond the grave; occult possession and speaking in tongues among followers of Cuba's religious cult, *Santería*.

I was fascinated by the differences between the two territories which had been united as *el país de los milagros* : the bureaucratic, exasperating country familiar to the Cuban in the bus-queue, and the magical island, shaped like a crocodile, which the foreigner recognised as Columbus's paradise. The domain of the disgruntled *habanero* attracted me. Cuba was a good story. Incongruous since the 1960s as a Communist state off the eastern seaboard of the United States, it was now almost the only one left on the globe. How was the country adapting to its new role as a lonely standard-bearer of the Red Flag? What lay in store? I thought that I might at last see history in the making in Cuba. In China, I had arrived in Tiananmen Square, Peking, too late to witness the pro-democracy demonstrations there, and their bloody suppression. By the time I reached the Square, all I found on the flagstones was a chalk silhouette: not, as I tinglingly imagined, the work of a daring human rights pathologist, but actors' marks for a pageant intended to divert the restive Chinese. Disappointed as I was, I discovered that an inspired piece of political navigating had delivered me to a Communist capital at a turning point in the fortunes of Marxism. It was just my luck that the world-famous wall which came tumbling down that week was not the one which I had been photographing but the one separated from me by two continents, in Berlin. Despite my efforts to catch up with the upheaval in Eastern Europe, I was *in situ* too late to take away anything from those events apart from a mock-onyx coat-hanger which Nicolae Ceauşescu of Romania had kept in his hunting-lodge. I was determined that I wouldn't miss what some analysts would subsequently call the 'slow-motion collapse' of Cuba.

So much for the land that European Communism had abandoned. As for the other place which occupied the same spot on the atlas – the paradise island – it had been a beguiling mystery ever since the phrase 'Fly me to Havana' had insinuated itself into my childhood. There's a period quaintness, of all things, about those words today. If you were born in the 1960s, they were part of the background noise of events, leaking out of the radio and the television. Memory insists that they belonged to an age of cod wars and three-day weeks. But while other headlines and slogans seemed homespun even at the time, 'Fly me to Havana' gave off a more exotic whiff. It wasn't an entirely agreeable aroma. It was hot cockpits and desperate men and gun oil. You knew that the phrase was somehow associated with the dark and disapproved-of world of 'terrorism', that it was as much a threat as an instruction. There was no mistaking the menace in the first half of the hijackers' command. But the second half – where was this place with a name like a murmur? Even if you didn't recognise the echo of Nirvana in it, you supposed that it must be somewhere of an ambrosial desirability, that it could move men to the lengths of snatching aeroplanes. What little you gleaned about it tended to point in the same direction. While not, strictly speaking, overflowing with milk and honey, it seemed that Havana was practically the birthplace of rum and tobacco – defined one way, Havana *meant* cigar – a more rakish combination by some margin. Elementary research established that Havana was virtually the West Indies. To a childhood imagination reared on pirates and *Treasure Island*, the fact that Havana's grid reference was on the Spanish Main gave the place an added frisson. It was only later that you discovered how similar the city had been to the shanty-echoing, tropical bolthole of the mind's eye. The infamous Bluebeard had known Cuban waters well, and Robert Louis Stephenson had modelled the desert island of his story on an outcrop of Cuban terra firma.

Nonetheless, what was chiefly graspable about Havana at this early stage was its remoteness. You ate cod, and you sat in the darkness when it wasn't one of the days that the three-day week fell on. You could no more imagine yourself going to the place where the pirates lived and the hijackers went than you would dream of going to the moon. This was at the time when men *were* going to the moon, of course, and science fiction was enjoying a boom. All the same, the prospect of saying 'Fly me to Havana', even to a travel agent, was as unlikely as employing the expression 'Take me to your leader.'

Havana was as exotic as a foreign language. It was as odd as the curious tongue that our mother tried on us, the one which made us stare at her in the kitchen and laugh at her uncertainly, not quite recognising her while she was uttering it. She was speaking Spanish. This came from Spain, we knew, but it was also spoken in South America, where she had spent her childhood. She had been a little girl in Colombia. And when her parents had sailed home to England, they had broken the journey in Cuba, in the deep harbour of its capital city. It appeared that Havana wasn't as remote as you had thought. It was as remote as your own flesh and blood.

Twentieth-century Cuba wasn't a distant Valhalla for freedom fighters – or at least, it wasn't only that. It was the tremulous foreground of international affairs at what was coincidentally a key time in my life – my birth. American-backed Cuban guerrillas went ashore on their native soil in April 1961 in an unsuccessful attempt to reverse the Cuban Revolution – the original Bay of Pigs invasion. I spent it in the womb, an innocent party but an interested one, nonetheless, given the way things turned out for superpower relations. The Cuban missile crisis of October 1962, which *was* the way things turned out for superpower relations, found Khrushchev and Kennedy daring each other to be the first to blink over the deployment of Soviet nuclear warheads on the island. It found *me* displaying a sang-froid beyond my years, leisurely awaiting the arrival of my baby brother. But both he and I would have handled the situation very differently if we'd only known what was going on out there. The Russians at length cancelled their plans for installing the bomb in Cuba. Khrushchev had blinked, or come to his senses, first. Nevertheless, matters involving the island overshadowed the early lives of my generation, whether we were aware of them or not. And they had repercussions for years, because the missile crisis was the closest call of the Cold War. It was the nearest we had come to the bomb dropping on us.

In time, though, the effect of the crisis grew fainter – in Europe, at any rate. From where we were standing, it was only the shock wave of a bomb that had *failed* to go off. Cuba slipped back into the role of glamorous oddity. It was a trick question in a board game ('name the largest island in the Caribbean'). It was a tropical Xanadu of cigars and sugar cane, presided over by a Kublai Khan in green fatigues. I refer of course to Fidel. Like most people, I suspect, I associated the idea of Cuba with her leader, a swaggering, somewhat doleful figure in a beard, or so he appeared. Together with his comrade-in-arms, Che Guevara, Castro was the most fashionable Third World figure of the sixties. The pair of them appeared on the walls of student bedsits more dependably than damp – Che, who was John Lennon to Fidel's Paul McCartney, or perhaps Keith to his Mick, featuring on the lion's share of the merchandising and spin-offs.

Four or five years ago, I happened to be reading the autobiography of the celebrated television cameraman, Eric Durschmied, who had interviewed the then renegade Castro in Cuba's Sierra Maestra mountains in 1958. I realised with something like a start how rarely you *heard* from Castro. Durschmied's scoop had lost little of its exclusivity in the long years of Fidel's far court. Castro complained that his arguments weren't given a fair share of airtime in the West, and he probably had a case. But the radio silence out of Havana increased your curiosity about Castro and his island republic. Here was a leader who had been around for as long as you could remember – as a matter of fact, longer – a man who was frankly implausible as a shrinking violet or wallflower, and yet whose *presence* nonetheless seemed so incorporeal.

It was part of the exoticism of Cuba that the man who represented the country, to me at any rate, was reducible to a kind of joke shop disguise-kit and an olive tunic, and his country to a series of improbable Routier symbols: a green cane, a rum bottle, a voluptuous silhouette. That said, by the time I was reading Durschmied's book, I knew that it was not prudent to take Cuban images at face value. I understood that there was a worm in the cane, and that if Cuba was paradise, then it was paradise lost. The reason the board-game poser worked every time was that Cuba wasn't what you thought of as the Caribbean. It wasn't sun-loungers, natty shorts, an indolently compliant constitution drawn up for the benefit of lotus-eaters and tax exiles. People you knew *went* to the Caribbean. As for the beautiful girls in the fashion shoots, you understood by now that it wasn't only the walls that were distressed, (those walls, by the way, were practically toppling with rot and distemper. They weren't simply distressed any longer. They were devastated – they'd lost everything – they were *ruined*.) Even the rum bottle and the salsa seemed less about celebrating life in Cuba than consolations for it. On any true Routier map of the world, Cuba would have been represented by a shaky outline, on which the great epicure's reeling cartographer, handkerchief to his nostrils, would have written 'Here be savages!'

By 1990, I was thinking of going to Havana. When I told my mother, she mentioned the spectacular, gloomy cemetery she remembered from her childhood visit. I promised to pay a call on it. She envied me my trip, and for a time we talked about her accompanying me as my interpreter – Our Mam in Havana. But by now I was a grown-up journalist – if that's the phrase I want – coining the headlines and slogans of the media myself, or rather, I was helping in a small way to circulate them. Chaps like me didn't take our mothers with us on assignment. By this time, it was well within the bounds of possibility to approach a travel agent and say 'Fly me to Havana'. A single telephone call, or a stroll down the high street, was all it took. I suppose that this demonstrated the truth of a particularly hackneyed slogan: it *was* a small world. It was getting easier to get to everywhere else. And, as a result, everywhere was getting to be a little more like everywhere else. Since the world was dwindling, there was all the more urgency to see a place like Havana while you still could, before it turned into somewhere else. It was a small world, but it was an even smaller *second* world. The Communist bloc was shrinking. Having been to China and a couple of countries from the Eastern bloc, I got it into my head that if I saw Cuba and, say, Vietnam, I would have an historic full house, a *fin de siècle* flush.

By the 1990s, it was many years since Cuba had welcomed unscheduled arrivals; what with younger Cubans attempting to flee on rafts, unscheduled *departures* were more the order of the day. Indeed, in July 1996 a scheduled flight *to* Havana put down in the United States instead after a passenger claimed there was a bomb on board. Havana was just about the last place you expected to be hijacked to now. Anyone sentimental enough to divert a plane there had to ask himself whether the guards at José Martí airport would still recognise a fraternally toted AK47 when they saw one. The preferred mode of arrival was with a visa. Holiday-makers from Britain could enter Cuba on tourist cards, issued through travel agents for £15 each. But I would need a press permit, which meant contacting the Cuban embassy. I would also need the embassy's help in setting things up for me in Havana: putting in requests for interviews on my behalf with the kind of people who expected to be asked formally and well in advance; arranging permission to visit out-of-the-way places and organisations which could be ticklish about unannounced callers. Having travelled in Communist countries before, I knew that this was likely to mean a 'programme', an itinerary which was choreographed by government handlers and disclosed to me item by item, as tantalisingly as a striptease. It would mean my reporting to officials regularly, on the pretext of picking up last-minute reschedulings and cancellations. This would be instructive in its own way, I told myself, and I was curious to find out how much access the Cubans were willing to grant. Besides, it would be impossible to see half the people I wanted to see without going by the book. In any case, I expected to be left to my own devices for long spells in Cuba, no matter how time-consuming my official itinerary.

You can tell a great deal about a country from its embassies. Stepping into one is the equivalent of planting your foot on the soil of the place you are planning to visit, and not only in the legal sense. If you didn't already have a good idea of what Rwanda might be like in the bloody spring of 1994, there was a clue in your passport when it came back from the Rwandan embassy in Nairobi, the authorising stencil of Norah Kamikazi, Premier Secretaire, franked gooseflesh-raisingly across your visa. And an atmosphere of under-the-counter entrepreneurship was exactly right, in retrospect, for the place where you went for a Vietnamese visa in London in 1991. The embassy subcontracted out its accrediting chores to a Chinese restaurant on the Chiswick High Road, where the proprietor would let you have a *carte* in the back-kitchen for the far from take-away price of £96.

The Cuban embassy was in High Holborn, where it met the theatre-strip of Shaftesbury Avenue. One wet morning in March 1995, three months before I planned to fly to Cuba in order to spend the summer there, I had an appointment with the press attaché. I was also intending to submit my passport details for a visa. The receptionist was a young Englishman with what might have been an unsuccessful Che goatee. At his elbow was a brick-thick biography of Castro. A middle-aged man was standing behind him. The receptionist said he would let the attaché know that I had arrived, but I would have to go to the consular section to apply for my visa. 'Go out of here. Turn right. First on your right,' he said. The consular section was in Grape Street. The street was little bigger than an alley, really. There was room for a car, but not for two to pass. There was a brass plate on the door. Inside, a woman sat behind a counter. Behind her was a middle-aged man – he looked very similar to the one I'd just seen at the embassy. It was the same man, in fact. While I had walked from the embassy to the consular section on the streets of London, he had slipped through a connecting door. The little piece of Cuba in Britain was a looking-glass set-up: an embassy and a consular section which turned out to be one and the same. This suggestion that the operation was a little grander than it really was, the comic transparency of that pretence, the petty bureaucracy, wasn't a bad introduction to Cuba, to official Cuba at any rate.

The press attaché was a small, dapper man who dressed in a blazer, like the smarter kind of sports journalist. We talked in a private room. On the far side of blinds that were as broad as planks, the rain fell into Grape Street. I explained why I wanted to go to Cuba. There was growing interest in the attaché's country among Western investors and tourists, I told him. I quoted the embassy's own statistics back at him: 20,000 visitors from Britain in the past 12 months, compared to 9,000 in the previous year. I said that I wanted to write something on Cuba's health and education services, which enjoyed such a high international reputation. I was laying it on a bit thick, as I was sure the attaché was aware. But he smiled emolliently, as I knew he would, and promised to wire Havana recommending that they approve my visa and 'help you with a programme'.

Though he had almost certainly forgotten, the press attaché and I knew each other of old. His name was Roberto de Armas. We had met in 1990, on the day I was due to fly to Cuba for the first time. I had been outside the embassy in London's theatreland at eight o'clock that morning, waiting for the Cubans to arrive for work, wondering if my visa would at last be ready. Perhaps it was my own fault, perhaps I had left it all too late, but with my plane to Havana practically boarding, there was still no sign of my permit. My plan had been to make a flying visit to Cuba that July. It was the season of shoe-warping heat and stultifying humidity. But carnival was celebrated then, and Castro would be making his set-piece address to the country on the 26th, a public holiday marking the anniversary of his first, unsuccessful attempt to start the Revolution – a botched raid on government barracks in 1953. It would be the first time *El Comandante* had given the speech since the fall of the Berlin Wall and the decoupling of the Eastern bloc from the tottering Soviet Union. What would he have to say? What would happen when he rose to his feet? Señor de Armas and I had already been through a q & a session about this trip, conducted by fax; I had, I remembered, briefly hymned the Cuban health system on this occasion, too. On the day that Señor de Armas and I first made each other's acquaintance, nothing could have surprised me more than his news that my visa was at last available. It could be stamped into my passport at once, he said. He asked if I had a hotel reservation. I had to admit that I hadn't. 'It's okay,' he said. 'You will be met in Havana, and you will stay in a mid-class hotel.' No other journalist from Britain had applied to cover Castro's speech, he told me, though a few London-based American correspondents had. He said that it was a critical anniversary. 'Not since the Bay of Pigs has Cuba been under such pressure.' The United States was turning the screw, making Cuba out to be the last redoubt of Stalinism, operating a propaganda campaign against her.

I had been wondering if I dared share with Señor de Armas a thought that preoccupied me, a silly question – would it be possible to speak to Castro? Señor de Armas said, 'Fidel makes his interviews for specific audiences and politicians. Recently, he has spoken to CNN and to the Brazilian and Spanish press.' Reading between the lines, *El Comandante* did not consider it was worth his while talking to the British and their then Prime Minister, Mrs Thatcher, who was best known in Cuba as the victor of the Falklands, a conflict in which Castro, like other Latin American leaders, had supported Argentina.

Like the country it represented, nothing seemed to change at the Cuban embassy. Five years after I had applied for my first press visa, they were still £25 each, and Roberto de Armas was still suavely overseeing them. Equally, though I had by now glimpsed Castro on a distant dais, I was no nearer an answer to my preoccupying question: 'Could I speak to Fidel?'

'Everyone wants to speak to Fidel,' sighed Señor de Armas this time, his back to rainy Grape Street. 'Put it all in a letter and send it to me.'

'And you'll wire Havana with my request?'

'Look, the problem is that Fidel won't have anything like press officers, people who advise him who he should speak to. Your only hope is to go where he is, at some function or reception. Maybe you will have a chance to talk to him then, I don't know.'

Every time I talked to Señor de Armas after that, I asked him what news there was from Havana about my programme and my request to speak to Castro. He hadn't heard yet, he always said. Once, he told me that he was going to put a copy of my letter in the diplomatic bag. Señor de Armas was the guest speaker at a seminar on Cuba held at a London college in the spring of 1995. The seminar was led by the bearded receptionist at the embassy. He belonged to the Cuba Solidarity Group. The Cuba Solidarity Group might have been run by Dave Spart, the character created by *Private Eye* magazine who spoke the musty rhetoric of the workers' struggle. The CSG was almost heartbreakingly Spartist, doggedly attributing all of Cuba's problems to the American embargo. The seminar was modelled on the workshops that CSG volunteers underwent before spending their holidays as part of 'work brigades', helping with the harvest in Cuba. Señor de Armas's appearance was scheduled for the afternoon. By then, we had already picked apart a documentary on Cuba which had been made by an unfortunate BBC correspondent – 'Most of the views came from?' asked the bearded man; 'The presenter!' chorused the class. Later, I had been for coffee with a man who thought it was a good thing that the Cuban state discouraged its own citizens from going into Cuban hotels. 'Tourism is very corrupting,' he told me.

The bearded man offered to take Señor de Armas's coat, and said, 'Is there anything you would like to say, first of all?'

'No. You've said a lot already,' replied the press attaché smoothly. He answered a question about Cuba's record on human rights by saying that his country was at war with the United States.

I asked if he thought President Clinton's undertaking to turn back Cuban boat people would increase tension in Havana. The bearded man, who was sitting on the corner of a desk, leant forward and murmured, 'Good question.'

'This summer will be different to the last,' said Señor de Armas cryptically. After the conference ended, I asked him whether he had heard from Cuba about my programme, and he said, 'Ah, yes, your programme. Now remind me ...?' After a time, during which he appeared to be deciding whether or not to remember me, he suggested it would be better if I called him at the embassy again.

One day I telephoned and he said that the Press Centre in Havana had agreed to plan a programme for me. 'You have to go there and ask for a man whose name is Igor.'

'And they know about my interview requests?' I said.

Señor de Armas laughed. 'Don't sound so worried,' he said. 'The impression you leave with me is that you're paranoid. You cannot start with traditional British things in Cuba. You cannot count that they will sort everything out in Cuba.'

'That's why I want to get the wheels in motion.'

'Relax,' said the press attaché. 'Go to the Press Centre. Have a good time in Cuba.' My visa was ready. I had a month to go to the consular section to collect it and a further three months before it wore off, like a charm or spell. I took this to mean that it was good for up to three months. But no: my visa – a sticker the colour of a ruby grapefruit, suggesting a certificate pasted into a confirmation Bible – was only valid for thirty days. It was renewable in Havana, according to the burly man who was behind the counter at the consular section when I went to collect it. 'At the Press Censure,' he added, prophetically. You thought about the rake-off that the Cuban authorities were making. Not only would I have to take out an extension on my visa, but I gathered I was expected to pay the Press Centre a registration fee of $60.

'What's the news from Cuba?' I asked the burly man.

'It's quiet.'

I thanked him for his help. 'Write well about Cuba,' he urged me in a perfunctory way, not looking at me but tucking a box-file out of sight beneath his counter.

A few weeks later, in early summer 1995, I took the train from Liverpool Street across the Essex marshes to Stansted airport. *Cubana*, the Cuban national carrier, was inaugurating direct flights from Britain. Now that foreigners were no longer taking aircraft to Cuba, the Cubans were bringing their aircraft to them. My travel agents, who specialised in trips to South America, had warned me to expect a lengthy check-in. When I entered Sir Norman Foster's clean, light rhomboids and saw a long queue, I assumed that it was for Flight CU455 to Havana and Kingston, Jamaica. But I was wrong: the line I wanted was far longer. It was slow moving as well as long; a crocodile of people for the crocodile-shaped island. In the travel pages of a Sunday newspaper a few days earlier, I had discovered that there were three classes on this flight. As well as Economy, in which I was booked, there were Tropical and Club. The travel agents had asked me to call by their offices to pick up my ticket – I realised why when I saw the size of it: it was like a car manual – and I took the opportunity of asking whether they could tell me the difference between the classes, 'Do they just turn the air-conditioning off in Tropical?'

'I think you get a few more cocktails in Tropical,' I was told. 'I think there are more stewardesses per passenger.' It was a little vague. I ought to have taken note, or even fright. When I reached the front of the Economy check-in, after three-quarters of an hour, the girl behind the desk looked at my rucksack, my laptop word-processor, my in-flight grip and the canary-coloured carrier bag which contained my radio, and said, 'You do know there's a weight limit on luggage?'

'Yes,' I said, not having given the matter a thought.

The weight limit was 20 kilos per head: the check-in clerk leafed through my ticket and pointed out the missable detail. My luggage tipped the scales at 43 kilos. It was more than twice as heavy as *Cubana*'s allowance. I was *over* by 23 kilos. The excess baggage charge was £11 per kilo, making my liability a total of £253. The sum was grievous in itself, but the worst thing about it was the shame: £253 was the sort of money you expected to spend on an air *ticket* – for that price, I could practically have booked the seat next to mine for my bags. The idea of lavishing such an amount on my luggage made me feel like one of those cruise-going widows who insists on the biggest cabin in order to accommodate her Pekinese. The weight was nearly all books, although I had also packed half a dozen cans of food, and several cartons of Marlboro, which were left-over bribes and checkpoint-inducements from a journey to Africa for 'Channel 4 News'. I said, 'Couldn't I go Tropical?'

The check-in woman said, 'It's full. Anyway, the weight limit's the same.'

I began removing what I thought I'd want on the flight from my grip, with the intention of leaving the bag behind. Perhaps this was the necessary third thing to go wrong, I thought superstitiously – following the loss of my notes in Bradford, the disappearance of my Spanish tutor. But then a man in uniform appeared at the desk and told the woman to waive the excess charge on my bags. She was astonished. But he insisted. 'We don't want any more delays,' he said.

The first time I had made the trip to Havana, five years earlier, the airlines who had wanted me to fly them there included Aeroflot of Russia; Iberia, the Spanish flag-bearer; and Czech Airlines. But it would be wrong to imply that there had been fierce competition among them to sell me a seat. No-one was really bothering with the Cuba-bound traveller then. The only place where you were likely to come across advertisements for trips to Cuba was in the back pages of left-wing political weeklies, where tour firms attempted to sell their Cuban excursions on the strength of the cycling and comradeship. I had decided to fly Czech Airlines. The Eastern bloc lines were both cheaper than Iberia by about £100. The decider was that Aeroflot was dreadful whereas the word-of-mouth about its Communist competitor was that it was merely poor. With stops in

Prague and Montreal, Czech Airlines could get you from London to Havana in 22 hours flat.

The *Cubana* plane was a DC10. The bulkhead illumination panels – showing whether or not to wear seatbelts; the state of occupancy of the toilets – were faded. The no-smoking icon, a red cross through a puffing, ash-heavy fag, looked like the kind of thing you might see nailed to a weathered post in a forest. My fellow passengers included Jamaicans – and some Cubans – going home; middle-class, almost middle-aged couples; honeymooners; families. There was a show of sandal and British hot-weather togs. The flight crew looked sleek, suggesting that there was something in the argument I'd heard from my Cuban tutor that theirs was a coveted living where he came from. A safety film was running on a pull-down screen – it had been dubbed, I would have sworn, by the same hammy tenor who made the Spanish language cassettes I'd been cribbing.

Nominations were closing for the vacant leadership of the British Conservative Party elsewhere in London. When I had last heard, it was a two-cornered affair involving the Prime Minister and one of his former Cabinet colleagues. It was curious to be on the point of leaving a country where the leader could soon be leaving office – the people having nothing to do with it, one way or the other – for another where, you sensed, the leader would never concede power without a fight – again, the people having no say in the matter. I supposed that the exchange of countries also renewed doubts about my news judgement.

There was one bar of soap in the toilet, the size of a communion wafer. Most of the signs were in German. I went through the cabin. In Tropical, they looked as though they were as packed-in as we were. Extra legroom, if any, would be measured in millimetres. I asked a Cuban stewardess what was different about Tropical. 'It costs more,' she said, with almost baffling candour.

Dinner was stringy beef in insulating tin. The cruets were perhaps ill-judged sachets bearing the likenesses of old tubs of the air: stringbags, flying boats. Even allowing for the miles on the DC10's clock, it was impossible to believe that the salt and pepper were genuinely left over from the golden age of flight. A steward brought round a box containing more sachets. You made your selection from a choice of coffee or tea, and held onto your foil-wrapped beverage until the stewardess followed up behind with a kettle.

The captain tannoyed for a doctor. I discounted almost at once the romantic idea that the co-pilot had stopped a hijacker's bullet in the thigh: we were flying to Havana already. All the same, I wondered where we were going to put down if we had to. By this time, we were over the Atlantic Ocean. Disappointingly, we heard no more about the emergency. It was probably just a touch of air-sickness, a non-German speaker who had taken gratefully to a cubicle only to get into difficulties with the instructions.

It was dusk as we descended towards José Martí airport: despite the long flight, I found myself wishing it was later. I wanted the *Cubana* jet to circle Havana until it grew dark, so that I could see whether power cuts really did make the city flash like a Christmas tree at night.

2

The Hotel England

WHAT I WAS LOOKING forward to was not touching Cuban soil again but experiencing the Cuban climate. Stepping onto the wheeled staircase in Havana was like being swaddled in freshly steamed laundry, though not so aromatic. Beneath the tang of aviation fuel was a characteristic pungency of sulphur. They had vamped the airport since I was last there. Disembarkees were confronted by a bank of television monitors playing rock videos. There was an air of prosperity – at least, compared to the shabby aspect the airport had worn before. Perhaps it was the fleet of air-conditioned coaches, waiting to ferry the new visitors directly to the beaches of Varadero.

Before, I had taken a taxi from José Martí into Havana: a Japanese saloon nose-diving and ski-jumping in places where the road was rutted, the driver making a fist and crying 'Fidel!' This time, I was being met. I was looking for Julietta. She was a graduate of English who from time to time had acted as my translator during my last visit to Cuba. She had been recommended by another foreign journalist. Julietta was 23, pretty, petite, with a black cloud of curly hair falling over her left eye. When I had got through to her on the telephone from London, she had offered to come and collect me from the airport. However, it was her father, Roberto, whom I spotted first: a big wave, a diffident smile, spectacles. I walked round the barrier and there was Julietta. She was lighter-skinned than her father: a *mulata*. It was a balmy evening, about 30 degrees, and she was wearing shorts and a T-shirt. I gave her the bottle of scent I'd brought for her.

Roberto's Lada smelt strongly of petrol. Gingerly, I committed my luggage to its reeking boot. I hoped he didn't notice my expression because it was a considerable sacrifice on his part to have picked me up at all. He was using up precious, rationed fuel, and all I had for him in return was a copy of *National Geographic*: well, he *was* a geographer, I told myself uncomfortably. History suggested that there might be a black market value for *National Geographic* in Havana. It was famously a boy's first primer on the opposite sex – all those bare-breasted tribeswomen – and the regime had adopted a very unCuban prudishness, sweeping away the blue movies and mucky postcards that visitors, including Graham Greene, had enjoyed. *National Geographic* was closer to porn than anything the Cubans had (although, notwithstanding Greene's adventures, I found it difficult to imagine that there could be much call for 'adult' books in the Cuban capital: it was like picturing wine gums getting off the ground in Bordeaux). *National Geographic* had currency as intellectual property, if nothing else. Foreign newspapers and periodicals were unobtainable except in one or two hotels. But I couldn't see Roberto hawking my gift on a street corner. He was a committed supporter of *la Revolución*, a decorated hero of Cuba's adventures in Angola and the head of his local Committee for the Defence of the Revolution, his CDR. The CDRs were the grass roots of the Cuban political system. The benign view of them was that they were a combination of parish council and coffee morning. They were also the eyes and ears of the regime. They were supposed to keep a lookout for 'anti-revolutionary activity'. One of my guidebooks said the people who belonged to the CDRs thought of eavesdropping as their civic duty. In the documentary I'd watched with the Cuban Solidarity Group and friends in London, the BBC reporter had called the CDRs a cross between the neighbourhood watch and the Gestapo, which had not endeared him to his audience.

A respected Western journalist in Havana calculated that half the working population of Cuba, two million people, had some connection to the security services. 'The capacity for duplicity is incredible,' he said. In his novel *Cuba and the Night*, Pico Iyer wrote of Havana, 'The whole city was a circle of informers.' You could be forgiven for thinking that you were back in Romania after the events of Christmas 1989, when the secret police, the Securitate, were still at large, and people told you that every fourth citizen was on their payroll. However, other foreigners in Cuba took a more relaxed view of state security. Diplomats – though *they* were certainly all spied on – would tell you that the regime was too busy trying to keep the population fed, and distracted from rioting, to maintain round-the-clock surveillance on everybody. This insouciance was almost certainly justified where holiday-makers were concerned. However, there were modest files on foreigners such as businessmen and reporters even before they had arrived, thanks to Cuba's embassies, where their visas had been prepared. Despite Señor de Armas's teasing about my paranoia, it was a fair assumption that the Press Centre kept tabs on visiting journalists. Simply by means of the programmes they devised, they could tell where you were and who you were seeing for considerable lengths of time. The same was true of the agencies responsible for overseas entrepreneurs. Perhaps the security services used what they were told by hotel snoops and CDR snitches to help them triangulate a foreigner's position, to work out where he stood. There might be nothing of interest in it for them in the end. But they represented, at a conservative estimate, a substantial proportion of Cuba's productive capacity – the country's GDP might have been poor, but the black economy was resilient, and spying was one of the biggest invisible sectors – and the spies had to find *something* to do all day.

As for Roberto, the CDR boss, a decent and honourable man, I didn't imagine for a moment that he was spying on me. Given his history of conspicuous service to the Revolution, it was probably enough that he and I were friends. If he found nothing in our friendship to trouble him, then there could be nothing for any patriotic citizen to be troubled by, Fidel himself might have concluded. At most, there was about him a watchfulness which might have stemmed from caution. It was like an involuntary action, an instinct that he should keep his distance. Perhaps Roberto recognised that our friendship had the potential to compromise him as well as me. Supposing for the sake of argument that he *was* expected to make my business his business: how would it look if he was seen accepting a beer from me in a hotel, or a few dollars at a filling-station? Even if there was a sinister side to our relationship, it felt preferable to have things as they were rather than be observed by informers who weren't constrained by any ties of friendship.

From the back of Roberto's Lada, I saw cranes at the roadside, and men working with concrete which appeared to consist entirely of dust. I couldn't tell if I was breathing in traffic fumes or the vapours from the Lada's fuel tank. Roberto told me about his current project. 'I am compiling a geological museum,' he said. Every day he pedalled to work to save petrol, and put in eight hours or more, sifting rocks. Just what Cuba needs, I thought, another museum. The country was very well supplied with archiving of every sort, and despairing guidebook writers could always fall back on a museum for their 'Things to do' listings concerning towns which were otherwise entertainment black-spots.

The roadway was fringed with long grass and palm trees. Most of the housing on the outskirts of Havana was single storey, with bleached and peeling walls. Exhortatory hoardings proclaimed '*Socialismo o Muerte*', Socialism or Death, but there were also newer ones for mobile phones. We went through Revolution Square – there was a likeness of Che Guevara on one building. We talked about Julietta's success in graduating, and her elder sister's, in becoming a wife. Everything they told me was in response to my questions, until Roberto eventually asked me how things were in Britain. They were better informed about world events than, say, many of the Americans living 90 miles away in Miami, though their perspective on some of those events was curious. They were familiar with the ructions in British politics, for example, but they thought the most significant thing about them was the resignation of the Foreign Secretary. It was as if they were talking about a frock-coated grandee from the days when his office ran half the globe. Absurdly, you felt flattered by proxy.

We pulled up outside the Hotel Inglaterra. In the crowded lobby, Roberto and I had incriminating drinks. I haven't done the arithmetic, but I would think that Havana (pop. 2 million) has more famous hotels per head than any other city in the world. There is the Ambos Mundos, the Two Worlds, where Ernest Hemingway wrote *For Whom the Bell Tolls*. The Riviera on El Malecón, Havana's seafront, its paint stripped by the blow torch of the Cuban sun, was built by the Jewish godfather, Meyer Lansky: on the eve of the Revolution, his staff walked off the job and Lansky had to cook the dinners while his wife waited table. Like the Hotel Capri, where George Raft had once looked after the casino, the Riviera had been a favourite watering hole of the Mob before 1959. The Nacional, with its sand-blasted Moorish turrets, was a home from home for visitors including the Windsors, the Churchills and most of Hollywood. I met an elderly ex-bellhop who could remember Johnny Weissmuller swimming lengths of the Nacional pool and Alexander Fleming taking the lift. 'Fleming didn't tip,' said the ex-bellhop lugubriously.

On my first visit to Cuba, I stayed at the Habana Libre. One of the city's landmarks, it appropriately resembled the rusting radiator of a classic American automobile. The cane furniture and tropical foliage of its vast lobby were notoriously frequented by secret police, informers and prostitutes. Until the Revolution, the hotel had been the cosmopolitan Havana Hilton; afterwards, one of its upper storeys was for a time Fidel Castro's quarters. 'A bazooka was ... under the bed, sticking out,' according to Marita Lorenz, who wrote an account of being Castro's mistress, and of being put up by the CIA to poison him at the hotel. She was unable to go through with it, as she sorrowingly told him. 'Nobody, Marita,' Fidel said sadly, 'nobody can kill me.'

The Libre was, I suppose, the sort of 'mid-class hotel' that Señor de Armas had had in mind for me, although $57 a night for a single room didn't strike me as a mid-class tariff. I was told at the desk that bookings for carnival and the 26 July celebrations had been driving prices up, which wasn't the sort of thing you had bargained on hearing on your first morning in Communist Cuba. The hotel had had no idea that I was coming, of course. I had asked the taxi-driver to drive me to

the Libre simply because I had heard of it. It was where other visiting
journalists were putting up. An American photographer told me that
he didn't care for the place. He had stayed there before, and found it 'a
cave'. 'The guests can be seedy and the food is terrible,' he said. He
was right. The Libre was cavernous. My fellow patrons included pasty
Russians, buying round after round of drinks for the girls in the
shrubbery. It was as if they sensed that goodwill exchange visits to
Cuba would soon be a thing of the past. And the photographer was
also shrewd on the subject of the food at the Libre. I ate there as little
as possible. By coincidence, that was what the hotel apparently had in
mind for me too. When I went to breakfast at the second-floor buffet, I
was rebuffed by the waiters in their too-tight jackets, who insisted that
my room key was insufficient proof of residence, and demanded the
accompanying card. It was on the 14th floor, marking my place in *Our
Man in Havana*, so I opted to breakfast outside the hotel instead. I
walked down the street, La Rampa, towards the sea. Halfway down, a
youth in a white shirt and bow tie was brewing coffee at an open-air
counter. People waiting for buses gathered around his sweltering
percolators. I had two servings of hot sweet *café cubano* in an
earthenware cup the size of an eyebath. The coffee stall was outside a
restaurant with mirrored windows. Inside, a couple sat at a Formica
counter. Behind it was an empty refrigerated display case. Two men in
shoelace ties were serving cakes filled with some kind of cured meat. I
spent a dollar on one and almost finished it.

The Habana Libre was in Vedado, the city's downtown, such as it
was, a district of airline offices and government buildings. On the whole,
the hotels in the old city, Habana Vieja, had more to recommend them.
The best place to stay was the Inglaterra – the Hotel England – which
overlooked Parque Central. It was the oldest hotel in Havana, built in
1875, and at least as famous as its competitors. Its patrons had included
Federico García Lorca. Greene put it into his novel. In *Dreaming in
Cuban*, by the Cuban-born writer Cristina García, the Inglaterra was
the scene of trysts between Celia, the *Fidelista* old lady of her story, and
her Spanish lover. It had been the billet of choice among correspondents
who covered the collapse of the Batista dictatorship. It seemed like a
good place to sit back and wait for the Castro regime to fall.

The Inglattera was flanked on one side by the blackened statuary of the Gran Teatro. If your room was on the right-hand side of the hotel, a noise from the street – the raucous and persistent raspberrying of a trumpet on a Friday night, say – would draw you to your balcony, and you would look out upon a maiden fixed in an attitude of suffering upon a marble column, while the serried air-conditioning units on the wall above your head wept in sympathy with her. The hotel was bordered on its other side by an old Spanish townhouse. If your room was on the left-hand side of the hotel, your balcony was adjacent to the one on which a cockerel unfailingly halloed the dawn.

The Inglaterra took the least likely bookings in Havana. As well as Western men bashfully entertaining their rented dates to dinner, a sight you became accustomed to across the city, you would see hearty blond cyclists, and the only Africans I ever came across in the city. The hotel's facilities were limited. There were no minibars, but a man at reception with a wall eye and a Nehru jacket would give you the key to your own mini-safe. It was in the wardrobe and the rental was $1 a night. There was no swimming-pool, but a rooftop bar where you could pass the balmy hour of dusk as pleasantly as anywhere else in Havana. It was unjustly neglected, and sometimes you would be drinking there by yourself, apart perhaps from one other European, with a long drink in his hand and a short, curvy Cuban in his lap. The food was nothing special. Like most hotel cuisine in Cuba, it had the tang of a house-clearance sale. The kindest interpretation to put on this was that a hint of disinfectant from over-zealously maintained kitchens had been allowed to lace the washing-up water, tainting the plates; or else it had somehow permeated the scrupulous shrink-wrapping which was the bedrock of Cuban portion-control. There was never any problem getting into the Inglaterra's dining-room for breakfast but you would always wish you hadn't. The meal consisted of a plate of sweetmeats including an imitation WI cupcake; a sandwich featuring tumescent salami; a little spinnaker of pale bread with corrugated butter; and a sachet of mango conserve. It was washed down with a foul concoction of orange *and* banana juice. But breakfast only cost $3. And you could always wander down the tree-lined boulevard, Prado, to the Hotel Sevilla instead. There was fresh bread at the Sevilla and urns of coffee, though breakfast was $5. The management turned off the air-conditioning at ten sharp in order to drive out laggardly patrons, and you were grateful for the tobacco-redolent zephyr created by an elderly waiter passing your table. The Sevilla, too, was famous as a location in *Our Man in Havana*, which scholars will one day recognise as a kind of fictionalised brochure of the hotels of the Cuban capital.

All the same, I preferred the Inglaterra. The Sevilla was more expensive, and its courtyard bar, boxed-in by the flesh-toned walls of the hotel, was a flagrant pick-up joint. Moreover, it lacked the melancholy comedy of its neighbour. The Inglaterra struck you as a family hotel which had seen better days, where the waiter asked you for help with his English and the phone went at dawn with a random wake-up call, just as you had disciplined yourself to tune out the noise of the cockerel's alarm. You didn't begrudge the hotel its unbilled extras, however. The word the waiter had got stuck on, throat-lumpingly, was 'knowledge'. And when the phone bounced in its cradle like a baby at six in the morning, you picked it up to hear an electronic rendering of 'Happy Birthday to You'. I was only a few days shy of my birthday the first time I experienced this, and wondered in my bleary condition if this were not some handsome, albeit mistimed, gesture from a grateful management. But no: all guests were apt to hear the same refrain in the early mornings, whether they were celebrating anniversaries or not; indeed whether they had asked to be disturbed or not. In the lobby of the Inglaterra, teardrops of red and green were projected through stained-glass windows onto tiles which had been shipped over from Spain. A sentimental ballad, *'Reloj No Marques Las Horas'*, could be heard on the public address system. Julietta said that it meant 'Don't let the time go', but my limited Spanish suggested that it translated literally as 'My watch doesn't mark the hours', which didn't seem a bad anthem for a country where the public clocks had all been allowed to run down or seize up. There was a bronze of a flamenco dancer by a grand piano in the ground-floor bar, and sometimes a blonde pianist at the keys. She was quite something. She was got up in wispy white confections even though she was a broad of a certain age, and indeed breadth. Her accessories included an absurdly dainty white clutch purse.

The Inglaterra wasn't always a comfortable place to stay. There was the shock of a tapping sound on the windows of the dining-room at night. You looked round, wondering at the noise – hoping that it was the wind, knowing that it wasn't – and could just discern, through the smoked and treated glass, a hungry man's imploring face.

I walked down the Prado to El Malecón. There were oil streaks on the tarmac. Above the teeteringly-stacked rubbish bins at the kerbside, the air trembled with rankness. There was gratuitous-looking wooden scaffolding. It seemed so insubstantial you thought it had hardly been worthwhile putting it up. A sign claimed that constructors were erecting a new hotel in the ruins of an old Spanish building. Only its beautiful columns were standing: they were pitted and engrimed with decay. Reminded by the architecture of wedding cakes, I spotted one, on a pushbike being wheeled down Prado early enough to thwart the sun's effect on icing sugar. I had once attended a wedding reception for *habanero* teenagers at a pigeon-fanciers' club, where guests' glasses, abandoned for some reason on the bottom tier of the wedding cake, sank through the icing up to their stems.

People hissed as I passed. It was the favourite way of attracting attention: as Norman Lewis has written, it was normal to be stopped on the street in Havana by strangers wishing to share their thoughts about anything that had caught their attention. In front of the Sevilla, a tout from a local nightclub pushed a flyer on me. 'Best disco, I like it,' he said in English. He asked me where I was from – *why* do people do that? We all need to know, for some reason. I said, 'London.'

'Ireland?'

'No. *Inglaterra.*'

'Ah. What you name?'

'Stephen,' I told him.

'Francis!' he exclaimed delightedly.

On the Malecón, there were a couple of new fast-food cafés, and what looked as though it was going to be a car showroom when it was finished. Another cake was being nursed in the sidecar of a motorcycle-combination by a little boy. It was more lurid, with piping of a nosebleed-in-the-snow hue. The boy's father, astride the puttering motorbike, looked Asian. But when I flagged the pair of them down, to take their picture, he told me he was a *cubano*, a resident of Havana's modest Chinatown. The cake was for his son's classmates, he said.

A young man fell in with me and told me a story about being a soccer player. He agreed with me that some of the *hamburguesa* joints, and the car showroom – '*la casa para los coches*', as I put it – were new. He wanted money but a policeman foiled him by calling him across to check his papers. A line of cyclists went past me with a susurrus of slack chains. Among the girls, the fashion appeared to be for gynaecological Lycra. Julietta told me that she wouldn't wear it, she was too skinny. She thought that Lycra was only worn by women trying to hold in excess pounds. A beautiful girl with Nefertiti plaits was wheeled past me by her boyfriend, astride the handlebars of his bike.

I was going to the Centro Internacional de Prensa on La Rampa, the 'Press Censure' to which I had been so unguardedly referred by the visa clerk at the London embassy. The clean, airless vestibule was hung with self-consciously artistic photography – nudes with dock leaves – and rather intense works of modern art, in which, for instance, Bob Dylan and Jimi Hendrix might be looking at a Daliesque clock-face. There was an air-conditioned café in the basement where you could drink coffee and watch Mexican soap operas on the barman's television set.

My attempts to get journalistic endeavours off the ground had always foundered at the Press Centre. I had never quite managed to get accredited as a visiting reporter on previous visits. The centre's representatives and I had danced a minuet of futility every day – all told, I calculated, we had completed a masked ball of pointlessness. Each morning I would go in, ask where my accreditation had got to, and be advised that it was pending. I would ask about interviews, facilities, access, and get stalled or brushed off.

This time I approached the front desk and asked for Igor. Señor de Armas had said I would be looked after by Igor, not the sort of name you forgot. A wiry man appeared wearing a *guayabera*, a short-sleeved shirt with breast and hip pockets much favoured by Cuban officialdom. Was this Igor? No, this was Señor Almeida. He said that nothing could be done until I had filled in accreditation forms. I had to provide photographs. Foolishly, I'd not thought to bring any: I would have to go to an official photographic studio and sit for the state portraitist. I had pulled on whatever came to hand that morning and was dressed in full Englishman-abroad fig. A man on the street cried out 'Sherlock!', presumably a generic term for my countrymen: I'm not sure that the sleuth of Baker Street ever ventured abroad in floor-length green cotton trousers, long-sleeved shirt, and a sun-hat bearing the legend 'Australia' – it was a present and was mirthfully set off by corks on yellow strings. I was perspiring, but I found a handkerchief, and then a smile for the photographer – unlike my fellow subjects, Cuban men, who were done up in dully gleaming suits and shirts with abstract designs where the buttons would ordinarily have been. They returned the camera's fixed look.

Almeida's full name was Eugenio Almeida Bosque. His brother Juan had been one of a handful of rebels who hid in the Sierra Maestra mountains with Castro before the Revolution prevailed. They were known in Cuba as 'the Twelve', which was also the title of a biography by a writer called Carlos Franqui. The book had helped to establish them in Cuban mythology as a cross between the Apostles and the Dirty Dozen. Juan was now a provincial governor. His brother settled himself at my table in the Press Centre. He was accompanied by a woman, Ivette, young and dark and pretty. 'Welcome on board,' said Almeida. He had a copy of my letter to Señor de Armas. Several lines had been picked out in a green marker pen. Almeida said the embassy had told the Press Centre all about me. I said, 'What did they say?'

'That you're the best after me,' he said with a wolfish smile.

I was apparently serious, responsible. I had been to Angola – that was good. 'You can write whatever you want,' said Almeida. 'Talk to anyone you want. We are on your team. Don't think of us as from the state. You must talk to dissidents, people at the bus-stop. They are years ahead of officials. Write whatever you want. All we ask is you *don't* write that you didn't get cooperation, otherwise we will be hanged!' We laughed. We smoked – in Almeida's case, the aromatic, filterless Cuban *Popular* brand. He had told me to talk to dissidents! I couldn't quite believe I had heard him correctly. Foreign journalists and diplomats to whom I repeated Almeida's remarks couldn't quite believe them either, although everyone understood that dissident writers and activists were on the itinerary of every visiting journalist, the unofficial 'programme' which he performed in parallel to any routine organised by the Press Centre. Almeida was only acknowledging what was accepted practice among the foreign media. But that was still saying quite a lot – wasn't it?

I suggested some drinks. Almeida called for beer. He had a broad, broken-looking nose. He had been a revolutionary since the mid-fifties, he said, a student in the Soviet Union and a servant of the new Cuba in some tantalisingly indistinct capacity overseas.

Ivette produced a list of my schedule, my official 'programme'. On Wednesday, I had an appointment at the Institute of Biotechnology, she read from her hand-written notes. Friday would find me interviewing a man from the sugar ministry. A nickel official was pencilled in for Thursday week, and so it went on. Almeida leant over the table, keeping one arm over the back of his chair. He said, 'And now I will tell you what to do at the weekend.' He jabbed a forefinger against my notepad. I should take in Varadero, the Tropicana cabaret and *Santería*, he said. 'This is the best introduction to Cuba.' The resort of Varadero, seen at first hand, would give the lie to accusations of 'apartheid'. Yes, it was true that Varadero was beautiful and luxurious and denied to ordinary Cubans, said Almeida. But the Cubans had proved themselves a race more than capable of revolution. I supposed that he was speaking about 1959, though Cuba had a history of revolt: the island had eventually ejected the Spanish at the turn of the twentieth century, the last possession of Madrid to do so. If the Cuban people were smarting at the 'apartheid' of Varadero, surely they would rise up against the place – why not? demanded Almeida. It occurred to me that perhaps they were kept too busy looking for food, or else too listless from failing to find any, but I didn't want to be having this argument now. 'I don't know,' I said.

The reason, said Almeida, was that the Cuban people understood the necessity of the tourist income for their way of life, their economy. Tropicana, Almeida claimed, disproved the image of Cuba as a Communist fun-blackspot. We didn't get around to *Santería*, though his argument there might have been that this flourishing cult answered allegations of religious intolerance. Almeida had already admitted to being a follower himself so perhaps he was only expressing a personal enthusiasm. The reason that we failed to discuss religion was that we were interrupted by a middle-aged Briton with a pudding-bowl hair-cut. 'Did I hear you say you're from ITN?' he asked me. He introduced himself as Tom, and said that he did quite a lot of work for 'Channel 4 News'. I did a double-take. I'd never seen or heard of him before. Should I say something? Suppose I outed myself as a Channel 4 News-man and he said he'd never heard of *me*? It would be his word against mine. It might sow doubts about my own authenticity in the minds of Almeida and Ivette. Tom said he was doing something for RDF. 'Ah, German TV,' I said, and immediately thought better of it – didn't I mean ZDF? 'What's it about?' I asked, without giving Tom a chance to correct me.

'A breakthrough in the neurological industry,' he said. 'We're doing a special.'

'That sounds interesting. I'm looking at medicine myself,' I said, with a gesture which was meant to allude to the programme set out on various pieces of paper around the table. 'What's your particular angle?'

'Oh, well, I don't want to give the game away,' said Tom, only half joking and actually rocking back on his heels. Tom and I made a pretty picture of journalistic paranoia. I almost wished Señor de Armas could have been there to see it. The itinerant hack was terrified of showing himself up (as I had been a moment ago); terrified at the thought of losing his scoop, as Tom was; and yet loath to be alone, terrified of his own company – which was Tom now, inviting himself to my hotel for a beer. 'And then we might eat something?' he said, as though adding a clause to a contract between us, an unwritten compact in which we had tacitly agreed not to do anything to undermine each other's rickety credibility.

I had to leave my passport at the Press Centre while my accredit-ation was processed. It was a Friday and I thought it best not to be parted from it all weekend so I returned in the afternoon. I ran into Almeida: he welcomed me to Cuba again; again, he put himself at my disposal. The effect of his courtesy somehow wore thinner the more he displayed it. But he had good news for me. My press pass was ready. Perhaps this was another straw in the wind – the accreditation that had previously eluded me was ready on my first day back in Cuba.

One morning when the phone went first thing at the Inglaterra, and I picked it up with my eyes closed, expecting to hear 'Happy Birthday to You', a voice said, 'Steve? It's [pause] Tom here.' He said he'd called the hotel several times but I was 'never bloody there'. I laughed indulgently, liking the image of myself as a hack tirelessly out on the story. But I had to reproach Tom, pointing out that he had failed to keep our appointment for a drink. It seemed he had telephoned and asked for me and been put through to my empty room while I was sitting at the bar waiting for him. Tom said he was staying in Miramar. He had his own room. 'Ver's a table,' he said – there was a mittel-European inflection on his 't's, I now noticed – 'it's OK, but it's not really a work table.' I saw him frustratedly composing shooting schedules, call-sheets, at his wobbling occasional furniture. 'You have to lock the door by leaning through a grill. Ver lock is on the inside.' He was like one of those implausible German agents parachuted into Piccadilly during the war, able to converse pedantically about Lyons corner houses.

Tom and I bumped into one another from time to time around Havana. He had found a great restaurant, he told me at the Press Centre: he drafted a minutely detailed map in his notepad, illustrating where the restaurant was in relation to several more landmarks than were strictly necessary. One afternoon on La Rampa, he wondered if he might borrow a few dollars. He made a scrupulous note of where he should send the money. We got on well enough, but it was a slightly wary relationship, at least on my part. Perhaps there is an atavistic trace of the pirate in the roving journalist (public opinion surveys routinely bracket reporters with vagabonds of one sort or another, after all). Tom and I had both come to Cuba in search of booty. He might sketch me a chart, and I might briefly top up his war chest, but in the end I considered that it was every man-jack for himself.

3

Fidel's Bed

YOU COULD STILL SEE authentic American-style diners of the 1950s in Havana, but many had gone the way of the Cafetería Biltmore. It had red leather-topped stools in front of the long stainless steel counter, and behind the griddle, a *naïf* mural of surfside scenes: a man in low-slung bathing briefs; the landing of a monstrous marlin. A cook with a pink lump on his cheek – it was a burn but it looked like a quid of bubblegum which the cook had misplaced – said no when I asked for *café, frescos, cerveza*. All he had were *croquetas*, he said. They appeared to have been made to a recipe consisting chiefly of paper and didn't even detain the flies long.

Julietta and I had lunch at a place off La Rampa, the Cafetería Maraka. It had been stripped out and done up and air-conditioned, although the designers had retained the signature counter. We asked for ham and cheese sandwiches, which was as well since ham and cheese were the only sandwich-fillings you found in Cuba. The order came in leathery French bread. The Maraka had a display cabinet in which more sandwiches were stacked on shelves, like shoes. I was still getting re-acquainted with Cuban time and humidity. I drank a black coffee, ordered another, and looked for a lift or hit in a brace of my foxed Marlboro. But I felt far from revivified as I stepped into the soupy afternoon. The sappy laces I had threaded into my loafers in London now had the consistency of wood pulp. Julietta was helping me to look for a place to stay. We were going house-hunting in Havana. *House-hunting in Havana!* The very idea was preposterous. The houses seemed unattainably grand, for all that it was a shabby grandeur. In 1982, the United Nations had placed them on its World Heritage List. They were familiar from countless fashion spreads and liquor promos and perfume campaigns, and no matter what was in the foreground of the shoot, it was the ravaged pastel *casas* which unfailingly drew the eye. The *edificios* and tenements had stolen the scene from every model or piece of merchandise unfortunate enough to be cast opposite them. As I was leaving London, a toiletries house was promoting a cologne named after the Cuban capital. In magazine ads, a louche young man in pomaded hair was seen reclining on a balcony in a linen suit and co-respondent's shoes. Partly because of the way the photograph had been cropped, your eye was drawn to the shutters behind him and the diamond motif on the wall bordering them. Even when you attempted to concentrate on the louche man, whose cheeks were presumably tingling with the advertiser's product, you became involved with the doodle-pad swirls of the railings on the balcony in front of him.

Havana had been built around a knot of plazas in the sixteenth century. Each square had its own function or association. Armas was military; the Franciscan and Old Squares were commercial; the Cathedral Square was religious. The common reference was religious, too. The scheme of things became apparent at Easter when the plazas were revealed as stages of the cross. The last surviving crucifix was on the corner of Mercaderes, opposite an old bank, and Amargura del Buenviaje. Christians coming from San Francisco Church passed it in processions along Calle Amargura. The oldest municipal space, Plaza de Armas, was named after the castle in one corner of the ceiba-shaded square. It was the oldest fortress in the Americas. The Governor of Cuba had lived in the plaza in the days of Spanish rule. The layout of Havana accorded to the blueprint drawn up in Madrid for Spanish colonies in the New World: a main square with a government house and a church. The road immediately outside the Governor's residence was paved with wood to preserve the gubernatorial ears from the tiresome noise of carriage wheels on granite. Elsewhere in the old city, what was underfoot was St Miguel stone, named after the place where it was found in Cuba. Many of the houses were made out of 'sea stone': fossilised shells and sponges and bi-valves visibly leavened the building materials. Old Square was where General Fulgencio Batista, Cuba's last pre-revolutionary leader, had developed an underground car-park, in one of his few contributions to the architectural heritage of Havana. The Cubans were intending to dynamite it.

A typical *casa* of Habana Vieja , dating from the eighteenth century, was three storeys tall. A visitor of the period, provided that he was a caller of means, would have been made welcome in an airy vestibule. The rest of the ground-floor would have been given over to shops and warehouses, with perhaps a small restaurant. The visitor's horse would have been tethered within the whitewashed walls. A tiled mezzanine floor served as office-space and quarters for domestic slaves. Their owners lived upstairs, where they had their dining-rooms as well as their bedrooms. They could follow the life of the city – military parades, parties – from the detachment of their balconies.

In their own way, the *casas* of Havana were the last word in gracious living: they had the glamour of the crypt. Perhaps because they had achieved World Heritage status, it didn't seem fanciful to compare them to other wonders of the past, and to feel that taking a flat in Havana would be an act of *lèse-majesté* comparable to cultivating an allotment in the Hanging Gardens of Babylon. So, you trembled at the threshold of Havana because the buildings were devastating. But you also trembled because they were devastated. If they were as glamorous as crypts, they mouldered like them too. In a Habana Vieja street such as Teniente Rey, which commemorated an Irish mercenary who had served the Spanish Crown in Cuba, you might see scaffolding erected between two buildings, and scratch your head about which was keeping the other from falling over. It was not uncommon to find that a Havana entranceway disclosed missing tiles, metal struts exposed in a calcified staircase, the tang of urine. Fleapit billets weren't altogether unfamiliar, and I knew enough about the city not to expect too much in the way of amenities. But the kind of considerations you took for granted choosing accommodation somewhere like London became urgently germane in Havana. For example, it was a definite plus if a place had water; it was a definite plus if it was in one piece. You were keeping up with the Garcías if there were slightly fewer of you than there were of them: the *edificios* were oppressively overcrowded. And a regular supply of electricity was an almost nannying mod con. In Britain, you talked about slumming it when what you meant was sleeping under canvas in the New Forest or spending a week on a friend's sofa. It was no slight on my prospective neighbours in Havana to recognise that living with them was going to entail slumming it in a less jocose way.

Just as you had to accept that your basics were frills to a *habanero*, you realised, with something like relief, that it was useless to comb the city for the kind of features you looked for in property at home. There was no advantage in being handy for the shops since the shops had nothing in them, though it paid to be within walking-range of a dollar shop, a diplostore, if you thought you might require bread or milk or other luxuries. In London, you plotted the distances from a prospective address to the Tube or the bus-stops. But in Havana, public transport had been dramatically scaled down because of fuel shortages. When they could find them, citizens strapper-hung from the hot metal ceilings of buses which had been built in Eastern Europe to withstand sub-zero winters. The buses, known as *camellos*, were essentially prefabs which had been hooked up to the cabs of articulated lorries. The *camello* routes were not a concern to me, since I was happy to walk everywhere, and had a dollar in my pocket for a taxi when I grew weary. The ironic *habaneros* said it was another uncanny feature of Cuba that cabs never went where Cubans wanted to go: drivers always had pressing engagements in other directions when they were hailed by people with *pesos*. The fact that I had hard currency begged the question from Julietta of why I wasn't doing what other foreigners did, and staying in a hotel, or in the landscaped, thermostatically-temperate precincts of Miramar, the smarter part of greater Havana where the diplomats and businessmen and resident correspondents had their homes. The answer was that I feared a hotel would go through my cash without necessarily filling up my notebooks; Miramar struck me as remote and suburban. Of course, that wasn't the whole answer. There was another reason for staying in the slums, and it had to do with slumming in another sense, which is defined forgivingly by one dictionary as 'going about the slums through curiosity, to examine the condition of the inhabitants'. I simply assumed there would be more to say about a place that was nothing to write home about.

First I had to find my place. There were no classifieds in the back pages of *Granma*, the Communist Party daily, advertising this des res or that flatshare. But Julietta had asked around and found me a couple of apartments to look at. One was on Calle Industria, which was practically around the corner from the Inglaterra, in the elegant decrepitude of Centro, Central Havana. Julietta had heard of the apartment through her sister's boyfriend, whose family lived a few blocks away from it. It was on the second floor of a stew and it belonged to a black cabinet-maker, or at least he was the one who was asking $150 a week for it, winking at me and sweating and wiping his hands on his trousers. Property ownership was a complicated business in Havana. In 1959, the Revolution had recognised the rights of people to the houses they lived in. Formally, there had been so little movement in the city's housing market since then that the British slump of the 1990s was by comparison a hiccup while contracts were exchanged: it was illegal for Cubans to buy or sell property, I was told. In fact, though, there had been almost constant activity. Households might not have been able to sell up but they could swop, and the addition of new family members by birth or marriage was made possible, in the absence of new housing stock, by DIY partitions and extensions. I liked the cabinet-maker's neighbourhood, and I didn't mind the saws and nails and wooden offcuts lying about his place, but the front room, which overlooked the street, did so only by means of a narrow window raised barely eighteen inches off the floor. You would have to lie on your stomach to watch the world go by. The apartment was a conversion – perhaps the cabinet-maker had done the job himself, to give himself a workshop. I found myself complaining that I wanted a room with a view, like a guest at a British seaside B&B.

Another apartment we looked at was on 25th and O, where old, dilapidated Centro gave way to modern, dilapidated Vedado. Julietta pointed out the *edificio*. There were balconies with balustrades, and beneath the balconies, what looked like random blotches of black paint from an aerosol can, as though a neighbourhood graffiti artist had been using the building as his palette. The blackness was streaks of damp. In fact, Julietta had meant the shorter *edificio* next door. It was an eight-storey pile of crumbling concrete, with concrete-and-iron balconies, and it was similarly autographed by the damp-tagger. The place was difficult to date. It wasn't Spanish colonial and it hadn't been put up in the post-1959 era of Comecon either, notwithstanding the vision of drab utility which it presented. It had probably gone up in the thirties or forties, during what was effectively the American protectorate of Cuba. An orange sign over a side door depicted Abel Santamaria, a martyr of the failed attack on the Moncada Barracks in 1953, and a small bronze plaque said that the block was a national monument. I thought that it must have figured in Cuba's revolutionary history because, architecturally speaking, it made few claims on posterity. On the ground floor was the Bookshop of the Centenary of the Apostle: it had been named in honour of Cuba's great patriot, José Martí, sometimes referred to as the Apostle, and it claimed to specialise in 'Marxist classics'. Inside, the *edificio* was dark. There was an ammoniacal reek and a cockroach lying on its back on the stairs. On the first-floor landing was a broken fusebox, and beside it a blackened breeze-block. There was some evidence that small fires had been laid inside the breeze-block – was it, I wondered, a shrine to *Santería* spirits who watched over the building?

There were metal grids in front of several doors. These barriers had romantic antecedents in Cuba. They went back to the 'courting grilles', dumb chaperones which interposed themselves tantalisingly between daughters of the house and gentlemen callers: this type of amatory window-shopping had come over with the Spanish. However, the spars and girders guarding these thresholds appeared to have been welded into place with less welcome visitors in mind. Number 402, directly opposite a particularly impregnable-looking portcullis, was the apartment we had come to view. We were greeted by a handsome black man in his twenties. Nico was a friend of Julietta's from university. He showed us into a bright, airy sitting-room. An open door gave onto a tiled balcony. On the other side of the room, a woman with hennaed hair and a slight moustache was bracketed at a dining-table by a pair of twins. 'My mother,' said Nico, 'Hilda.'

'And your brothers?' I suggested. No; the boys were entirely unrelated, it seemed, but Nico, Hilda, and the anonymous twins enjoyed the idea disproportionately. Hilda and Julietta hugged and kissed each other.

Three china ducks were taking flight up a wall. On a wooden table was a television set under a shawl, like the cage of a talkative bird. There was an old upright General Electric refrigerator as big as a wardrobe. A small, dark kitchen led off from the sitting-room. There was a gas cooker and a sink, and beneath it, rags screening a stash of old bottles and canisters containing a pungent fuel which might have been paraffin. I tried a tap in the sink and it ran water: as I say, in Havana that wasn't as workaday as it sounds. It was commonplace to see people hauling buckets up to the balconies of *casas* from the street or queueing at standpipes. Indeed, a line had formed across the street from Hilda's *edificio* where a standpipe had been put up on the edge of a patch of wasteland. Hilda said there was water in the building from half past seven in the morning until eleven, and again from early evening. She talked in a gabble, and I was grateful that Julietta was with me. Hilda was like one of the characters the Cuban novelist G. Cabrera Infante describes in his novel *Infante's Inferno*: 'There was something of the crow, magpie or parrot in her strong Havana accent.' There was no problem with power cuts, said Hilda, because the *edificio* was on the same electricity circuit as the Habana Libre, in Vedado proper. You could just make out the hotel from the balcony. I noticed that Hilda's left eye was a smoky blue because of a cataract.

I liked Hilda and Nico and I liked the apartment. It was as well cared for as the *edificio* was run down. It had a telephone and a shower, which I negligently assumed was the same thing as saying that I could keep in touch with people there, and keep clean; I assumed it was the same thing as saying that it had a *working* telephone and a *working* shower. The apartment was close to useful places like the Press Centre and government buildings. But the next street along was Calle Infanta, a thoroughfare named after the daughter of a king of Spain, and one which bore the signs of Havana's Spanish past. From the balcony, I could see the green copper coronet on top of the statue of Carmen, whose church dominated Infanta. And the Malecón and the sea were only a few hundred yards away.

We agreed that I would pay Hilda $100 a week in rent; she would clean, do my laundry, and cook the odd meal for me. Looked at one way, I could have got away with less. Looked at another way, it wasn't much, but at least I would be giving them hard currency. Hilda said that she and Nico would stay with friends in another apartment in the *edificio*. I said, 'You must stay here.'

'But you are paying for the apartment,' said Hilda. 'It is yours.'

I felt guilty. I felt as though I was evicting them. They would both still come and go as they pleased, and stay in the apartment whenever I was away. Julietta said they had come to the same arrangement before, with another foreigner. In due course, as it happened, they moved back in full-time. I salved my conscience with the thought of the foreign currency that I would be giving them. It seemed that I put up little resistance to the corrupting influence of Cuba's black economy. You saw this corruption plainly in the case of the teenage *jiniteras*, the jockeys or prostitutes, who solicited on the Malecón and the Prado, and the Western men who squired them. But it was insidiously present in every transaction that took place between Cubans and foreigners, and the sign of it was the sense of almost seigneurial power that having dollars conferred on the stranger.

On my first day in the apartment, I came by early from the Inglaterra to drop off my things, and I asked Hilda if she would mind cooking dinner for me. I wasn't sure of my plans but I liked the idea of not being alone on my first evening at 25 y O. 'What do you want to eat?' she said. Having dined in the hotel on what tasted like salt-barrel chicken and pork, leftovers of Soviet cuisine, I felt like fish. Nico was deputed to go out and look for some. 'What else do you want?' asked Hilda. She was doing my washing. A dishcloth was secured over her cleavage with a pair of clothes pegs, to keep her blouse dry while she pounded my clothes in a battered crucible. I would like rice and vegetables, I said, perhaps some bread. Hilda said I should give Nico dollars for the food. I had a $5 note, which was too small, she said. I didn't have anything else apart from a $50 bill. Nico said he would bring me the change, so I gave him the $50.

When he came back from shopping in the late morning, his T-shirt was blotted with perspiration. He presented me with a copy of his accounts. It appeared that I had been charged for tomato juice, to the tune of $6.70, which struck me as somewhat discordant; bread and vegetables were a dollar each; and the fish was a whopping $14.20. Julietta was visiting, and my surprise must have shown: fish was very expensive in Cuba, she told me. It was on the ration, she said, apparently contradicting herself – but only small fish: with thumb and forefinger, she described the dimensions of plankton.

Hardly had my key turned in the lock that evening when Hilda took my elbow. The fish was almost ready, I must bathe at once. Reluctantly, I put the bottled beers I'd bought from a dollar shop into the refrigerator and collected my towel. Nico was on the balcony, talking to a pretty, dark-haired girl. When I opened up the shower tap, no water emerged. I tried the lower tap, the one which was apparently meant to fill the bath, in case I had misunderstood Hilda, but that was dry too. I wrapped the towel around me (surprised that what had been a cotton bathroom sundry in London had transformed itself, in the humidity of a Havana summer, into a furry loincloth, even before it had been used), and reported the outbreak of dryness to Hilda. The look on her face suggested that I was a poor *extranjero* who couldn't even run a shower by himself. But when she tried the taps, she was forced to concede that the water had stopped. 'The pump was running at six.' Hilda looked embarrassed. She kept an old oil barrel full of water in a corner of the bathroom. There was a polythene sheet draped over it to keep the water clean; a shadow marked the spot where the sheet touched the water. Hilda filled a bucket from the barrel and heaved it into the bathtub together with a little red plastic scoop.

I washed myself from the bucket. My liquid soap dispenser, which didn't travel well judging by the flight from London, in the course of which it had evacuated itself into my rucksack, was now as unyielding as the taps. And then all at once I was covered in proud ejaculations of scented goo, and struggling to rinse it off with the shallow scoops I was extracting from the bucket. The water was cold: as sweaty as I was, I flinched at it. But it was the only way to get rid of the soap. I tipped the bucket over my head.

The water supply hadn't stayed on as long as usual, Hilda said as she dished up. 'It all depends on the janitor. If he's going out he only puts the pump on once a day.' Or perhaps the pump had run out of fuel, or had broken. If so, there wouldn't be any water in the morning either. The telephone had been off all day, added Nico: he drew a line across his throat. The men were here to fix it, but like everyone else who worked for the government, they were lazy, he said. 'I hope they will fix it today. Maybe if I offer them some dollars …' The phone worked sometimes and at other times it didn't, I found out: you never knew which it was going to be. The Cubans made sardonic cracks about their telephone system: when a woman told a man to call her, she was giving him the brush-off, so unlikely was it that he would ever get through to her by phone. Listening at the earpiece of Hilda's telephone was like using a stethoscope: you monitored the phone's sickly pulse. When you made a call, you heard the dials clicking over at the exchange as heavily as tumblers on a safe.

Dinner that first night was delightful: a herby, fleshy swordfish. I was unable to finish my helping. There was more in the icebox, said Hilda. I opened the icebox door: it was a haunch – a side – of fish! No wonder it had cost so much. Hilda left that evening with a saddle of swordfish, and Julietta, who had invited me to her home for dinner in a few nights' time, took away a cut of the same carcass, which she said her mother would prepare.

The gusto of my neighbours posed the greatest threat to a night's sleep. Surrounded by their television sets and their *salsa* and their animated conversation, you felt that staying in the *edificio* would be like overnighting on the bleachers at Malaga airport: the tannoy effect of television speakers, all pumping out Spanish; and the blare of radios and hi-fi's, like holiday-makers' cassette-players. The doorbell went late at night. By the time I'd answered it, the corridor was empty. The bell rang again an hour later. By now, I'd noticed a spy-hole in the door: I was in time to view a woman's figure retreating down the landing. The fish-eye effect distorted her figure, no doubt, but I was still left feeling regretful that I hadn't made it to my door before she had left it. I supposed that she was a friend of Nico. He seemed to do well for attractive company. The dark-haired beauty I had seen on the balcony with him earlier that evening apparently enjoyed a reputation as a singer in most of Latin America. I would be celebrating my birthday in the morning and Nico had asked me, 'Would you like her to sing "Happy Birthday" for you tomorrow?' It was an inviting prospect after the reveille I was used to at the Hotel Inglaterra. I'm going to enjoy living here, I thought.

I woke before my alarm went off. Another way of looking at it was that I *slept* before my alarm went off, perhaps for several minutes. For the most part, the night had rung with televisions at the limits of their volume specifications, strangled dogs, model bad children, insomniac carpentry. And I got up to find that Hilda had been right; the taps were still dry. I shaved in cold water from the oil barrel. The next *edificio* was so close to Hilda's that I found myself looking directly into the eyes of the people who lived there. Their heads were the same size as mine; perspective had no need to make them to scale. Through the broken shutters of the nearest window, a man was putting on his flip-flops. It was still dark in the next bedroom along, where a boy was lying face down on a mattress, the sheet pulled down, exposing his back. Hilda didn't care for her immediate neighbours at the next *edificio*. They fought, she told me. She let herself in at about eight o'clock, chattering about butter – '*Mantequilla! Mantequilla!*' – and entered the bathroom with a cluck of distaste. Leaving the WC as I would have wished to find it without the use of a flush had felt, in what was after all a stranger's house, like trying to dispose of evidence. There seemed to be a critical volume of water for a simulated or manual flush, and it was some days before I learnt to calibrate the bucket-loads for this purpose. Until just the right volume had been introduced into the bowl, the water level simply continued to rise – well, no, *not* simply; *complicatedly*, with potentially alarming *complications*. Then suddenly the saints of the

sewerage system were appeased and the grimly brimming swamp was
Moulinexed into a whorl, a chute, of water, which corkscrewed out of
sight.

Outside the *edificio*, the *camellos* dragged themselves up the hill in
low gear. Or they rumbled on the spot at the corner of the street,
where a set of traffic-lights was suspended from lampposts in a web of
cables. In the absence of entry-phones and door-buzzers, people yelled
up from the street to attract the attention of friends living in the
apartamentos. The standpipe on the far side of the tip dribbled onto a
concrete slab when no-one was filling a bucket from it. The pipe was
overlooked by a dun-coloured apartment block where artisans sat on
their balconies, whittling geegaws or souvenirs which it was impossible
to imagine anyone purchasing. A severe-looking bearded man had the
balcony facing Hilda's. The craftsman occupying the crossword square
down-two and three-right from his was bare-chested, and plate-
stacker thin. He looked as gaunt as Gandhi, in fact, but seemed to go
about his work with a light heart.

Hilda had lived in the apartment for a year. She had moved a lot,
she said, because of problems with the electricity supply in Havana. 'I
don't know if I'll stay very long. I'm like a gypsy.' Everybody minded
their own business in the block, but there wasn't complete privacy. The
family in the adjacent flat – in the next building, the ones I had seen
when I was shaving – were a nuisance, according to Hilda. I could
vouch for their noise but I liked the women of the house, who chatted
to me when we found ourselves watching the world go by from our
respective balconies, in the Havana custom. Sylvia, a pretty 23-year-
old whose husband was away in the army, told me that there were five
adults in their *apartamento*, and four children. But an infinite variety of
women seemed to rotate on and off the balcony: co-eds in afros; pert
mulatas in shorts; mothers in curlers. Nico told me that their *casa* was
shared by five families, who had only one room each – it served as
kitchen and *habitación*, bedroom – and the use of a single bathroom
between them.

Hilda owned number 402. She said, 'Before the Revolution, we
were paying rent to the owners of the building where we lived. When
the Revolution began, they gave houses to the people who were living

in them.' Hilda was in her thirties in 1959, married to Nico's father. He was managing his own small business. He died of a heart attack in 1984. Hilda lived on a pension of 67 Cuban pesos a month: the black-market exchange rate was 35 pesos to the dollar. Nico wasn't working, though he had recently held down jobs as a photographer and a roadie for a salsa band. Hilda and Nico had to find 9 pesos for electricity every month; 11.45 for the telephone; 3 for gas; 2.40 for water. There was also a kind of service charge of 1 peso a month on the *edificio*. Everyone chipped in when the pump broke down.

The hardships of Cuba's 'special period' were offset by the *bodegas*, the ration shops. There was one outside Hilda's place, on the corner by the traffic-lights. There always seemed to be a queue, mainly of elderly people, outside it waiting for it to open, or for the number of customers inside to dwindle so that they could take their place. Cubans were entitled to a daily bun. There were also four pounds of rice a month on the ration, and ten ounces of red, green and black beans respectively. The allowance of salt was three to four ounces; of coffee, a four-ounce packet per person twice a month. Proteins included a pound of fish and seven eggs a month. There was milk for children and pregnant women. The children were given a cereal mix, 'Cerelac'. What people received from the ration was very little, said Hilda as she brewed coffee. 'At the beginning of the month, or when the food comes, people queue for it because sometimes there are thefts. If the food is stolen, they won't replace it.' Nor was the ration free. Eggs cost 10 Cuban cents each, for example; fish was 90 cents. The ration provided for subsidised cigarettes and matches, and bars of soap, when they were available. 'Sometimes there are months when you don't see soap,' said Hilda wistfully. From time to time, there were savoury biscuits and sweets for the children. There was cooking oil 'when it comes'.

'You're supposed to have a ration book for clothes and shoes. But it's only useful for baby things and for toys. Men get razors sometimes. There are meant to be sanitary pads but they hardly ever turn up. Women are crazy about it because they have to use pieces of cloth instead.' The *bodegas* seldom stocked shampoo, and never toilet paper. 'But *Granma* is good and strong,' laughed Hilda. 'Cubans say *Granma araña*, *Granma* is scratchy.' There was one bottle of rum per household per month, for 20 pesos. The state bestowed its secular blessing on marriage by giving newlyweds a cake, three boxes of beer, and a ration for clothes and shoes. When Hilda's sister got married, the Revolution gave towels.

Hilda said, 'I remember how things were before the Revolution and it was a period of tensions, of very severe measures. I'm glad that there haven't been any assassinations or bombings since 1959. On the other hand, I've seen some changes that are difficult to accept, changes in some people's behaviour in the government, which is not the way Fidel told the people it would be. I'm talking about people who don't have the principles that they should have.' Hilda placed her faith in an improvised creed of her own devising. She was baptised a Catholic and went to church every week, although she didn't take the host – 'I don't practise religion,' was how she put it. She kept a glass of water in the bathroom for the refreshment of her late husband's shade.

Hilda's bathroom cabinet wasn't the only venerated feature of the building. A pamphlet entitled *Abel Santamaria*, by Ricardo Villares – 'a biographical sketch of the second in command of the assault on the Moncada Barracks. The most generous, beloved and courageous of our youth' – listed Abel's address at the time he first met Fidel: 'the apartment was on 25th Street between O Street and Infanta Street'. In other words, it was my building – that explained the bronze plaque. The pamphlet said that the *edificio* had been built by the Electrical Workers' Pension Fund. It was 'one more in the attractive festival of real estate ... in the metropolitan area looking on to the drink bars, gaming the [*sic*] houses, and sex paradises'.

In the pamphlet, Haydee Santamaria, Abel's sister, who had shared the flat, recalled Fidel's first visit: 'Abel brought him up one day. I remember I had just cleaned up and he was walking around dropping ash on the floor. I thought to myself: he's going to muck up the whole place, this fellow. When he went away, I asked Abel: "Who was that chap you brought, Abel?" and he began talking to me about Fidel ...'

Other things went on chez Abel besides social calls and careless cigar smoking, however. It was the office of an underground propaganda-sheet, *El Acusador*, 'which made insulting attacks on

General Batista'. Fidel, a contributor, showed that he meant business
by installing his desk in the flat.

I got to know 'the attractive festival of real estate' to which my
edificio had been such a prestigious addition. I walked up Infanta, away
from El Malecón, taking care to avoid what Cubans call the fool side
of the street – the one on which there is less shade. A dog was stretched
out on a front step with its front paws pointing directly ahead of it, as
if it was dreaming that it was diving. A man was sitting on a kerbstone
with a tray on his lap, giving his full attention to a tiny flywheel which
might have been a part of an old cigarette-lighter. Another man, with
his shirt off, was cutting the grass which bordered a memorial obelisk.
His mower, like the lighter, was driven by old wheels. I passed what
seemed to be the entrance to a monastery. A gaunt, grey-haired
Franciscan monk was talking to a man behind a pair of glass doors.
The great wooden doors of the Carmen church, further along, were
locked. There were drying, evil-reeking pools of wetness on the marble
step. A lank-haired beggar sat with coinage in his palm. Medievally, a
staff was at his side. He appealed to me to give him '*dineros*', and when
I shook my head, he moved as if to rise up and follow me until he got
his due. I walked to the side of the church, to Calle Neptuno, to see if
there was another entrance. All I found was a boy firing a homemade
catapult. I decided that the friar I had seen might be able to help me
enter the church. '*Habla usted inglés, Padre?*' I asked him.

'A very little,' said the friar in a funny sing-song voice. He retreated
into an office and returned with a postcard showing a view of the
church from the street. I thought that this was as close as visitors could
come, now, to admiring the building – relations between church and
state had been uneasy since the Revolution: the official position was
that the regime never penalised anyone for a religious conviction, but I
had read about expelled priests, careers blighted by religious
attendance. However, the friar asked me to follow him.

The church was airless. A fanlight in the dome appeared to be the
only source of light. There was the granite face of a great neglected
altar; the Christ of Nazareth in blue; a single lit candle in front of the
Virgin; Spanish tiles to decorate a pillar. I thought that what saved
Carmen from being oppressive, in its gloom and opulence, was the

neglect in which it languished. When I said goodbye to the friar, he asked me not for money, as I might have expected, but vitamins.

I went in search of 'the drink bars, gaming the houses, and sex paradises' promised by Villares' pamphlet. The legitimate sector of the catering trade (all proceeds going directly to the government) was represented by restaurants like El Conejito (The Little Rabbit), a refrigerated barn inexplicably done out in a Tudor motif. There was a massive Welsh dresser against one wall. The barman stood in the neon glow of a baronial fireplace, in which no fire would ever be set. Bottles of drink were arranged on a trestle-table in front of him like prizes in a tombola. The Merrie Englande theme did not extend to the waiters' uniforms, which comprised gingham waistcoats and Doc Holliday ties. The stout mestizo who waited on my table had a frilled shirt front and a denture-wearer's grimace. The other waiter was more genial. He had a napkin folded over his forearm, and looked on in a moved way as the house trio picked out 'Guantanamera'. El Conejito had immaculately laid-out tables and, incongruously, one of those arcade games in which you use a crane to liberate a toy animal. The barman, waiters and musicians were drawn to the crane game, the brightest thing in the room.

The rabbit, the speciality of the house, was surprisingly good: salty but gamey. The beer was so chilled that it wouldn't come out of the bottle. The Indian-looking waiter tonged more ice into my glass of water, which was already a floe of cubes. It was like a lateral-thinking puzzle: I wasn't touching the water, preferring beer; the waiter was professionally obliged to keep the water icy; but the ice was melting, topping up the water level. The waiter's poser was whether to let the temperature of my water rise, or risk overflowing my glass onto the table. Either way, he would be falling down on the job.

The best places to eat and drink were the *paladares*, the private restaurants. Familes set out tables and chairs in a backroom, put on a bootlegged pop cassette and some pork escalopes, and made a few dollars for themselves. The *paladares* were still illegal, although they were later tolerated – and taxed – under reforms opening up self-employment. Julietta and I went to El Colonial, which was in an *edificio* around the corner from mine. At the end of a corridor on the third floor, I pressed a buzzer and a panel slid back in the door. It was like being admitted to a speakeasy. We went through a lounge to a room dimly lit by red bulbs. There were five rude wooden tables, like school desks. Our only fellow patrons were a garrulous engineering student from Honduras – 'Is she your girlfren? I have three girlfrens in Cuba! I also study in Japan' – and his companion. El Colonial sold more than food. In an alcove was a glass display case containing a single leather shoe, a tin of polish, and an indeterminate aerosol can. A set of shelves held an empty phial of aftershave, bottles of shampoo and 'Khasana' deodorant. The place seemed to double – or even treble – as a shoeshine parlour and beautician's.

The Revolution had closed the gaming houses; it was some time before I found my way to my first illegal cock-fight, where owners rubbed their birds down with rum like seconds massaging prize-fighters, and the spurs were made of talons shaped into lethal points over a naked flame. As for what pamphlet-writer Ricardo Villares called 'sex paradises', Nico was looking into that for me. The government maintained that all the brothels had been closed down after 1959. But a friend of Nico's had talked of going to one recently. It was in Miramar. You paid $20, watched a show, drank some rum and chose a girl. Pressed for an update, Nico said, 'The news is sad.' The friend who had bragged about the place was out of town. I would have to be patient. If I did but know it, I was looking out onto sex paradises from the balcony at 25 y O, just as the pamphlet had said. There was the Cabaret Las Vegas at the end of the street, where the girls danced to salsa till dawn, and an *edificio* a block or two away where a woman called Olga was madam to beautiful prostitutes.

One of the difficulties of writing anything approximating to a travel book about Cuba was that it was hardly *possible* to travel in Cuba. Trains were slow and haphazard, buses irregular. When I needed a set of wheels, I sometimes flagged down a Creole limo, an ingenious Cuban invention. It was effectively a stretch Lada or Zil, created by welding two such East European saloons together. The cars generally had many miles on the clock before they were spliced into one, and were not entirely reliable. Hermes, a fat man with *Santería* bangles on his wrists, drove a bright yellow Creole limo. It got a flat tyre before we had covered a hundred yards in it. Another driver came to our rescue, lending us a tyre so that we could get to the nearest *ponchera*, or ad hoc tyre-bar. When the puncture was repaired, Hermes looked for the taxi-driver who had lent him the spare, in order to return it. I sat and waited for him. From time to time, in the tree-dappled sunlight of Vedado, I would see him waddling hotly between the houses, carrying the tyre in a fireman's lift.

Nico persuaded me to give some work to a friend of his called Ramon, who claimed to have experience of driving a taxi. Unfortunately, Ramon revealed little of this to me. It didn't help that his gutted-looking Lada handled so poorly. It – or perhaps Ramon – screwed violently to the left out of second. The horn would sound for no clear reason, and when you were least expecting it. While Ramon was executing an illegal three-point turn under the disbelieving eyes of the police in a loading bay off La Rampa, the horn locked on. Ramon had to lift up the inlay in the middle of his steering wheel and tighten a nut with a screwdriver before he could shut the noise off. He didn't seem to be a natural taxi-driver: he had very little idea of where any-where was; he demonstrated no sense of purpose about getting there (spending his time peering down side streets, apparently on the off-chance of spotting his friends); and he parked without a thought for how his positioning might leave his passengers. Reading that back, he sounds like a *model* cabbie, in fact, and I can see that it's a crying shame that he isn't in London, doing the Knowledge. Without a great deal of regret on my part, I let him go.

Marooned, I was thinking of walking to the corner of La Rampa in search of a tourist cab when a man leant across from the driving seat of his Lada and hissed, 'Taxi?' He told me his name was Nestor. I said I was a '*periodista inglés*'. 'I better be careful what I say,' said Nestor, who was short and looked like the American film actor Cliff Robertson. 'You aren't going to believe what I do for a job,' he said, and I briefly nursed the hope that he was a member of Fidel's domestic staff. 'I am a lawyer. But it's better for me to drive a car.' The journalistic standby of interviewing your cabbie was more defensible in Cuba than in other countries, because there was a good chance that he wasn't a cabbie at all.

Nestor said there were many problems in Cuba – I heard this so often that it took on the ring of a mantra, which wasn't perhaps so wide of the mark: the state-licensed media similarly repeated that the country faced *problemas*. I asked Nestor why there were so many. 'Partly, it is some people in Miami, they want Cuba to fail. Also people here. We need changes and I cannot understand why the changes are so slow. But the government says, "We go slow in order to hurry."'

The temperature had dropped and there was a freshening breeze, prelude to a storm. I had heard the first, distant boom of it outside Hilda's *edificio* and now Nestor and I were driving in the direction of a flash of lightning. He tried to interest me in an apartment for rent. It was in Miramar. 'Water-cooled,' said Nestor, and for a moment I thought he was talking about an air-conditioning system, but then he said 'water hot', and I realised that hot and cold running water was something to get excited about in Cuba – as it admittedly was in Britain until comparatively recently.

I showed Julietta the pamphlet by Villares on Abel Santamaria and Fidel, my predecessors as tenants of 25 y O. She said, 'You can see the apartment. It's number 603, two floors up. It's a museum now.'

I tracked down the keys to Abel's old place. They were in the care of several middle-aged ladies, whom I found sitting in the adjacent flat. They didn't get a lot of visitors, they told me. One of them opened up the museum for a dollar and let me wander around. Fidel's desk was still there (*buró de trabajo de Fidel Castro*). There was a sofa, and Abel's refrigerator, fuelled by kerosene, and, in a wooden cupboard over the sink, an incomplete china dinner-service: *piezas de la vajilla de Haydee Santamaria utilizada en el apartamento*, according to a small typed notice. I bounced on the double bed which Fidel had slept in (*cama de Abel Santamaria utilizada tambien por Haydee. En ella descanso en varias ocasiónes Fidel Castro*). It felt unsprung. I lay back on the off-cream coverlet and stared at the eau-de-Nil walls, the mottled mirror of a low dressing-table, the matching bedside-tables. It was very unshowy, not at all like the trappings of Cuba's Spanish rulers in Plaza de Armas. Having said that, Fidel's disavowal of a personality cult was hard to

accept when you saw that his most prosaic relics – the plate he had
dined off; the bed in which he had slept – were among the treasures of
the Revolution. There was a curiosity-value to them – I had been keen
to see them, after all – and perhaps a certain fugitive valency, the ghost
of a charge that they carried as Fidel's ex-effects. How could I deny the
force attaching to familiars when I was too superstitious to use the
bombastic piece of junk I had taken from Ceauşescu's hunting-lodge
for its intended purpose of hanging clothes? As befits a land of
miracles, Cuba was the home of resonant keepsakes, a place where
Norman Lewis was shown a tuft of Catherine the Great's pubic hair
pressed between the leaves of a scrapbook. The Cuban faith, *Santería*,
I presently discovered, was a bran-tub of sinister jumble. As I left
Fidel's old apartment, I saw that a fragment of the original upholstery
of his sofa had been mounted behind glass, like a scrap of a saint's
garment.

4

The Cult
of the Saints

JULIETTA'S FATHER WAS A FRIEND of a *babalao*, a *Santería* priest. Roberto agreed to use his influence with the *babalao* to see if he could get me into a *Santería* ritual. One Saturday evening, I came in to find a note from Julietta telling me to call her urgently. On the telephone, she said, 'We are very lucky, there's a *Santería fiesta* tonight.' We had been 'highly recommended' to the people who were giving the party. Julietta said the *babalao* had given her father a warning to be passed on to me. She said, 'There are a couple of things he says you must know. One, no pictures. You understand? Don't even bring your camera. The other thing is, don't wear black.'

Despite myself, I laughed.

'It's not funny,' said Julietta.

'Why can't I wear black?'

'It's not good to wear black. This is what the *babalao* told my father. When these people are in a trance and they see someone in black they will see it as a sign of the Devil.'

'Well, I've got a pair of white trousers—'

'Don't wear all white, either. I'm going to wear a mixture. I shall wear a brown skirt.'

It seemed that there was also a third thing. Although the party had begun at around four that afternoon, it would only just be getting going by the time we arrived. There would be plenty of food. 'But you should eat before we go,' said Julietta. 'There's something wrong with the food.'

'Wrong?'

'It's poisoned. Well, not quite poisoned, but it will contain aphrodisiacs, things like this, to help put the people in a trance.'

I changed into a grey T-shirt, white trousers, desert boots. When Roberto and Julietta picked me up, I asked them if they thought I could get away with a black belt. Like the voodoo of Haiti, *Santería*, the cult of the saints, is a profane marriage of the animism and ancestor worship brought to the Caribbean by slaves, and the Roman Catholicism imported by Europeans. But unlike voodoo, *Santería* was something I had never heard of outside Cuba, even though as many as 75 per cent of Cubans are to a greater or lesser extent believers – an astonishing proportion. You couldn't know much about Cuba without knowing something about *Santería*, I felt. There were worshippers among people of all shades, but Cubans said the most ardent tended to be the ones with the darkest skins. In Oriente, the province on the island's eastern coast, you saw *Santería* dolls by the roadside. Followers revere dozens of gods and goddesses, sometimes called *orishas*, who are the doppelgangers of saints in the Catholic pantheon. St Anthony, for example, has an alter ego known as Eleggua. St Francis's double is called Orula. St Lazarus's is Babalu-Aye. Saints' days are kept as faithfully as they are in the Catholic calendar, and celebrated with *fiestas* at which dancers re-enact the lives of the *orishas* to the hammering beat of drums. However, the *orishas* are not immortal. They live on fresh blood and depend on their human acolytes to procure it for them.

Santería has its own pop-eyed perspective on the old, old story. God was Olofin, the great architect, sometimes known as Olodumare. Christ's job was to finish Creation. He was effectively God's foreman. He took a wife, Odudia, who was the goddess of the underworld and, for some reason, a stern taker of the pledge. The history of Afro-Cuban religion isn't all so winsome. Some followers belong to small sects comparable to masonic lodges, complete with their own secret handshakes. They practise *brujería*, or black magic. Some groups were like mutual-preservation societies, mafias. As late as the turn of the twentieth century, initiation rites required would-be followers to kill the first passer-by they came across. Because of an official black spot on all religions which lasted until the 1990s, adherents used to worship covertly. Now religious repression had eased, and the Revolution even tolerated a *Santería* shop on the foreigners-only sunspot of Cayo Largo. As to my own religious beliefs, you could say that I was a Christian, though not a confirmed one – I had walked out of my confirmation class at church. An *un*confirmed Christian was what I was. The longer I had gone without being confirmed, however, the more I thought about becoming confirmed: in something – I wasn't sure what. All I could say for certain was that I was no longer as confirmed as I had been in being unconfirmed.

We went to the *fiesta* in Roberto's Lada. He turned onto the Malecón. An electric storm was X-raying the horizon. While Roberto concentrated on the road, Julietta turned to me and asked for money for petrol. Her father had been entitled to 75 litres of fuel a month back in 1990 but the last refill he was allowed had been three months ago, and that was only 25 litres.

Refuelled, we drove on to the house where the party was being held in Vedado, on East and 21st. The place where Fidel Castro first lived in Havana, before he moved into my *edificio*, was just around the corner. The street lighting wasn't working, and the branches of the trees hung low over the pavement. Perhaps 250 people were at the *fiesta*, which was taking place on the roof. There was a covered outbuilding – a shack – in one corner, and everyone was drinking and there were tables of food.

The house was an *ile ocha* in the language of the Yoruba people of East Africa: a house of the *orishas*. In Spanish, it was a *casa templo*, a place where worshippers kept a shrine to the saints. The Spanish had tried to eliminate the Yoruba faith. They insisted that all slaves were baptised as Roman Catholics as a condition of their entry into the West Indies. Catholic Cuba in turn was prepared to defend their rights to marriage and personal safety. It also recognised the rights of freed slaves to hold property. Some cross-fertilisation beween Rome and Nigeria took place on the plantations in the eighteenth century, when 'sugar priests', poor Catholic chaplains from Spain and the United States, ministered to some of the 700,000 or so slaves shipped over from East Africa. At the same time, the domestic servants of the colonial planters passed on something of their religious lore to the mistresses and children of the planters' houses. But the flame was kept alight – or rather the *orishas* were kept watered with blood – by the *cimarrones*, the runaway slaves. The Cuban Office for the Capture of Maroons reported thousands of them between 1795 and 1846. Like Castro's guerrillas in the Sierra Maestra, the *cimaronnes* had lived in fugitive communities, known as *palenques*. The emancipation of the slaves encouraged the drift of the *cimarrones*, the custodians of the Afro-Cuban faith, into the towns and cities. The fortified *palenques* were succeeded by peaceable mutual aid societies called *cabildos*. The Catholic Church encouraged the *cabildos*, as a means of social control. The faith of the *cabildos* became known as *Santería*, because devotions to the *orishas* were performed beneath the images of Catholic saints.

Julietta was saying, 'All *fiestas* are in honour of saints. This one is dedicated to Babalu-Aye, St Lazarus. You know, he was raised from the dead.' I had to bend close to her to hear what she was saying because of the crush of people and because drumming had started up in the outbuilding. Juiletta said, 'They are calling the dead with *Ija*, the mother drum.' The outbuilding was the size of a sitting-room, but as Roberto, Julietta and I worked our way through the crowd, I wondered if there would be enough space for us. Inside, it was suffocatingly hot. The shack smelled of sweat and the sweetmeats which were laid out on an altar in one corner. There were dishes of coconut and pineapple and strips of meat; a bowl of water sprinkled with petals; several yams as thick as the trunks of baobab trees; and dolls representing the saints, including a Christ-doll in a gold foil cloak. Hanging from the clapboard ceiling were halved coconuts from which coxcombs of feathers protruded. There were three drummers – the *Ija* was accompanied by the 'children drums', *Okonkolo* and *Itotele*. The beat grew louder. A fat black man was urging the women near him to dance. Beside him was a paler man who was wearing a waistcoat over a skinny torso.

A woman with chequered teeth handed me a glass. I remembered Julietta's warning about Mickey Finns – about aphrodisiacs and not quite poisons – but I had the impression from the way the woman was looking at me that she wasn't going to move on until I had accepted the drink. I assumed it was rum but it didn't taste like rum, not even the Cuban hootch, *chispa de tren*, train sparks, or the trachea-shredding stuff they got on the ration in Havana. This was sweet but with a sour aftertaste. Later, I discovered that it was a confection of toasted corn, bitter orange and honey. It had been spiked with the blood of animals which had been slaughtered in the house: a ram and a goat had had their throats cut, and the blood had been allowed to pour, and then to drip, into pails, and the sacrifice of the ram had been dedicated to St Lazarus, Babalu-Aye, and the sacrifice of the goat to Fidel.

The crowd in the shack began chanting in time to the drums. I couldn't make out the words but I could tell they weren't in Spanish. Julietta was talking to a young woman who was standing close to the altar and sipping a bloody cocktail. The woman was wearing a good suit. She was a doctor. 'They are singing "The land is shaking",' reported Julietta. 'It's about earthquakes in Oriente – they have earthquakes there. It's an old African language, I think.' She was beginning to sway to the rhythm of the drums. The woman with the keyboard teeth returned, carrying a bowl of food. Dancers scooped out handfuls of what looked like nuts, and swallowed them. The woman came to me. I took a handful – they *were* nuts, covered in a sticky caramelised paste. Roberto looked uncomfortable at finding himself in this shack with these dancers and dolls and plumed coconuts. Perspiration glazed his face. I could feel a pearl of sweat cultivating in the groove of my upper lip.

Suddenly there was a moment of the kind you sometimes experience in a crowd of people, when you can tell by their movements that something extraordinary and disturbing is going on but you can't tell what it is. It might be a fight or it might be a death. On this occasion, it was something in between the two. A hunched black man was gesturing at the dancers around him with his left hand. His nails were two or three inches long and discoloured. He could have been brandishing a hand of plantains. His eyes looked as though they were being squeezed out of his head. They didn't blink. They had the sheen of the taxidermist's about them. The man couldn't have been more than 45 but he was stooped, shambling around and mumbling. I gathered from the look on Julietta's face that she didn't recognise the language he was mouthing any more than I did. 'This man is possessed by the spirit of a dead man, from ancient times,' she said. 'Maybe the dead man was old and this is why he is bent.'

The skinny man in the waistcoat cried out. His green eyes were starting from his face. He was swaggering to and fro in front of the drums. These men were not like the zombies of Haiti, drugged and prematurely buried and brain-damaged as a result, but nonetheless entirely mortal. The men at the *Santería* party were not undead but dead, or rather, they were the temporary hosts of the dead. At least, that's what everyone at the *fiesta* believed. In the middle of the floor, the man in the waistcoat was aiming a blow at the hunched man: it seemed an antic gesture rather than an assault, but even so the hunched man stopped a haymaker in the shoulder. There was no sign on his face that he'd felt a thing. He was shambling around as before. He was shambling across to us, in fact. He raised his hand to Julietta's face. He was touching her forehead and uttering words from a language he didn't know: a dead language, a language of the dead. She looked anxious. Now the man was staring at me, with those gross dead eyes. I tasted the sourness of my drink all over again and wondered what else had been in it besides rum, and whether whatever it was accounted for the pats of cold sweat which were piebalding my shirt.

The man in the waistcoat was raising his voice. He was shouting. The crowd was opening up around him. He was pointing in my direction. The hunched man was backing away from me. The drums stopped. The man in the waistcoat and I were facing each other across a clearing of floor. He was pointing and shouting, repeating the same incomprehensible phrase. The woman doctor was saying something to Julietta. Julietta grabbed my hand. 'We must go,' she said. Her father was walking away, on his way out of the shack. Julietta looked at me. 'We must go.' She was pulling my arm. As we went through the door, I looked over my shoulder in time to see the hunched man falling on his face.

When we were outside, Julietta explained, 'The man was saying that there were strangers at the party. He was saying "open the door for me" in an African language. The doctor said we had seen enough. She said we should go because things were not good for us, and they might get worse.' My clothes were wet through. I had an overwhelming urge to sit down and realised it was because my legs were shaking.

I asked Roberto if he would put me in touch with his friend the *Santería* priest, the *babalao*. I wanted to know more about what I had seen at the *fiesta*. A week or two after the party, Julietta called me to say that everything was arranged. She said, 'You must take gifts to the *babalao* – pork, olives, and rum. My father says the rum he likes best is Caribbean Club; the five-year-old.' A *babalao* lives on the gifts of supplicants. Apart from cash, he expects considerations in the form of animals, clothes, fruit, 'gifts for the saints'. It costs a lot of money to become a *babalao* – as much as 10,000 Cuban pesos, the equivalent of about $300, or almost three years' average wages – and the initiation is tortuous. Novices have to undergo a peculiar form of semi-isolation, during which they must dress entirely in white and swear off palm wine, red meat, and anything else liable to provoke passion or rash action. At the end of nine months, they spend seven days sitting in a chair and are fed and bathed by the select of the faith, the made-*babalaos*. They are not allowed to see anybody else. I had heard stories of sacrifices and other rites accompanying initiation. Understandably, perhaps, *babalaos* look for payback.

Roberto said that his friend, whose name was Enrique, or Kiki for short, lived on a smart avenue about 15 minutes' walk from the house where the *fiesta* had been held. I wasn't able to find fresh pork because of rationing but I bought a tin of luncheon meat at a dollar shop and hoped that it would do. When I arrived at Kiki's house, there was a tall, slim man of about 40 in the drive. He had light brown skin and a receding hairline. He was wearing shorts and a T-shirt bearing the slogan '*Palacio de la Salsa*'. He surprised me by saying, 'Hello, I'm Kiki,' and smiling. I was expecting – I don't know – a whiff of sulphur, witch doctor's weeds, a scowling apothecary.

We climbed stone steps to his front door. They were arranged in a spiral staircase. Kiki twisted the top off the bottle of Caribbean Club I had brought and tipped the first nip over the threshold of his house. 'For the *Santos*!' he said. In his sitting-room were a cane suite, a cane basket full of tousled magazines, and a poster of a teenager in a bathing costume. 'My daughter,' he purred. 'She's a model.' On the wall next to the swimsuit-spread was a wooden mask with a blue chin. It represented Olokun, a god from under the sea, according to Kiki. The effect of divine five o'clock shadow was achieved by an inlay of painted seeds. 'This mask comes from Africa. There are only six of them in the world. This one came from the ancestors of my family,' he said. He poured two glasses of rum. 'It was 400 years before I could have it.'

'How did you get it?'

'An African woman came here with a cancer. I gave her a doll to cure it,' he said blandly. 'An African messenger came directly to bring me the mask. I have been offered $10,000 for it but I refused. I said it was priceless.'

'Is it safe to leave it on your wall?'

'People don't understand what it is. They don't know the secret of the mask.' A god from under the sea presumably had a special meaning for Kiki, who moonlighted as a scuba instructor. He took me to his chapel, a backroom screened by a *mariguo*, a curtain of secrets, (it was a canopy of fronds above the door, like a grass-skirt hanging up to dry). On a wooden bench was a plastic bust of a Red Indian. Kiki said he had recovered it from a shipwreck. Seven people had died after the ship went down during the Mariel boatlift of 1980, when President Carter had allowed thousands of Cubans into the United States. Kiki said, 'I went down to pick up the bodies and the first thing I found was this head. I had a revelation about this Indian. He thanked me for saving him and said, "From now on I will be guiding you and taking care of you and your family."' The Indian's name was Tonka: 'He gave me the name in the dream.' On the nape of his neck, Tonka was franked 'Chicago 1966'. We drank a toast to Tonka.

Kiki said that he communicated with St Francis – Orula. When the saint allowed him to, he said, he sold amulets containing beads and ivory to the sick for $250 each. 'They are very precious. I've given five to people and they all got over their illnesses. I only have two left.'

'How do you know when Orula wants you to sell another amulet?'

'He tells me.'

The credo according to Orula was that you've got nothing if you haven't got your health; good fortune is more important than knowledge; and it's nice to have a roof over your head. Kiki showed me a shell. 'When the animal that lives inside this comes to the world, it has a home already. It's one of the most important things that people should look for on earth – a place to live, also someone to love and money to give to their loved ones.'

On the bench was a statue of a saint. His bloodstains were represented by red paint. Around the walls, there were bloodstains to a height of three feet which appeared to be genuine. I said, 'How did you become a *babalao*?'

'It was through my ancestors. I have belonged to this saint since I was seven. Then I became a *babalao* in 1970. Now I am 51 – oh yeah!' added Kiki, noting the surprise on my face, 'this religion keeps you young, you don't feel stress.' In the sitting-room, a clock cuckooed the hour. Through the *mariguo*, I could see a tall, attractive woman – Kiki's wife – moving in the room. Kiki and I had more rum. I said, 'So what happens when you become a *babalao*? I've heard many stories. What about sacrifices?'

'Yes, there are sacrifices,' Kiki said. 'The saints have to be fed.'

'What happens?'

Kiki smiled. 'Do you know what is the meaning of *babalao*? It means the father of secrets.' Popping an olive into his mouth, he made a goldfish face.

'Okay, well, what powers do you have?'

'It's a bit difficult. There are powers, but I don't know when they are going to come. They are given through the saints. A man might come to see me about a problem with his wife. Orula could say, "If this man has accepted a woman, why change things later?"'

'What about punishment? Can you punish people?'

'Orula says that the man who doesn't have a good principle will never have a good end. He will receive the punishment that God has for him.'

Kiki told me that *Santería*'s critics in Roman Catholicism secretly practised live sacrifices themselves. Priests slaughtered sheep on the stones that made up 'the cardinal points' of new church premises – 'it's strictly confidential,' he said. He explained what was happening at the *Santería* party I'd attended. When the man in the waistcoat, the trancee, had shouted, 'Open the door for me,' it was because he was possessed by a saint. Kiki said, 'The saint wanted the spirits of the dead to come to the *fiesta*. Because you were a stranger, not a *Santería* man, the saint believed that you were blocking the way. He was angry with you.' Kiki gave me a look of mock reproof. It was easier all round if everybody accepted that I had known no better. Otherwise my solecism might have to be regarded as an insult to the dead.

The bottle of Caribbean Club was empty. 'So, would you like me to give you a consultation?' asked Kiki.

I had never had my fortune read, or cut a Tarot deck, or held hands around a Ouija board. I had preferred not to know. I was always afraid of the palmist blenching and sprinting from her caravan, of the Reaper glowering up at me from the divining baize, of the shattering tumbler. I said, 'Sure. When could you see me?'

'What about now?' said Kiki. He left the room. When he came back, he had changed out of his shorts into a pair of baggy white trousers, and he was wearing a white bonnet like a chef's toque. He instructed me to sit on a wooden stool. He squatted cross-legged on the floor in front of me. By his feet was a polythene-covered book. It was like one of those feint ledgers sold in stationers for inscrutable accountancy tasks.

Kiki was fingering what might have been a chunky rosary – pieces of ossified coconut shell strung together on a metal chain to make a necklace. Kiki lifted the necklace to my forehead, pressed it to my skin for a moment, and let it fall to the floor. He studied the configuration of its coils on his reed mat and made an entry in the book. He added characters to a column composed entirely of '0's and '1's. He said he was able to discover things about me by the way the coconut rosary landed on the floor. 'This chain has 256 possibilities. There are 101 stories,' he said, and I wondered where I had heard that last expression before – wasn't it part of the come-on, the tout's rubric, for an old black-and-white television series about New York, 'The Naked City'? The principle of divination was known as *ifa*. According to the lore of *Santería*, God once told a favoured *orisha* that the best way of understanding him was in the patterns created by the apparently haphazard fall of shells or nuts. God would reveal the destiny of anyone who asked sincerely. Studies of *Santería* said that it could take a *babalao* up to 15 years to master *ifa*, which explained why men like Kiki could call themselves the fathers of secrets and charge top dollar. Kiki went on, 'In this book, all the signs are written. You can refer to it. Illumination comes through the necklace.' He read the binary runes. 'You had ancestors in Cuba.'

'My mother once stayed here as a girl,' I said doubtfully. 'She remembers the great cemetery of Havana.' Kiki placed the necklace against my brow again, dropped it, and did more of his occult bookkeeping – this happened three times in all. From this, Kiki, or Orula, was able to tell that I had a brother and sister (true); ancestors born in Germany and Poland (not that I know of); and a quarrelsome disposition. Kiki now produced a cloth bag which contained a snail shell, a pebble, a charm-bracelet-sized elephant made of ivory, and a bone – a goat's bone, he said. The shell represented money, 'the first money that people had in the world'. It also stood for shelter, as it was a 'snail's house', and travel. 'It's from other lands. It has travelled from one continent to another.' The pebble denoted 'the years that have passed. So that this stone can be as it is now, a thousand years have passed.' The elephant meant health. 'It is the animal which lives longest, but it is also very fragile.' The bone meant death.

Kiki said, 'Take the shell and the pebble in your hands and shake them.' The principle was the same as Find the Lady. I rattled the signifiers together, then made a pair of fists, and we discovered which symbol was in which palm. He tried to explain the science of it – the left side of the brain governs the right side of the body; 'Bad things go in the left side and go out by the right side. Even if you think you're shaking these things at random, you have the powers of the world in your hands.' I couldn't wholly follow it, which may or may not have been intentional on his part. I may have been a little drunk. The shell ended up in my left hand, the pebble in my right. Kiki closed his eyes. Presumably speaking on behalf of Orula, he said, 'The person is very interested in taking many trips to different countries around the world. Do you love the sea?'

I repeated the crap-game shake, this time with the shell and the elephant. The elephant turned up in my right hand. Kiki said, 'You might have some problems with your liver. You must take care of it. You get furious sometimes and this can be bad for it. You have to take some medicines. You must eat some sweets, some desserts, and jam with your breakfast. Once a month, you should clean your body from the inside with a laxative. At this time, you should lie on your right side so that the salts can work.'

I didn't like to mention it but Orula was beginning to strike me as a bit of an old woman. Kiki had an almanac of his predictions and *pensées*, and he read to me from it. True, some of Orula's sayings appeared insightful. His warning to 'be careful of people in the sea', for instance, could be interpreted as a reference to the perils faced by the Cuban rafters, *los balseros*, the thousands of would-be Miami immigrants. But elsewhere the divinity who is honoured with *fiestas* of animal sacrifices, blood-drinking and supernatural possession, sounded like a Jewish mother. His guidance included: avoid eating late; take care of possible operations on the stomach; mind how you go with countryside work.

I shook the elephant and the pebble. When I opened my fists, the left contained the pebble, the right the elephant. 'There's something interesting here,' said Kiki. 'Orula says you're the favourite bird of God.' It seemed that I had been born with *ashe,* meaning a kind of divine current. The other birds hadn't. 'They were envious of you and so they threw paint over you.' However, God held a kind of ID parade in order to pick out his favourite bird. Kiki said, 'When you went out for the selection, God spotted you and said that you were his favourite bird.'

Ashamed now of my unkind thoughts about Orula, I shook the elephant and the bone. It came out like this: elephant, left hand; bone, right. Kiki said, 'If you see a person who's hitting somebody you shouldn't get involved in this. It's none of your business. All this fury can turn on you. You have to be careful not to be lost in any place, in a place where you can find some friends who are drug addicts. You must be careful not to get involved in any situation about drugs. It could be fatal for you.'

'That's a pity. I was planning to write something on drugs.'

'Orula is never wrong,' said Kiki.

I shook the pebble and the bone together. This was to give me an insight into my desires, according to the *babalao*. The bone appeared in my left hand. 'God said to you, "Ask me something," and you asked God to let you live in a tropical country and to give you a *mulata* to marry you.' Kiki laughed, and so did I. From his squatting position, it was easy for him to roll around the floor, which he did. 'These are the wishes you have,' he said, slapping me quite hard on the leg.

Kiki wanted to show me his patent laxative; it was in an old rum bottle on the porch. His sitting-room was now occupied by a large, sad-eyed man. Kiki introduced us. The visitor was Ricardo, who was 43. He was as big and harmless as a harem eunuch. He had qualified as a *babalao* two months earlier. 'I helped him. I was his godfather,' said Kiki. I asked Ricardo why he had decided to become a *babalao*. He didn't say anything. Instead his lip trembled and he started to cry. I looked at Kiki – what had I said? Ricardo buried his face in a hirsute forearm. He was so overcome that he had to take himself off to the doorway, where he stood breathing heavily for several moments with his back to us. Kiki said, 'Ricardo was diagnosed with cancer. He asked Orula for help and now the problem is gone.'

'I see. That's terrific.'

'Yes,' said Kiki, 'Orula told him to change his doctor.'

Ricardo nodded. 'You see, after what happened to me, I wanted to devote my life to the saints. This religion is good for you,' he said, and asked me huskily for one of my cigarettes.

I didn't know that I would be seeing Kiki again. Kiki knew, though – or at least that's what he told me when we met, nine months or so after my consultation with Orula. Kiki said it was something he had learnt from 'the white part of the chain': his necklace had made its own gnomic contribution to Orula's almanac, or letter, for the New Year, and the letter had duly revealed that I would be coming back to Cuba – 'and here you are!'

It happened that I was back in town, and had found myself climbing the corkscrew of smooth stone steps leading to Kiki's house, and parting the beads which served during the day as his front door. I liked Kiki's company. He was good fun to get drunk with on a hot Havana afternoon. And there was a lot still to learn about *Santería*: having exposed myself to Kiki's coconut rosary and his fortune-telling keepsakes, I found my appetite whetted. As for Kiki, he insisted, 'If you came back to my house it was because the gods wanted to give you certain powers. That's what I will give you tomorrow. I will make certain combinations with the gods to see what you want and what your objectives are in the future.' He was wearing a singlet which read 'Instructor'. I had the impression that he had just pulled it on, having been roused, in the middle of the afternoon, by the cleaning lady. It was three o'clock and he had as much beard as the stubbled mask on his wall. He went on, 'I think you need an amulet. It will contain power for you. It's necessary to make a sacrifice of two cocks. Since you're travelling across the seas it seems a good idea if it is an amulet from Yemayá, the saint of the seas. I will have to call another *babalao*,' he said. It was as though he were reminding himself to telephone an electrician. He produced two glasses and a bottle of rum.

It seemed that my amulet would 'receive' the blood of the two cocks, which would be offered to the queen of the seas. But before anything else could happen, another cock would have to be sacrificed to Eleggua, the saint who opens the way. And I would have to be 'cleaned' with a dove. 'A dove is a symbol of peace,' said Kiki. 'The dove will be sacrificed to Oggun, the god of the force of the earth. This saint lives together with Ochosi, the saint of intelligence. He has great wisdom. These forces are the key to any objective you might have. After this ceremony with all of these saints – including Osun, the warrior – we will be able to make the sacrifice to the goddess of the sea. And we can ask the coconuts what your future will be. It's a very beautiful ceremony.' He sipped his drink with a faraway look.

I thought, *cleaned with a dove*?

Kiki said, 'After what I will give you tomorrow, you will be a very rich man. I hope you will buy me a beer after that.' There was more to it than buying Kiki a beer. When he told me how much the ceremony would cost, I repeated, 'Two thousand dollars?'

'No, no, two *hundred*,' said Kiki. 'Two thousand dollars?! *Caramba!*'

We started to laugh, but I had the feeling that Kiki would have charged me $2,000 if he thought he could. 'This ceremony is important because it will open all ways to you,' he told me. 'All ways are closed to you and thanks to this ceremony, all ways will be open. You should always carry the amulet with you.' Kiki impressed on me how much supernatural access I would be buying for my $200. Armed with my amulet, I would be able to stop by the beach for a chat with the sea anytime I wanted. The only additional outlay for which I would be liable was the price of a quarter of sweets. He said, 'The great power you have is to go to the sea and talk. Drop seven candies into the sea. Relax and talk to the sea.'

I had brought some books, including one about *Santería* which I'd come across in the University of London library. I dug it out from the bottom of my rucksack. Kiki pored over the book and looked up in delight at one of the plates in the middle pages. 'Is exactly! Is exactly!' he exclaimed in English. He held the book open on a page featuring a Nigerian shrine which had been photographed in 1940. He rushed to a cupboard by his top step. He knocked on the cupboard door, as if he was seeking permission to enter. He opened the door to reveal a shrine identical to the one in the book. It was a coal bunker of blackened gourds, half-empty medicine bottles and otherworldly raffia work. 'The saints are like animals in the circus,' said Kiki. 'Any time they do something for us, we have to give something to them.' He came back to where I was sitting, took a gulp of rum, went over to the shrine again and spat out the rum in a fine spray. He gave me a paperback about the rituals of *Santería*. There was a bloodstain on the spine.

I told Kiki about the loss of my research during rioting in Bradford. 'The man who did this to you may have bad luck,' he said, and refreshed our glasses. I felt disappointed. This wasn't the ringing prediction of pestilence and sores for which, I now realised, I had been hoping. I sensed that revenge probably depended on the man who had robbed me putting himself at the mercy of the sea and Yemayá, something you couldn't count on in a resident of land-locked Bradford.

Kiki appeared to have put on a little weight since I had last seen him. Perhaps Cuba's special period was less arduous for *babalaos* than it was for other people. I asked him how things were. He said, 'The saints say that Cuba is the country of corks. When the cork sinks, everybody thinks that everything is lost, but suddenly it rises to the surface. Everybody thought Cuba could be lost this year, but the cork floated again. We are going to have relations again with the United States, the United Kingdom, Canada and great capitalist enterprises.' It was Kiki the likeable, plausible fortune-teller whom I heard predicting recovery for Cuba. 'Any moment now, people will have problems crossing the streets because they will be full of cars. Food and jobs will come again. Before this year finishes, great improvements will take place.' However, I recognised another side of the *babalao*, the priest as huckster, as Kiki boostered a new business venture, 'Did you know we have an English enterprise taking care of the Marazul Hotel in the eastern beaches?' he asked. 'It's now called the Via Coco. Food and drinks are included in the price.'

That night, I saw a man on Prado whose brown face and forearms were covered in pustules, like the kind that form on old fruit. Perhaps the man was some kind of augury for my session at Kiki's the next day, but what exactly did he portend? I wasn't scared, exactly. I knew that Kiki would have to answer to our mutual friend, Roberto the CDR boss, if anything happened to me, and the Press Centre might feel compelled to bestir itself on behalf of an accredited foreigner who was offered as a sacrifice. On the other hand, I wasn't keen on the sight of blood: I'm the only journalist I know with war-zone experience who has to bite down hard on a sweet just to get through his shots. Thank – thank *what*? I was going to say 'Thank God', but perhaps I should be thanking the *Santos* – Kiki hadn't told me exactly what the rites entailed. I had a suspicion that they were blasphemous – but weren't followers of *Santería* baptised, didn't they consider themselves Christian?

*

When I arrived at Kiki's house the next morning, a man in a brightly coloured shirt and tan shorts came to see who was calling. This turned out to be Billy, a friend of Kiki and a fellow *babalao*. He explained that he had come to help Kiki with my 'ceremony'. He regarded me warily. A dark-skinned woman was sitting in a cane chair. I knew that Kiki's parlour doubled as his waiting-room so I assumed that she had need of his gift. Her name was Marisol Peteira, she said, and when I asked her what her consultation was about, she told me she had come with her husband, about his eyes.

I asked Billy how long he had been a *babalao*. Three years, he said.

'Why did you want to become one?'

'It's in my family. My grandfather was also a *babalao*.' Billy said one side of his family had come from Italy, the other from Spain. They had worked in the sugar industry. He was lighter-skinned than Kiki, and quieter, more guarded. A wiry man emerged from Kiki's backroom – his chapel or surgery. It was Marisol's husband. From another room came the sound of a cockerel clucking. I looked in the direction that the sound was coming from. There was an open doorway which gave onto a kind of back-kitchen. I couldn't see a cockerel but I did see Billy. He was crouching in front of a sink in a white bonnet and placing pieces of fresh coconut on the floor. He was putting them in front of what appeared to be a half-section of terracotta roof-tile. Candles and nightlights were burning by the tile. Kiki appeared, wearing the white slacks and tunic which I had seen him in before. He was affecting necklaces of beads and the familiar Mr Pastry millinery. The *babalaos* invited me to join them in the scullery. Kiki was fiddling with a small raffia bag which was hanging from a peg. After he let go of the bag, it carried on moving by itself and I understood with a small lurch of revulsion that it contained the dove.

Billy was chanting. He had some coconut in his hands and was breaking little flakes of it off in his fingers and sprinkling the flakes over the terracotta tube. He also sprinkled water from a dish onto the floor. I couldn't follow what he was intoning – presumably it was in the Yoruba language. Kiki put his hand in the raffia bag and pulled out a grey bird: it looked more like a pigeon than a dove. He held the bird tightly in his palm, so tightly that it was unable to move a leg or wing. The bag continued to twitch – perhaps it held more than one 'dove'. It reminded me of those novelty laughing bags that you used to be able to buy from joke shops. Kiki gave the pigeon to Billy. Billy in turn held the bird up to Kiki's forehead, just brushing its wingtip against his skin. He also brushed it against Kiki's throat; Kiki turned round and Billy touched the pigeon's wings against Kiki's back. Kiki faced him again and Billy pressed the bird against his palms, knees and ankles. He continued to chant. I recognised the name of Eleggua. At one point, Billy double-checked my name. 'It's Smith? Smith Stephen?'

Kiki called his wife. The attractive woman I'd once seen from Kiki's chapel, through the veil of privacy-preserving fronds, nudged and prodded a girl of seven or eight into the room. I was introduced to the *babalao*'s wife and to Cynthia, his youngest daughter. They were both brushed by the pigeon. It attempted to flex its wings but remained pinioned by Billy. Cynthia recoiled as the bird beat against her bare shoulders. Finally it was my turn. Billy pressed the pigeon into my palm and I inhaled the close odour of pet shops. I noticed as he continued to dab me with it that its feathers were soiled. I turned my back on him the wrong way, turning anti-clockwise, and had to come back on myself and start again.

Billy was holding a short-bladed, plastic-handled knife. He screwed the pigeon up tightly, as if it was a piece of grey cloth he was wringing out. He held it a couple of feet off the floor and jabbed it in the neck. I had been bracing myself for a tangy geyser but instead the blood fell to the floor in a tidy, steady flow. Billy, still chanting, waved the bird over the terracotta pipe, marking it abstractly in blood. He plucked out a tuft of feathers. It was the bird's head. He flattened the corpse on the terracotta.

Kiki was holding a saucer of what looked like chalk. He rubbed his fingers in it and smeared the powder on his forehead and hands. He clapped his hands over the pigeon's corpse so that the remnants of the powder fell on it. The rest of us copied him. Kiki said the sacrifice of the 'dove' was to propitiate the dead, and alert the *orishas* to my impending initiation. The dove was also supposed to 'clean my health'. 'Your aura is dirty, but it can be cleaned with the animal. This changes the colour of your aura. You were very white and now you're red.' The chalky powder we had dabbed on our hands and faces - *cascarilla* - was also part of the cleansing process. It was made from eggshells. 'The sun turns them to dust,' said Kiki, clapping his palms together. 'So, this was the first ceremony.' He raised his eyebrows. I was looking at a showman or barker, whose expression said that I hadn't seen anything yet. Throughout the ritual, he had alternated a look of reverent concentration with one of larkiness.

Now Billy led me into the chapel. Kiki had made a few changes, I noticed. A pair of dolls, one black, one white, stared down malevolently from the top of a wardrobe. There was a Spanish bull-fight poster on the wall. I stood in front of a shrine composed of Kiki's charred familiars – gourds, a conch shell, what appeared to be a small gin trap. Kiki came in holding a cockerel upside down by its talons. 'Hold this in your right hand,' he said. I squeezed the bird by its brilliant yellow gaiters as tightly as I could, imagining it getting free, flailing at me with its bony claws and strutting around Kiki's chapel, kicking over his tarry icons. In fact the cock barely stirred. I knew that its reflexes were making its feathers move rather than any breeze through the open shutters, but only because of the lowering noonday stillness – the ceremony was taking place on a Sunday, at what would in England have been the church-going hour. I took the cock to the window for a breather and found I was swallowing nothing but thick, damp air.

I had begun to feel I could master the rooster when Kiki returned with a pigeon and told me to hold it in my left hand. He showed me how to wrap my fingers around its middle. I held on so tight that I was afraid I was hurting it. I could feel its heart contracting and relaxing. There was shit on its feathers where it had soiled itself in Kiki's grabbag. Unlike the cockerel, which was facing the floor, the pigeon had a more natural vantage. It was looking directly in front of it. It wagged its head. Kiki said, 'This cock and dove represent the spiritual quality inside you.' The idea was to create a 'circle' with the two birds, with me at the centre of it. 'In the left hand is the dove and in the other hand is the cock. In the beginning is the circle. Everything in the world is the same as the world. In the world, everything is about three. When you sit down at a table, you have a spoon, a knife and a fork. You also have three lives: child, young man, and old man. The world of the Catholic church has the Son, Father, and Holy Ghost. Three true essences. Three in one body: head, trunk and limbs. It's the same with you and two animals.'

While I was gripping the birds, Billy frisked me, or rubbed me down, with slices of coconut. He touched me in what Kiki described as my six most important places: my head; my throat; my back (home to an important *Santo*, Ikuako); my stomach, or at least my belly-button; my solar plexus; and my knees, feet and hands, which seemed to count as one place. Kiki said that the ceremony was to give me a 'special power', courtesy of the four warriors of *Santería*: Olgun, Ochosi, Osun and Eleggua. 'Billy talks with them through the coconuts. The coconuts receive the message about you,' he said. 'Now you must stand on one leg.'

Without loosening my hold on the ceremonial fowl, I took my left foot off the ground. I said, 'Why am I doing this?'

'Because Osun, the warrior, only had one leg,' said Kiki. 'You must be like him.' He took the cockerel from me and stabbed it in the throat. He put his thumbs on either side of the wound, directing a stream of blood over the venerated *objets* of the shrine. He dispatched the pigeon with his knife. He and Billy ripped feathers from the birds and let them fall on the bloody gourds in a blizzard of tawny and grey feathers. The chapel suggested the scene of a pillow fight which had gone tragically wrong. The *babalaos* were kneeling in front of the shrine, disembowelling the cockerel and the pigeon. When they had finished, they swabbed the floor with handfuls of feathers. I was told to get on my knees and join them. The browns and whites of the entrails, the unexpected blues, were as thick as oil paint. Until now – perhaps because of the skittishness I'd seen from time to time on Kiki's face, or the sheer incongruity of what we were up to – it had been possible to keep what was happening at the *babalao*'s house literally at arm's length. Even at this stage, had I been raised on a farm or brought up by butchers, I daresay I might have found less to question in what was happening. As it was, kneeling over the gore, sweating from the stifling closeness, it seemed to me as though, with every ineffectual stroke of my mop of clotted feathers, the ceremony was emerging as more dubious. Only the engrossed, methodical Billy gave any impression of believing in what we were doing.

Kiki said that I would be left alone in front of the shrine. I must knock on the floor. This was because 'when we were born it was from the earth, and we are going to return to it. Earth gives birth to us and we have to return to it,' he told me. 'Dust to dust.' In our morning's work so far, the Egun, the dead, had been squared, and the saints warned to expect my initiation. I now had the power of the warriors on my side. The ritual was approaching its climax with the third and final 'movement'. This was *asiento*, the central ceremony of initiation into *Santería*, in which the *orisha* becomes seated in the head. 'This is a confidential ceremony,' said Kiki. 'Not even the Africans know about it.'

Billy told me to kneel on a raffia mat which faced the open shutters. In front of me was what appeared to be an earthenware casserole dish. A string of blue and white beads had been wrapped around the handle. Inside the bowl were grey, shiny stones, an old rusted blade like a fishknife, and three metal figurines of saints. There were several smaller bowls beside the casserole dish, including one made out of a vegetable husk of some kind. It contained a dark, viscous solution. Almost submerged by the liquid was a tight cluster of blue and white beads. It looked like one of those Liquorice Allsort sweets covered in hundreds-and-thousands. 'This is your victory,' whispered Kiki at my shoulder. It was my amulet. He removed it from the bowl and turned it over in front of me so that I could look at it properly. On the bottom was a discoloured yellow oblong – it could have been a tooth or a toenail. 'Ivory,' said Kiki.

I heard him taking a swig from a bottle. He drew breath – and spat a fine spray over the back of my neck. It smelt like rum. 'It's necessary to clean your head,' said Billy. He knelt down on my left, his chef's hat level with my face. He started to rattle a maraca. I had the impression of a feather duster on my right. The feathers were rustling independently: Kiki had his hands around another cockerel. Unlike the first one, this bird had pale talons. It was also clucking wretchedly. Billy and Kiki began chanting. Again I didn't understand much except references to the *orishas,* and a version of my own name. I felt Kiki's hand against my back, pressing me forward. Out of the corner of my eye, and then in the reflection on the surface of the vegetable bowl, I watched him raise the short-bladed knife to the cockerel's throat. He pushed my head over the bowl. The cock clucked. I felt the movement of its feathers against the back of my neck, and my hair stood on end. I was staring into the casserole – the stones, the figurines – and there was a gentle pressure on the crown of my head. Blood ran onto the figurines, a thin but distinctly red stream. The cockerel's blood was coursing over my head and into the pot. I kept my chin tucked into my chest, to stop it running down my face.

I felt – I felt *relieved.* If there was a right way to have a cockerel sacrificed over your head, then this was it. Kiki and Billy, or perhaps the *babalaos* of centuries ago, had devised the ceremony so that the kneeling initiate, the *aleyo*, didn't witness the dispatching of the bird directly, or see the blood as it fell on him, or even – such was the angle of his prostration – or even smell it. And since *Santería* didn't acknowledge luck, in the sense of pure chance, it must also have been by design that the *aleyo* also found himself in the medically approved position for conditions of light-headedness – with his head between his knees. I was thinking about how lightly I was getting off when there was a cloudburst of blood: it splashed onto my head and over my ears and down my neck and made the collar of my shirt wet. Kiki had slashed another rooster but this time it wasn't a clean kill. There was blood running off me and into the dish, as before, but there was also blood on the floor. Kiki was spilling it – it was going wide of my head by as much as a foot or so. Kiki was spilling it but so of course was the cockerel. I felt the draught of it above my head – it was still moving. Billy was still shaking his maraca. Above the noise, I heard Kiki grunting. After a moment, his hand appeared in my cramped field of vision. It was holding the second rooster. Its eye was closed in an expression of terrible resignation. Kiki dumped the bird by the casserole.

Now I could smell honey: I could smell it before I connected the smell with the thick liquid that was dribbling onto my head, thicker than the blood. It trickled into the dish, not mixing with the blood but pooling goldenly on top of it. The rooster which was by the casserole suddenly jerked, and brought its head down heavily in a saucer of holy coconut. Kiki pulled tufts of feathers from its breast and filled the casserole with them. He plucked more feathers and rubbed them into my hair and pulled a white hat down over my head until it touched my ears. 'You must wear this for two hours,' he said. 'The *orishas* are working under the hat. You must put down the money now. Shake the maraca and say a prayer to the *orishas*.'

I said a prayer but I'm afraid it wasn't to the *orishas*. If someone had asked me whether I believed in Kiki's religion, I should have said that I did, in the sense that I didn't doubt that it was sincerely held by those who espoused it, and also on the basis that there were more things in heaven and earth, etc. But left alone by Kiki and Billy to make my private supplication to the *orishas*, I asked instead to be forgiven in the event of a blasphemy. Comically, I fumbled for a rosary, a cheap thing in a cheap tin casket from a souvenir stall in Rome, never blessed or consecrated and never used according to theological instruction. I hadn't approached the rite expecting spiritual insight, but as things turned out, it had brought me closer to something I half recognised.

We sat on Kiki's cane suite. He poured rum. Billy said to me, 'You're a *Santero* now.' He looked at me thoughtfully over his glass. 'You know, you should drink less.' He claimed that this was a truth revealed to him when Kiki spat rum over the back of my neck. 'You need a clear head,' he added. Criticism of drinking struck me as a bit rich coming from priests who expect offertories of alcohol. Billy said, 'I want to know something. Are you more interested in writing about this religion than joining it?' I was interested in *Santería*, I explained to Billy, because it was an important feature of life in Cuba, and so little known in the wider world. I liked the idea of being a *Santero* but I felt like an imposter. On the other hand, it had been Kiki's idea. I didn't have a guilty conscience about the *babalaos*, least of all when I remembered the $200 I was paying them.

It was time for me to receive the amulet. Once more I was kneeling in front of the hollowed husk, the blood and the thicker honey. There was a sickly sweet smell, as of an air-freshener not quite masking a deathly stench. 'You may kiss the amulet,' said Kiki indulgently. I fished the Liquorice Allsort from the cloying goo and put my lips to it the way you greet a moustachioed great-aunt. I put it in my pocket. In the room where the pigeons had hung in Kiki's grabbag, he washed my hair. It was like a visit to a cowboy trichologist: tawny feathers and dried-on blood came away in his hands.

Kiki's wife served lunch. It was delicious: chicken. It was all part of the ceremony. The flesh of sacrificial animals had to be eaten by everyone taking part in the ritual. Kiki said we must remain seated until the last of the lunch things had been cleared away by his wife. He swallowed a juicy slice of mango. 'You are only at the first level of initiation,' he told me. The process normally took nine months. I said that, unfortunately, I didn't have nine months. Kiki said, 'It is possible that I can arrange the next step for you. It involves the sacrifice of a goat, we could do it in one week.' He saw the look on my face. 'It costs *less* than for today,' he said. It was Kiki the huckster. It wasn't the ineffableness of the rites practised in his back room which struck a kind of awe into you, I decided, but their transparency. On the one hand you accepted that he and Billy were working from a lore which had been passed down for generations. On the other hand, they seemed to be making it up as they went along: clean the mess up with a scrap of plumage; we'll slaughter a goat – it's a good price! Here was the amiable dubiousness I had caught a whiff of on the chapel floor, among the pretty innards of the birds and the useless blotter of feathers.

5

Guinea-pig Roulette

AN OLIVE BUICK RESOLVED itself out of the noonday glare. On the main road into the eastern city of Santiago de Cuba, it slipped towards us in a slow flare of chrome. Its fins, its duck's-tail trunk, displaced the slack air as it passed us. Pitching lightly in its wake, in the punctured steam-pudding can of our Lada, Cecil the taxi-driver turned to me and said that in his view the Buick had probably been a '57. Had I noticed its creamy roof? It had the distinctive markings of the popular *blanco y verde*.

Apart from Fidel Castro himself, and the swooning, swoon-making *casas* of Havana, the vintage American car was the most recognisable emblem of the Cuba of recent times. Indeed, besides the historical one-off of Castro, there was no more singularly Cuban image than the voluptuous leviathans of the road, such as the Buick outside Santiago. Notorious for bingeing at the petrol pump, they were all the more remarkable for enduring the country's petrol-rationing. In other countries, you might find copies of most of the sights that made Cuba what it was – not the real thing, but likenesses all the same. There *were* slums in other parts of the world, of course, albeit not the toppling theatre boxes of Habana Vieja. There *were* other plantations of tobacco, though none produced a finer leaf. Cuba wasn't the only place where history had acted as a matchmaker between the races, with perhaps unexpectedly pleasing results, though there were differences between Cuban women and other products of mixed relationships, a difference you could *hear* in the contrast between the words *mulata* and 'half-caste'. But nobody drove American cars any more (least of all Americans, whose garages and lots tended to be full of oriental vehicles). The world was divided into countries which ran about in thrifty, paperweight hatchbacks, and those you suspected would be forever uninitiated into car technology, but nobody drove American anymore. Except Cubans. This marked them out as different. It also gave the clue to exactly when they started being different. The venerable Plymouths and Chevvies and Studebakers on Cuba's roads would have told any Martian who had the back-numbers of a good car magazine that something dramatic had happened in the late fifties. No other Cuban landmark was capable of doing this. Essentially by chance – the timing of the Revolution; the implacability of Washington's embargo – Cuban motoring had stood still, sometimes literally, since the acknowledged heyday of the American automobile, a time when a United States Secretary of Defense could say, 'What's good for General Motors is good for America.' The classic American car had covered the ground between the Jazz Age and the Space Age. If by the end – and from the rear – it suggested a piece of friable Telstar technology, it could trace its history back to Prohibition and the Mob. Gangsters could almost have stepped out of the *blanco y verde* Buick. Indeed, the car's logbook, if any, might well have disclosed a hoodlum among its previous owners, for racketeers had been running Cuba right up until the Revolution. Now it wasn't alcohol that was a precious black market commodity but gasoline, high-octane moon-shine. Cuba's backstreet siphon-shops were the new stills and speakeasies, selling petrol which had been ripped off from barracks, police stations, tourist car-pools. Yes, you thought to yourself, a man could drive like a prince in Cuba. But better still, he could drive like a mobster.

It was in Jazz Age Hollywood that the most celebrated designer of

American cars, Harley Earl, made a name for himself. Earl was the first head of the Art and Styling Section of General Motors. His urbane handiwork belied a rapacious sensibility. You looked at his baroque roadsters in Cuba and thought, 'They don't make them like that any more.' This was a tribute to their longevity. It was also a comment on their wood panelling, on the seating and upholstery which recalled the suburban sitting-room. You sentimentally imagined that Earl's boys used to assemble cars as though they were building houses. The truth is that the American cars of Cuba belonged to the first generation of automobiles which had been built to be discarded. Earl and his colleagues had approached their task thinking, 'We *won't* make them like that any more.' The life-expectancy of cars of the fifties was a year. That was how long it was intended that American motorists should hang onto them before yielding to the itch to trade-up to some-thing bigger, fancier – above all, *newer*. Earl was the architect of what he called 'dynamic obsolescence' in the car industry, and beyond. One of his colleagues explained this Indianapolis of turnover more silkily: 'We have not depreciated these old cars, we have appreciated your mind.' No-one would have been more surprised than Earl to find that his throwaway models had become great survivors in Cuba, and that what car-fanciers appreciated about them was the way they grew old gracefully. The joinery finish of the interiors was also misleading. It disguised the true source of inspiration for Earl and his acolytes. They weren't interested in suburbia. They were reaching for the sky. Earl's imagination was seized by aircraft, and he was particularly struck by the Lockheed P38, the Lightning. From the outside, at least, you could see that the American cars of the fifties, with their spoilers and cones and after-burners, had been dreamt up by the people who brought us the space race, and the arms race too, or at least the West's contribution to them. It was poignant, then, to watch a Buick cruising along a highway, in Cuba of all places. Historically speaking, you knew what was coming next.

Earl retired in 1959, the year of the Revolution. Soon Americans were no longer driving cars like his and Cubans were driving nothing else: within a few years, the embargo had come into effect. At the same time a number of road accidents, and pressure from consumers' groups, had alerted Americans to the fact that their cars were too unwieldy for their brakes and suspension. It seemed as though the manufacturers had been rather literal-minded about the mayfly life-cycle of their products. They hadn't built them like they used to, they hadn't built them to last; they had barely built them to hold together. What had been good for General Motors was no longer any good to America. The Buick I'd seen in Santiago had effectively been written off as scrap thirty years earlier.

The ancient cars said a lot about Cuba, and her relationship with the United States. Long after models had been judged too dangerous for Americans, they were still apparently good enough for Cubans. This told you that impoverished drivers on the island didn't have a choice, but it also lent them an air of bravado. They had become the coolest motorists on earth. Spoilsport lobbyists might have exposed the fraud behind all that boxily reassuring bodywork, but it had proved impossible to strip the style out of it. Had fashion given Cubans the last laugh over their adversaries in the West? The sedans and coupés had come to represent Cuba – when you thought of them you thought of Cuba, and vice versa. But at the same time, they were 'Yank tanks', quintessentially American. When you thought of them, you thought of the United States too. They contributed to the appeal of Cuba with their air of mothballed incongruousness, but also with those American designs that refused to die. Whoever deserved the credit for the unique place of the American car in Cuba, it was capable of evoking ruefulness in onlookers. The Buick on the Santiago road was a symbol of Cuba's straitened present, and of the long-lost, recent past of the United States. When you watched Havana traffic, it brought to mind drive-ins and dairy queens and Blueberry Hill.

The government agency which among other things was responsible for dealing in American vehicles was Cubalse. A man called Vicente Caballero agreed to show me around the state pound in Havana, and we set off to look at classic American cars in my taxi, a Lada – a Lada, at that, in which the cabbie's laundry was hanging from a handrail. Señor Caballero astonished me by saying that Cubalse had only sold 20 American cars in the previous 12 months; that $10,000 or so wasn't a bad price for one in good condition (far too little, I'd have thought);

and that he only had a handful to show prospective purchasers. I said, 'Who are they? Americans?'

'Some Americans. Canadians, Europeans. If the customer is American, he has to take the car via a third country because of the embargo, so they don't come too much.'

'Do buyers insist on them being in mint condition?'

'No, some people want them just for the fun of it. Some buy the car and sell it later: they're not collectors but businessmen. Others use the cars for making films, or for publicity for their business.' But Señor Caballero added that it wasn't unusual to find cars in their original condition. Cuba had been a parts shop for the whole of Latin America before the Revolution, and you could still find authentic spares, he said. Even when motorists swopped old American parts for newer, more thrifty ones, they tended to hang on to the originals.

In Miramar, home of the well-appointed diplomatic residence – a flag, a fence, a satellite dish – Señor Caballero told the cabbie to pull up outside a dusty car-park the size of a football pitch. A puppy and a man sat in front of a guardhouse. One prize awaiting anyone who negotiated this security cordon was a column of new Renault run-abouts in citrus colours. The vehicles we had come to see were a sorry sight by comparison, occupying a far corner of the lot. A pea-green Cadillac was up on blocks, and bits of paper were attached to it like scraps of tissue staunching shaving wounds. The Cuban state wanted $2,900 for the car. There was a bulky Chevrolet Belair, made in 1957. Its black paintjob was bleached and highlighted across the trunk. It made you think of an old girl who couldn't see the back of her head in order to apply an even coat of hair dye: $8,500 o.n.o. The Revolution was asking $2,000 for a 1959 Cadillac Deville – a snip, but costly restoration was called for. The radiator had fallen onto the concrete, and in front of it was a pair of men's boots. It was as if the Deville, sensing its end under the tropical sun, the hot salt wind and, above all, the neglect and lack of flair of the Cuban state, had made sure of taking at least one Cubalse employee with it.

I said, 'What's the oldest car you've sold?'

'You can find American cars from the early 1940s. That's the oldest I've seen, though I've heard of cars before that date. We set prices according to a catalogue published in the United States. The cars are divided into six categories depending on the age and marque, the condition. The collectors have this catalogue too.'

'What would happen if I was buying a car?'

'First we would classify the car in one of the categories. We'd agree a price; I have a certain discretion. You would have to pay the costs of shipping the car back to your country. You would also have to pay taxes, insurance, import taxes.'

'You know, I'll bet you could sell hundreds of cars.'

'Yes,' agreed Señor Caballero. Cubalse was hoping to house the classic American cars under a roof, he said. It wasn't possible at the moment. But in another corner of the car-park, I noticed, the eggshell-thin bodywork of several Japanese vans was shielded from the briny mistral by a garage.

The mystery of Cuba's American cars was how the Cubans kept them going. I knew that there were workshops and parts foundries all over Havana, but finding someone who was willing to show me one was another matter. They were achieving respectability, as part of the decriminalisation of self-employment, but this only raised the worrying spectre of taxation in the minds of their proprietors. On Calle Aramburu, I saw a cream-and-berry 1948 Oldsmobile with the hood up and a giant black man tinkering beneath it. When I asked if he could point me in the direction of his local menders, he swayed from foot to foot, saying, '*No es facil, no es facil.*' (It's not easy.) Julietta muttered that no-one would want anything to do with my enquiries. Admittedly, we were a carburettor's throw from the police station on Salud: an astonishing sand-coloured fort like something out of Beau Geste.

The giant was saying that many spares were made on work premises out of hours, but I was distracted by the sight of a clip of bullets on the bonnet of the car next to his, on which several of his friends were sitting. Following my eyeline, he said, 'That's all right. They're hers,' and he pointed to a woman who was sitting beside the cartridges. 'She's a policewoman.' The woman smiled. This encouraged me in the belief that the police were relaxed about the informal car parts market. Yet, at least according to Julietta, it was hazardous for any motorist to let me accompany him the next time he so much as changed his points. I thought about whether she was really cut out for what we were doing. I had to remind myself to make allowances for her. She had grown up in a world of wait-in-line, keep your thoughts to yourself. Though she was in her twenties, and a graduate, economic facts of life in Havana dictated that she had never left home and sometimes it showed: her cravings for ice cream and milk-shakes; her impatience with the longueurs that sometimes went with work; her finickiness about food. One evening, Hilda had prepared chicken, bought for dollars from a diplostore. After a plateful, Julietta announced that she didn't really like chicken, before contrarily helping herself to another piece. She could only stomach certain morsels of the bird, she explained, 'and my Mummy always cooks those for me'. She was unable to cook anything herself.

My irritation was shaming, I knew. You could argue that it said something for Julietta that she would sooner go without than eat a dish she disliked. It was a small act of defiance against the special period. Perhaps Orula was right: my disposition was quarrelsome. When Julietta and I rowed, she would say that we were fulfilling our daily norm, a joke at the expense of Cuban economic planning as well as me. I would curse the heat and the humidity, like a pith-helmeted explorer in a B-movie, when what really bothered me was the fear of missing the story about Cuba. In more sanguine moments, something like my struggle to find a backstreet garage would remind me that I couldn't take the place for granted: Cuba's breezy, read-her-like-a-book disposition was the perfect disguise for her inscrutability. As for Julietta, she had once told me that she liked the idea of a career in journalism. Being a tour guide, say, might be okay, but once you'd seen a place, returning there endlessly with parties of holiday-makers would be dull. Later, though, she decided that she no longer wanted to be a journalist. 'You have to push people and I don't like to push people. I prefer to help people,' she said chasteningly. She was accustomed to taking the first 'no' she heard for an answer, and she didn't care to be near the things she had been brought up to find distasteful. Sometimes I wondered if there was more to her reserve than the reflexes of her personality and upbringing. Was it expected of her that she would guide me down certain paths and away from others? I didn't forget who her father was, or the words of the foreign journalist who had alleged about Cubans 'the capacity for duplicity is incredible'. Making as light of the question as I could, I once asked Julietta if she was spying on me. 'Not really,' she said. I teased her about her answer – she maintained it was innocent; an uncharacteristic slip – but I never quite got the doubts it raised out of my mind. I loved the idea that she might be my spy.

The guidebooks mentioned the old American cars but none of them told you what it was like to drive in one of them, much less to drive one yourself. This was probably because it was against the law. Foreigners were supposed to stick to air-conditioned *turistaxis* or rental cars from the state hire companies. That way, the dollars they paid for their transport went directly into official coffers. The authorities didn't want outsiders patronising Cuba's fleet of ad hoc Lada taxis, or coming to an understanding with the owners of the *particular*, the private, American cars. Drivers were liable to be flagged down by the Revolutionary Police and quizzed about any suspicious-looking passengers. They could face fines, or worse. Passengers, too, would be interrogated. It was a pleasing thought that you could break the law simply by *posing* as an old-time gangster. It seemed a risk worth running. The classic American car was a unique vehicle for exploring Cuba, in more senses than one. It was a time capsule, a working time capsule, and driving in one would be a kind of time travel.

The Doc was buffing his car the first time I met him in the summer of 1995. It was a two-door Dodge Colonel, and he was hand-kerchiefing a panel. It was the same affectingly superfluous act you could witness in the driveways of the British Home Counties any Sunday morning. The Doc was smartly dressed, in a *guayabera* and a pair of manilla slacks which matched the car's paint scheme. 'The car is from 1950,' he said in a booming voice. The Colonel was parked a block or so from my apartment, but the Doc told me he had driven in from out of town – from 'the provinces' as Cubans called anywhere outside Havana city centre, so that after a while you began to imagine the entire rural population of the Communist republic engaged in a permanent revolution of repertory theatre. A neighbour's daughter had come up to Havana to get married and the Doc was providing one of the wedding cars. After the couple finished signing the register in the municipal offices across the street, he would be driving guests to Miramar, a classy backdrop for the wedding photos. Judging by the way the Colonel had been looked after, it seemed as though it might be just the car in which to see more of Cuba, and the Doc the very man to explain how barely postwar jalopies like his were still on the road, while drivers in my country had got through entire lines of ergonomically designed runabouts and golfing-gondolas of the open road.

What I liked about Doc was that he wasn't really the wedding-car type, or the doctoring type either, come to that, although he claimed to be a specialist in 'internal medicine' at his local hospital. His real name was Dr Leandro Herrera Saiz. He became 'Doc' or 'The Doc' because of this, but also because of his resemblance to the American 'gonzo' writer, Hunter S. Thompson, the father of freewheeling narco-journalism, who was in the habit of prefixing his byline 'Dr'. Like Thompson, the Doc I met in Havana was bald on top. He wore dark glasses with big lenses. He was a big man with a roar of a laugh. The authors of what used to be called women's fiction might have discerned a capacity for cruelty in his eyes.

I climbed into the Colonel with a pair of girls in bridesmaids' finery. The Colonel had a green dashboard with a chrome inlay and its controls had to be clicked, or ratcheted, around – grooves had been cut into them at the factory. The big steering wheel was covered in tan hide, and at the base of the steering column, the word 'lighter' had been punched into the chrome over a pull-out lever. All the car's dials were rectangular. One illustrated 'Pounds … Pressure' (in English). Another said

AMPS
Discharge 40 0 40 Charge

although, like the rectangular milometer, which was stuck on 24, and the rectangular clock, which was stuck at 9.40, the ammeter didn't appear to be working.

The Doc seemed to be an experienced driver, although he had a disquieting tendency to maintain eye contact at all times during conversation. We discussed terms. I wanted to head out towards Trinidad, a city of such cultural riches that the United Nations had placed it on its World Heritage List. It was in central Cuba, but I thought it would be within the Colonel's range. We would go there for a few days. On a bosky avenue in Miramar, while the bridesmaids dimpled for the photographer, the Doc and I struck a deal: he would make the trip for $50, plus his expenses.

The Doc called by my *edificio* a week or so later. He had taken some days off work at short notice, one of the few perks that a consultant in Cuba apparently had in common with his counterparts in more developed countries. He was accompanied by his eldest son, Ivan, who was studying biology at college. 'It's a lot of driving. Too much for one person, I think,' the Doc explained. 'And we may have a problem, like a puncture. I hope not, but this is the land of miracles!' Julietta discovered from Ivan that the Doc had suffered a heart attack 18 months earlier.

In view of the laws against Cubans turning their private cars into taxis, the Doc said that if we were stopped by the police, I was to go along with his story that I was his patient, and he was driving me into the countryside for a consultation. 'Won't they think that's a bit suspicious in Trinidad?' I asked him. It was 500 kilometres from his hospital.

'We'll tell them that you're convalescing and you need a change of air,' he said. He was wearing a red-and-white-striped singlet which exposed hairy arms and a snowy chest. A pair of blue slacks, espadrilles and a cornball hat completed his ensemble. On the edge of the city, we passed a sanatorium and the Doc exclaimed, not very Hippocratically I thought, '*Para los locos!*'

People were by the roadside, bumming lifts. Several of them were in uniform. During the special period, it wasn't uncommon to see soldiers or policemen jerking a petitioning thumb. The Doc replied by holding out a cupped hand: 'We're full.' A woman was spark out – face down – at a roadside mango stall, though it was barely ten in the morning. We turned onto the broad *autopista*, the motorway. Directly ahead of us, the sun was catching the curvy buttocks of a girl in tight white shorts. She was riding pillion on a motorbike-combination driven by a soldier, and his kitbag occupied the sidecar. As we drew level, I noticed that although the girl's calves were smooth, her thighs were hairy. The scintillating whiteness of her shorts emphasised how darkly hirsute they were. 'Do you see her legs?' I asked Julietta.

'It's normal in Cuba,' she said.

'And the men like it?' I couldn't imagine the Cubans indulging their wives and girlfriends in what looked like a faltering feminist gesture – leaving half the leg unshaved. Though the Cuban regime prided itself on what it had achieved on behalf of women – more jobs, fair pay, better health care – equality between the sexes seldom extended across the domestic threshold. But Julietta told me that this was indeed the way the men liked their women. They were very aware of body hair on a woman.

'Really?'

'*Si.*' She explained that *piropos*, the Cuban version of leering remarks from building sites, often dwelt salaciously on the mooted hairiness of a passing woman. I noticed that Julietta also went unwaxed above the knee, although the hairs on her thighs were fine.

To one side of the highway, a turkey vulture made perfunctory passes over high grass and banana palms. Rushes stood in a lake, and there was a bleached chapel on a hill. Apart from a lone cyclist, who was inexplicably pedalling towards us in our lane, the *autopista* was deserted. Because of the empty road and the period automobile, it no longer seemed a tall order to be impersonating the Doc's chauffeured consultee. You imagined that this was more or less the same view that sickly tycoons and underworld invalids had glimpsed as they were driven across the island in the days before the Revolution, taking a little tropical sun on the orders of their physicians. The roads might look empty, the Doc said, but that only lulled Cuban motorists into complacency. Traffic accidents were the third biggest killer in the country. 'Number one is heart and brain illness. Number two is cancer,' he boomed. I caught a whiff of fuel. It made me homesick for Hilda's kitchen, the oil-soaked rags and canisters of paraffin beneath her kitchen sink. What I could smell was the cheap gas that Doc and

Ivan had switched to: it had meant a new engine for the Colonel. Or at least a *comparatively* new engine – a four-cylinder Toyota engine made in 1975. Doc told me that he now got 10 kilometres to the litre. Gas cost 25 cents a litre, less on the black market, but you had to know where to find it. He said the car was very economical on oil. 'It never boils over.' The temperature dial pointed unwaveringly to 'cool', and you felt sure that it would have done so even if it had been working. Nonetheless, I was disappointed in the Doc for replacing the engine, an original part in a car which had become an antique. I said, 'How rare are these cars, Doc?'

'There are only five of them in Cuba,' he said.

'How do you know that?'

'We showed the car at an expo in Varadero five years ago. We were told there were only four others of this two-door model on the island.'

Doc had paid 3,700 pesos for it. He'd bought it from a friend 20 years ago, when it was already 20 years old itself and in need of some work. The friend had since regretted the sale, Doc said, having seen what he had made of the car. He had fitted new door panels and replaced the nuagahyde upholstery when it had finally worn through, but the repairs had been in keeping with the original interior. The Colonel was recognisably the same car it must have been more than 40 years earlier, when it had been crated up and shipped out from the United States. Other drivers had offered him up to 20,000 pesos for it. 'In the expo, I met a foreigner who was ready to give me $25,000 – hard currency. I would have liked to have sold it, but you're not allowed to sell your own car. The state would have sold it for me and all I would have got in return was a pair of Ladas – no dollars! If a foreigner wants to buy a car and take it out of the country, he has to do it through Cubalse.'

It was impossible to find new tyres unless you had dollars. 'Before this trip, I swopped tyres with a friend. He gave me a tyre in good condition and I gave him a no-good tyre, just to keep his car on the road.' The tyres in the shops were American, embargo or no embargo. 'You can find everything here,' said the Doc. 'Nobody understands why.' The Doc earnt 400 pesos a month at the hospital. 'But I can make my monthly salary in two days on the road.'

He had contacts in the backstreet repairs trade. He told me he would show me 'the best-preserved car in Cuba'. It was in his home town of Alquizar, a collection of mud-splashed bungalows in Havana province. On Avenue 79, a young man was cleaning a 1959 Buick Invicta with a toothbrush. The car was broad and finny. It looked out of place between the rows of shacks, a World War Two bomber which had somehow come through an emergency landing without a scratch. Its electric windows still hummed thickly up and down at the touch of a switch beside the steering wheel. Wilfredo Vera told me that the Buick belonged to his father-in-law and he was making it ready for a bride. Like Doc's Colonel, the Buick earnt its keep as a wedding car. From the way the (still) brightwork was coming up, not only would the bride be able to see her face in it, she could also, if need be, apply her make-up and adjust her veil in it as well. Wilfredo lifted the bonnet to show me a new eight-cylinder engine: when he released it again, the catch dropped home in its greased coupling. I didn't have far to go if I wanted to see the old engine, according to Doc. It was in Angel's back-yard, awaiting salvaging. Angel García ran a 'Creole battery lab' at the back of number 8707, which was just across the road.

When a motorist's car battery went flat, he couldn't replace it because there were no new batteries. Or at least there were, but they were only available in dollar shops for more than $100 a time. So he would take his exhausted battery to Angel's yard, where Angel García and his men would open up the old battery, strip out the metal grids in which the chemical reaction took place, and put them in a metal crucible, a *crisol*. The *crisol* was on the end of a pole; this was tied to a wooden post – one of the props holding up Angel's garage – because the *crisol* was apt to become too hot to hold. The *crisol* was placed in the hollow of an old metal wheel where a fire was laid. A pipe running into a hole in the side of the wheel increased the air supply to the fire, so that the metal grids in the crucible would melt. Driving the air down this pipe was an electric fan reclaimed from a defunct washing-machine. The washing-machine fan in turn was connected to a tank or cylinder containing diesel, the tank being suspended from the garage roof. Once the metal had melted, it could be poured into molds, to be made into new grids. These were put through a metal mangle, to compact them, and left to cool in purpose-built wooden shelves, which looked like primitive CD racks. Then the grids or plates could be welded together, to form the matrix of another battery. While this process was going on, an oppositely charged element was being prepared with the use of a cement-mixer. Lead peroxide was placed in the maw of the mixer, where steel balls clangorously revolved. The balls ground the chemical into a powder, which could be sieved and eventually re-introduced into the battery casing.

Before Angel would allow a battery out of his garage, he measured its performance against a collection of coils thrumming in a corner of the garage which made your tongue prickle if you went within a few feet of them. The top of the battery would be replaced and then it could be sold again – for 800 pesos (the equivalent of $34), with a six-month guarantee. Angel's business had been clandestine, he said, a sideline to his day job as a mechanic in a government-approved garage. Reform of the employment laws meant that the Creole lab could come out into the open.

Angel had begun converting his yard into a battery plant five years earlier. He said, 'I've had to put the shop together little by little, according to what I could find.' I was marvelling at the ingenuity of the Creole lab. But Angel, in his broken boots, was ashamed of the improvised nature of it all. 'We could have done something much better but we didn't have the resources.'

My only reservation was about the health risks that Angel and his men might be running, with lead dust on their hands and in their faces all day. Did they wear masks, I asked him. 'Sometimes,' he said. 'We sometimes put handkerchiefs in front of our mouths. Or we have an electric fan. We've taken advice from a doctor about how to avoid accidents.' As we were driving away, I asked Doc whether he was concerned about the hazards the mechanics were exposing themselves to. 'I've been seeing a couple of them at the hospital with respiratory illnesses,' he admitted. 'But it's difficult. It's difficult for them to make a living.'

José Alfonso Gonzalez was rebuilding a 1950 Chevvy, which was up on blocks behind the tall metal doors of his garage. Like the '59 Buick, the Chevvy resembled an old plane, though this one had not had a happy landing. José said, 'The chassis is rotten so I've cut it up and now I'm going to put it together again.' He said the job would take him a week and he would charge 500 pesos. He was a handicrafts teacher and he was able to do the work because it was the school holidays. Everything about his workshop had a make-do, thrift-shop quality. He had made himself a polisher by finding an old engine, mounting it himself, finding an axle on which to fit the polishing wheel. Spanners hung from nails he had hammered at an angle into the door of his shed – his tool rack. José's most impressive cannibalisation was a machine which the Cuban military had sold as scrap. It was the stock or casing of a large, lethal pipe-cleaner: a device used to purge the gun-barrels of tanks. It gleamed from the shed, where it had been secured to a bench by a vice. It served as the stock of José's drill.

José earnt 250 pesos a month as a teacher, but 600 as a mechanic, and he was paying 60 pesos a month in taxes now that his enterprise was legal. He was married with two children. 'We have to work very hard and sacrifice ourselves a lot. The one who doesn't tighten his belt is eaten by a lion.'

I said, 'Is there such a thing as a write-off in your view?'

'In Cuba, cars may get written off, but only if there's absolutely no solution. If we can do anything at all, we will.'

'José is a magician,' said Doc.

We drove to the Zapata Swamp, on Cuba's Caribbean coast. We were going to Playa Girón, the Bay of Pigs, the scene of the abortive invasion of Cuba by exiles and mercenaries in 1961. A man on the hard shoulder was holding a pineapple aloft as though it was a trophy. He was hoping that we would pull over and buy it from him. On the liquefying horizon was the silhouette of a man in a cowboy hat sitting on horseback. We approached this apparition, watching it turn into a *campesino* offering limes for sale.

I had a compass with me, a cheap plastic thing which came with a thermometer. It was measuring the temperature inside the car at 36 degrees centigrade. But with the windows down and the quarterlights deflecting currents of air into the car – thanks to the Doc's patent spring-catches – it felt comfortably ventilated. The legroom was Tropical class. If I had a single quibble with the Colonel, it was over the matter of the colour. Light tan struck me as a poor livery for a Cunarder of the open road.

'It's not the original colour,' said Doc. 'Where we live, the earth is almost red, as you saw, so the car was always getting dirty. This colour is better for keeping it clean.'

'What was the original colour?'

'It had two colours,' he said. 'It was what we call a *blanco y verde*.' It would have looked like the car I saw that afternoon in Santiago with Cecil the taxi-driver.

As the Colonel approached the Australia sugar mill, where Castro had personally overseen the defence of the Revolution against the invasion, men stood at a junction with parrots on their fingers, like hitch-hiking pirates. They were trying to sell the birds. I said to the Doc, 'Maybe you know somewhere to eat?'

'Sure,' he said. 'Do you like crocodile?'

We stopped at Fiesta Campesina. It was all ersatz Treasure Island: the stalls were thatched in palm leaves. One was serving coffee which came with a cocoa leaf, and a sliver of sugar cane for a spoon. Prehistoric pike, *manjuani*, sweltered in two or three inches of water at the bottom of an ornamental pond. Disappointingly, crocodile was off. But there was *ruleta criolla*, Creole roulette. A stocky man was standing by a round wooden table. A bolt or swatch of sandy hair had been swept across his forehead and somehow fastened there. His name was Roberto Izqiardo. He offered to introduce me to the game. In the middle of the wooden table was what appeared to be a tiny yellow house with a sloping red roof. The house was the size of a shoebox, and the words *Ruleta Criolla* were painted on one of its walls. More miniature houses were set out around the edge of the table: sixteen in all. They were also finished in yellow and red, poster-bright colours which had weathered. At Señor Izqiardo's feet was a hutch. Ears of straw poked through its chicken-wire bars. Señor Izqiardo rummaged in the straw and pulled out a furball with claws at each corner: a black-and-white guinea-pig. His name was

Mario, said Señor Izqiardo. Mario straddled his master's palms. 'He's good, a one-year-old,' said Señor Izqiardo. He might have been talking about an Arabian thoroughbred instead of a kind of pert tumbleweed.

The idea of Creole roulette was that the guinea-pig was placed in the house in the middle of the table. I say house but it was no more than a shabby tin lean-to, a *trompe l'oeil* device like something in a conjuror's trunk. It could be whipped off in a moment, leaving behind only a wooden base – the floorboards of the house – and a guinea-pig, of course. Señor Izqiardo explained that he would set the table spinning through half a dozen revolutions and then snatch the 'house' away. The cavy would make for one of the houses at the edge of the table, like a roulette ball seeking its resting-place. Gamblers bet on which house Mario would scamper to. It was a $1 a time, and the prize was a bottle of Havana Club rum. I staked my buck on house number nine.

Ruleta criolla was a traditional peasant game, said Doc. He could remember seeing it as a boy. It was one of the attractions of the Fair of the Tangerines, which came to his hometown every year at the time of the tangerine harvest. It was a familiar sight at travelling circuses.

Señor Izqiardo raised the house in the middle of the table. He lowered Mario inside it. He replaced the house, and set the table spinning. It lumbered and creaked, but there was no sound from Mario. I wasn't concerned by this. I assumed that he was busy concentrating. My belief is that he did his best, but the disorientating effect of being spun around in a tin shack put him off his stroke. When Señor Izqiardo stopped the table and took the house away, Mario lost no time in making for a house bearing a number which was recognisably mine. True, it wasn't strictly number nine. Actually, it was number six – an understandable error for a rodent experiencing the effects of G-forces.

His owner told me that he was beginning to see British visitors. 'Two years ago there were none because there was no direct flight.' Now, Señor Izqiardo said, it was possible to catch a plane from Manchester to Varadero, or from London to Havana. 'But the majority of English people bring everything they need with them,' he added

They only buy very few things because they are very well
...d.'

...m the road, through the swamp, you could see the clear Caribbean breakwater. Crabs were tippy-toeing across the tarmac, splintering
under the Colonel's wheels, reminding me of Thing, the disembodied
hand from the Addams Family cartoons. Cubans caught them by
rattling a stick in a tin. The crabs sensed thunder, emerged from the
undergrowth expecting to drink rainwater, and were trapped. To see
them shuffling across the road of their own accord meant that a down-
pour was on its way. We went through a modest resort called Playa
Larga, where men were building a motel. Most holiday accommodation
was intended for foreigners paying in dollars. But Cubans could qualify
for vacations at the 'dollar-hotels' by working hard, emerging as the best
workers in their enterprises. The hotels charged them peso prices.
Julietta said, 'They keep two vacancies in most places. Enterprises
choose the two best workers and send them there.'

Just as the crabs had forecast, it began to rain. In fact, it was rainy
and sunny at the same time. The Cubans have a saying to describe
these meteorological conditions: 'The Devil's daughter is getting
married.' The Colonel was fitted with a windscreen wiper on the
driver's side only. In the rain, the view from the Doc's car was like the
one over the pilot's shoulder in a wartime newsreel. The drone of the
car's benzine-burning engine accentuated a resemblance to a Dakota.
The Doc wedged a piece of old green towel against the bottom of his
windscreen to collect the water that was getting in under the sill.

The shower had passed by the time we arrived in Playa Girón and
the air smelled of old leather. There were rows of white, empty-looking
motel *cabañas*. Long John Silver posed on a sign advertising the
'Pirate' motel, but we stopped at the Playa Girón Hotel. The reception
gave onto a concrete courtyard and a swimming-pool. I saw a couple
who looked European and a family who could have been Cuban, but
otherwise the place was deserted. Just outside the hotel bounds,
crowds of local children were playing lustily in a man-made lagoon. I
ordered a beer in the thatched poolside bar, which had its own pet
parrot. The Doc lost no time in putting it on his head. My image of
him as a gonzo quack suffered a knock, though, when he declined to

have a drink. I was heartened by his assurance that he loved beer, and that doctor or not – *not*, I found myself suspecting – he thought nothing of drinking six or seven beers when off-duty. He said he didn't want to fall asleep at the wheel. Beer can induce headaches, he told me – perhaps he *was* a doctor after all. 'When I was a medical student, there was a Bulgarian in my year. We were all training to be doctors.' The Doc looked around for Julietta. In her pink T-shirt and shorts, she was a squiggle of colour on the edge of the dazzling lagoon. Reassured that she was out of earshot, the Doc went on, 'This Bulgarian loved beer so much he used to drink it while he was pissing. We all did.'

I asked the Doc if he remembered the Bay of Pigs. He said, 'I was 11. I was watching television at my friend's house and suddenly we heard explosions. My father came to pick me up and take me home. He turned off all the lights and we all sat there in the dark, waiting until the bombing had finished.' This must have been 15 April 1961, when American bombers in Cuban colours strafed the island's four main airfields. Seven people were killed. Two nights before the invasion began, this softening-up exercise has tended to be overlooked in accounts of the Bay of Pigs adventure. Surreptitious and briefly deniable thanks to the Cuban markings on the aircraft, it was nonetheless the clearest case of direct American aggression against Castroist Cuba – the insurgents themselves, by contrast, could be described by the White House as Cuban nationals and mercenaries and so kept at arm's length, even though they had been trained by the CIA, and the United States chiefs of staff had been consulted over the invasion. The bombing raids also drew from Fidel Castro, in an oration for those who died in it, his first public declaration that the Revolution was 'Socialist'.

The Doc continued, 'We had two or three days without electricity. There was a blackout at night. There was a car going around with a public address system telling us that we shouldn't turn on the lights because they could be a sign for the aeroplanes.'

A Cuban family were at the next table, enjoying their incentive holiday. Finally you knew that they must be Cuban because their leisure wear looked as though it had been through the washing cycle once too often.

The Playa Girón museum was the size of a bungalow. There was an entire fighter on the lawn outside, a British-made Sea Fury flown by the Cuban air force against the invaders, and bits and pieces of engine and heavy ordnance. They were like self-consciously placed features or talking-points in the garden of a best-kept village. The three women on duty at the museum charged $2 admission. On a map, there were thick arrows pointing out the direction from which the invaders had sailed, from Puerto Cabezas in Nicaragua. A complicated family tree showed the chain of command of the invading mercenaries (under their '*Jefe de Brigada*'), stressing how well organised the mercenaries had been – they *hadn't* – presumably to magnify the achievements of the resistance. Shortly after midnight on 17 April, 1,297 men of the 2506 assault brigade landed in the swamp. The Cubans were ready. They had Soviet T-33 fighters and T-34 tanks. President Kennedy refused to sanction further bombing sorties to support the 2506, something which still rankles in the exile community in Miami. In fact, the brigade was abandoned by the Americans, and it surrendered on 19 April. After 48 hours on Cuban soil, or bog, it had suffered 107 casualties. There was no way off the island for the others and they ended up in Cuban jails, languishing for two years before Castro swopped them with the United States for $50 million dollars' worth of medicines. In terms of losses, Castro had actually fared even worse, losing 161 men and women. A photograph in the museum showed the single word 'Fidel' daubed on a wall – by the dying Eduardo García Delgardo, in his own blood, according to the caption. He was one of the martyrs of the Bay of Pigs. So was Rafael Morales Bonachea, whose sock was preserved with the other relics. However, deaths like these, his name scrawled in blood, enhanced Castro's standing. He felt confident enough to rule out presidential-style elections in Cuba, insisting that the ceaseless Revolution daily expressed the will of the Cuban people.

While we were among the display cases, I asked Julietta, 'What do you do for me?' Like all half-serious questions, it was a serious question: I was thinking of the numbers on my payroll, my swelling band of dependents – not just Julietta and Hilda and Nico and Nestor now, but also the Doc and Ivan. It was also a personal question, a seigneurial question.

'I take care of you,' Julietta replied indignantly. 'There are other things but I don't know how to translate.' It was the first time I had known her stumped. She went and sat in the back of the car, sideways on, her back against the mock-wood panelling.

The sun was drying out the swamp as we drove away from it. Steam rose from the grass. A luxurious shagpile of water vapour unrolled itself across the road and buried an oncoming bus up to its axles. I thought that the Zapata peninsula was a dreadful place to attempt an invasion.

On the road to the city of Cienfuegos, a Hundred Fires, we went through villages of single-storey wooden shacks. Towns were pinkly colonnaded. Buildings on busy corners were shaded brown to about waist-height, where they had been splattered with mud by lorries on rainy days. We stopped by a railway-crossing where an elderly man was selling twists of peanuts – roasted nuts in newspaper cones – for a peso. Doc bought ten. We had two cones each. Doc offered me a third and I accepted. 'Being European you eat a lot,' he said. 'It's okay! It's good to eat.' An old *campesino* trembled towards us on his bicycle. Man and machine were as skeletal as each other. The farmer had white five o'clock shadow. He was chewing on a cigar and wearing what Cubans called a *sombrero*: it was more like a stetson. As he drew closer, I saw that he was pedalling in wellington boots.

Julietta tried to sleep. When that failed, she flicked through a copy of a magazine which I'd brought with me from London. While Ivan drove, we did a quiz from the magazine, crossing off a checklist of experiences which any self-respecting reader was supposed to have under his belt by the age of 30. The fiercest critic of Cuba's revolutionary press could never have accused it of being titillating, and Julietta belonged to that tiny proportion of the world's population which hadn't read a word about the sexual peccadilloes of British royalty and Conservative politicians. 'What's a toe-job?' she asked me. Another poser raised by the quiz was whether the reader had ever said he loved someone even though he didn't. Another was 'Have you slept with a foreigner?'

We arrived in Cienfuegos to find a rain-emptied square. The main street, a scale-model of Havana's Prado, brought us to the bay, and the long straight road to the Hotel Jaguar. I remembered the road, and the hotel, from my first visit to Cuba in 1990. The guidebooks warned you of the way the house pianist at the Jaguar interpreted torch-songs. But what I recalled were a gauchely-spangled floorshow, a succession of mauve drinks on the house, a *cabaña* on the gnat-loud breakwater. We found the hotel next to a phoney French mansion, where I had once eaten in an empty restaurant. They didn't remember Angel, the hotel's director of publicity, who had made a point of my crotch-side seat for the cabaret. An eager student of English, Angel had also listened politely to my primer on Cockney rhyming slang: Gregory Peck, cheque; currant bun, sun; brown bread, dead. He had asked me for a tape by the Beatles. I wondered if he had ever received it. His old hotel was now full of Spanish tourists. They sat at the bar, watching a bull-fight on satellite television.

The road to Trinidad wound through the passes of the Escambray mountains. The Doc was at the wheel, but if he was worrying about the terrain which lay ahead, it was something he wasn't prepared to let the rest of us see. He was cackling at other road-users. There was an elderly cyclist with left-in-the-bath skin, and something clucking in his pannier as we drew level with it. The Doc leant out of the window and screamed, 'Thank you very much!' in English at the old boy, then turned to me and leered. I tried to imagine what his bedside manner might be like, and gave up. Not openly discouraged by me, he began to recite snatches of the English he had once learnt by rote. 'It is a fine day today. There are no clows in the sky. The sun ees shining. My wife and I walk over the river.' To one side of the road, vultures were attend-ing to the carcass of a dog – its face was set in a grimace but its ribs were already picked. I thought of a dinner in lawyers' chambers.

In Trinidad, there was a chapel in front of a graveyard on a hill, and a motel overlooking the city, the Las Cuevas. A lanky man occupied a gatehouse or sentry hut at the entrance to the motel grounds. Insouciantly, he waved the Doc's car away. According to Julietta, who was closer to him than I was, he added an insult under his breath. What had happened was that we had run into the barriers which prevented Cubans from going into their own hotels. The gateman was upholding unofficial Cuban policy, though, in fact, there was never any question of Doc and Ivan staying at the hotel. They were going to visit friends. Doc and Ivan were dropping us off.

At reception, Julietta complained about the gateman to the manager. He picked up a telephone and ordered the man to admit our companions. The sight of the Colonel, taxiing along the motel drive-way, was a reproach in itself. The Doc told us that he and Ivan had almost come to blows with the gateman. They had got out of the car and the two parties had squared up to one another. As he was recreating the scene for us, the motel's public relations officer sashayed up to us in the car-park. He was a stout man who carried his belly around carefully in front of him, like pottery. The Cubans stole a march on the West's premier hotel groups in appointing resident spin doctors, though I was surprised that a place like the Las Cuevas ran to one. We were emolliently invited to be the motel's guests at a 'special party'.

The Doc said he had better be calling on his friends. We expected him and Ivan to return later that night because they weren't sure if they would find running water in the city. It all depended on how the supply was rationed. They were welcome to use our showers, we said. I didn't forsee a problem in smuggling the Doc and Ivan in for a wash. The receptionist had given Julietta and me cabins away from the main motel buildings: they were on a terrace halfway back down the hill towards the main road, adjacent to each other. In the middle of unpacking my bag, I looked up and saw that Julietta was in my room. 'There's a connecting door,' she said.

We talked about what the Doc had said on the subject of the block-ade. It was easy to buy tyres if you had dollars, and yes, the tyres were American, blockade or no blockade. 'We have our own blockade,' he had added. I heard this cryptic phrase more than once. Cubans' fond-ness for puns and double meanings, together with a more recently acquired wariness, meant that discretion, or obfuscation, sometimes got the better of candour. The expression appeared to refer to the intransigence of the government. Julietta said the surly gateman was an example of Cuba's own blockade: he was kept in his job by the rigid shibboleth of full employment.

The motel's special party turned out to be a programme of traditional dances. The dancers wore traditional peasant garb, which included a surprising amount of gingham.

In the morning, I teased Julietta that she hadn't come into my cabin during the night. 'Well, you didn't come into mine,' she said, and sighed long-sufferingly. I had a girlfriend; she had a boyfriend, a Norwegian. He had come to Cuba as part of a solidarity brigade. Julietta had been doing a kind of community service in a fruit-picking camp when she met him. I felt ashamed for embarrassing her. I said, 'Actually, my door was locked.'

'Yes, I know,' she said.

We hadn't seen Doc and Ivan again in the night but they turned up just as we were going to breakfast. They used our showers. In the dining-room, the Doc heard me asking the waitress for a cup of hot, salty water. It was for an abscess on the roof of my mouth. 'I will give you a consultation,' declared the Doc.

'Say "Aah",' he said. I was sitting on the edge of my bed, beside the reading light. The bulb was bare: the Doc had removed the lamp-shade, which he was holding in one hand. He was standing over me on the bed, squinting down my throat. I thought, this would be a fine time for the management to discover that I had a Cuban in my room. Despite his bird's eye view, and the unshaded light, it was too dark for him to inspect my mouth. We went out into the sunlight and stood on the grassy slope beneath my cabin. This time he made an immediate diagnosis. He confirmed that I had an *afta*, a sore. I needed a solution of sodium bicarbonate called *violeta gencia*. 'Salt water isn't bad but you need a non-acid salt,' he said. 'This problem has to do with the psyche,' he said. Then he said, 'You should gargle with rum!'

It emerged that Julietta had washed out her panties and they had ended up in Ivan's towel, to dry. She teased him: 'You'd better remember to give those back to me, or you'll be in trouble with your wife.'

I asked her, 'Why didn't you wash them at home?'

She said, 'Didn't you wash yours?'

'I have a spare pair.'

'Well, I have a spare pair of socks,' she said defiantly, and it occurred to me that she wasn't wearing any underwear.

Trinidad had cobbled streets. The sewerage system was similarly antiquated, and water percolated through the stones. There was a story that the gutters ran down the middle of the streets because one of the city's governors had a right leg shorter than the other. He had the roads laid out to irregular specifications to give himself the appearance of poise when he was taking the air along the thoroughfares. The single-storey houses had high ceilings, and iron courting-grilles over their shutters where suitors had once come a-wooing. An old man was looking out from behind a fancy trellis like a buzzard in a budgerigar cage. From the balcony of the Romantic Museum, it was possible to marvel at a turkey vulture circling a Moorish bell-tower. Was there so much as a thermal up there, on this airless day? The museum owed its name to a fashion in lacquered furniture and not to ideas of courtly or sentimental attachment – Cuba was, after all, a land not of romance but of a more flesh-and-blood kind of love – though newlyweds were in the habit of having their picture taken on the balcony. Two French-women were filing through the museum's prettily cluttered chambers. They were living in the United States, and because of the embargo, had made a tortuous journey to Cuba by way of the Bahamas. They had been in Cuba for a fortnight, and were getting around in an old taxi. The heat and the travelling made them fractious. They stood bickering in pleasing voices at each other with their hands on their hips.

Trinidad had a museum devoted to the travails of the revolution-aries, the *Museo Lucha Contra Bandidos*, the Museum of the Struggle against the Bandits. Julietta surprised me by saying that she would like to visit it. She had told me on several occasions that her hero was Camilo Cienfuegos, the genial one in portraits of the Sierra Maestra rebels, so it was possible that she wanted to offer her devotions to him. On the other hand, perhaps she wanted to be able to tell her father with a clear conscience that we had included the museum in our itinerary. It occupied a building in the meagre shadow cast by the bell-tower. One exhibit was a scale-model of the scene outside the former presidential palace in Havana where an attempt had been made on Castro's life in 1961. Fidel had been speaking in front of the palace. A lint or cotton stretched between replica buildings represented the assassin's line of fire. He had hidden himself in an eighth-floor apartment on the corner of Avenida de las Misiones and Pena Pobre. Julietta was naturally familiar with the incident. There was an oral tradition of Cuban revolutionary history – everyone could recite the stories of martyrs and mercenaries. She said, 'The assassin had Fidel in his sights. He had a bazooka. But then he decided not to shoot. The police came in and found him. He told them it was as though Fidel had some powers which prevented him from firing. He said he could see that it would be wrong to kill Fidel.' In another case was an old electric razor, a Remington, said to have belonged to a CIA man. It had been recovered at Guantánamo. Perhaps Cubans put up with these tawdry relics – an old razor, a soiled sock – because of *Santería*, and its veneration of gamey keepsakes, a bloodstained gourd, a rosary of coconuts, an oxidised gin trap.

Doc put some more gas in the Colonel – 52 litres at 35 cents each. There was a dollar shop on the forecourt of the filling-station. It was selling 'Tulip' canned meat, litres of Castrol oil, and, at $84 each, American-made car tyres. Doc turned on the ignition, palmed a cassette into the incongruous hollow of the Colonel's dashboard player, and cried, 'Let's rock' – though what emerged quaveringly from the Colonel's hi-fi were the soupy strains of a Spanish balladeer. The purpose of our trip was to find a *farmacia*. The Doc was determined to tip some *violeta gencia* down my throat, in order to clear up my *afta*, and with it any lingering doubts that Julietta and I might be harbouring about his qualifications.

The red earth, the blanched hoardings with their exhortatory legends, the dusty, pink-washed towns, the *campesino* on his bicycle with his toothbrush moustache and *sombrero* – this was Cuba outside the cities. We were driving through a little town called Placetas when Doc spotted a *farmacia*. When he walked over to it, I saw for the first time what his clean singlet looked like from the rear. The Doctor was wearing a top worked with the device 'Shark Bait'. Inside the *farmacia* were shelves of bottles bearing the skull and crossbones. Other bottles were stoppered with scraps of metal foil, held in place by rubber bands. I had to drain the tepid contents of a soft drink bottle so that it could be filled with medicine. It cost 1.20 in Cuban pesos. The pharmacist who poured the *violeta gencia* said that he had never seen a two-door Colonel before. 'We're on the main road and we see cars every day, and this is the first time I've seen one of those,' he said, shaking his head at the wonder of it.

A man on a three-wheeled bicycle was pedalling a cake past the old Spanish courthouse in Santa Clara. A sign outside a playground praised Fidel. In a shabby snackbar, *Los Caneyes*, the Indian houses, flies were diving onto the counter and failing to right themselves. There were scores of them and they span on their backs at great speed. They looked like ball bearings. Outside, it was raining heavily. Perhaps the flies had been sent *locos* by the storm. They were as helplessly in thrall to nature as the jaywalking crabs of the Zapata Swamp. The front of the bar was tilted, inclined toward the drinker. 'It's so drunks can rest their heads,' said Doc.

On the road, there was the mottled grey of rain clouds and the greens of the fields, and just a splash of evening brightness from the lights of a town in the distance. I saw an *autopista* and said, 'When will it be finished?' assuming, from its desertion, that it was still awaiting topping-out. Then I saw a cowboy on a bike; then, on the horizon, a lorry. The *autopista* had been open for years. I asked Doc if I could drive the car. I had been itching to get behind the wheel since we left Havana. We pulled up and swopped places. Just holding the juddering wheel produced an electric tingle in my left hand. The configuration of the driver's seat, the steering wheel and the dashboard, pressed my face close to the windshield. I noticed the rust at the margins of the driver's window. There was a charred, laval look about the rubber fittings. Cars like the Doc's didn't deteriorate the way other cars did. Harley Earl and his imitators had built them with aeroplanes in mind, but in Cuba at least, they had outlived all the aircraft of a similar vintage (not to mention succeeding generations of cars), and the vessels they had come to resemble most closely – in terms of their longevity – were ships. You wouldn't have been surprised to find barnacles under the plates.

I was feeling better. The *violeta gencia* was doing the trick. The Doc had cured me – he *was* a doctor after all – and I had ended up being his patient. Unless the Colonel was pulled over at the last minute by a traffic patrolman, I had got away with driving around Cuba like an old-time gangster. The only laws the four of us had fallen foul of were the unwritten ones which governed where Cubans could go in their own country. The Doc reached over and put his foot on top of mine, nudging the speedo up to 100 m.p.h. I was dodging potholes, languorous strays. We overtook a car transporter, which had only one car aboard, a Lada. A man without his shirt on looked at us from the driving seat of the car. Standing behind the cab of the transporter was a man in a yellow oilskin with his hood up – perhaps it was this nautical association that gave the Lada-owner the look of a man in a lifeboat. Surely his trousers, if one could have seen them, would have been ragged.

6

Dreaming in Cuban

AT THE END OF JULY 1995, Havana ran out of money. By that I don't mean that there was a run on Cuban pesos. They remained as worthlessly available as ever. No, what happened was that the supply of dollars suddenly dried up. Bank cashiers turned you away from their counters. Tellers in hotel exchange bureaux directed you to each other's lobbies – fruitlessly, as it turned out. In an increasingly alarmed hurry, you would cough up for an air-conditioned *turistaxi* from Vedado to Habana Vieja in the hope of unearthing a few bills at the Sevilla, only to find yourself making the return journey, to the Capri, or the St John's – again without success – all the time eyeing the meter with more than usual watchfulness. It was like Weimar Germany in reverse. Instead of an overheated economy, in which everybody wheelbarrowed their loose change, there appeared to be a danger that cash transactions as you knew them would come to a halt. On the face of it, this was a pretty good sign of an economy which was cooler than it might be, although there was a rumour that the shortage of notes was due to unexpectedly high demand from tourists. I was down to my last few greenbacks and, unable to cash a traveller's cheque, facing financial embarrassment. The chequebook issued by my British bank was useless in Cuba. Hotels accepted credit cards provided that they weren't of United States origin – the embargo again – but when I asked receptionists if they could let me have some dollars against my plastic, they told me they couldn't spare them.

There is a fine tradition of the writer who travels light – a collapsible kayak and a billy-can of warm ants and he's happy – but I had by now accumulated precipitous overheads and purse-emptying outgoings. There was Hilda's rent to think of, and the money I gave Nico for the shopping. There was the $25 I gave Julietta every day she worked for me, and the retainer I paid Nestor for his loyal service and somewhat feckless Lada. When I thought about my costs, or reckoned them in a notepad, they struck me as a significant burden even without the disappearance of hard currency from the streets of Havana. Now that it was nowhere to be found, paying my bills looked even more difficult. I developed an almost Cuban yearning for a dollar. Objectively speaking, this was rubbish, of course. I could check into the Inglaterra again, live on tic while I waited for the fiscal dust to settle, and hope that I would be able to honour my credit card bill when I finally got back to London. But that would have meant abandoning the apartment and a routine, if not quite a way of life, to which I had become attached: the pretty sisters on the next balcony, *tranquilas* and come-hither in the morning and at dusk, though they fought with their men and children at night; the door-to-door salesmen, like the cake-man with his terrifically *combed* hair and shirt boxes full of eclairs; the green coronet of the Carmen church and the clanging of her bell.

All the same, so long as I stayed at 25 y O, without the credit-card facilities offered by a hotel, or the money-order security of the ex-pat stockades out at Miramar, it was a matter of some urgency that I put my hands on a few dollars. In this heightened state of financial awareness, I found myself speculating about what could have happened to all the money. Had an unrelenting CIA perhaps developed a new form of warfare, which left people untouched but destroyed all their currency? Anton Arrufat, a writer who had spent most of his career out of favour with the regime, claimed that Castro was mopping it up, taking it out of the system, so that he could spend it himself – perhaps on medicine or new buses, perhaps on other things he'd had his eye on. According to this view, the maximum leader was Cuba's miser, snowed in at his counting house by drifts of cash. When you tried to picture what Arrufat imagined, what came to mind was that familiar bearded figure up to his boot-tops in doubloons spilling from sacks, and surrounded by igloos of ingots. What came to mind was Castro the robber king, Castro the *pirate*, and you thought this was where you came in: Cuba and the pirates. Was Castro really snaffling up all the cash? In its back-handed way, the idea fed the myth of him as a super-man, capable of sucking all the value out of his country's economy single-handedly. In all the dirt that had been heaped upon him over the years, allegations of venality had never really stuck. There was said to be a retired European diplomat or soldier living in the Channel Islands who administered Castro's secret pelf. Precedent, for what that was worth, indicated that filching on the part of a Cuban president was by no means unheard of. Two of Castro's predecessors had taken the money and run. Machado hopped a plane to Miami in 1933 accompanied by five bags of bullion. Batista fled to the Dominican Republic on New Year's Eve, 1959, with $300 million in his luggage. Would Castro eventually take his place in the ignominious roll-call of world leaders found to have dipped in the till?

Perhaps the days of the vanishing dollars will not prove to be the most significant chapter in Cuban history. But to a foreigner who happened to experience them (and was spared the worst of other privations), they simulated what it might be like if the moment Cuba's friends had feared, and her enemies had prayed for, ever came to pass – the moment when Cuba failed. To the sympathetically-minded, there was a kind of Cuban dream. It was comparable to the more familiar American dream, but to some extent it was also the antithesis of it; to an American of a certain stripe, indeed, the Cuban dream was frankly the American nightmare. Within Cuba, the notion of a Cuban dream or myth arose out of the country's long nationalistic struggle: firstly, against the Spanish; then, in the twentieth century, against the United States – and, the man in the street might add, against Moscow and the Cuban government. Arguably, a sense of nationalism was the most enduring feature of the Cuban dream. The revolutionary regime shrewdly concentrated on this common aspiration in its propaganda. This accounted for the totemic bust of José Martí, the great – and manipulably late – Cuban patriot, outside every school, and for his likeness on every other hoarding. The Revolution in 1959 was nationalistic in character at the outset. It was not until after the Bay of Pigs invasion that Castro publicly identified it as Socialist, and Cuba's polarity was reversed, from inclining towards America to inclining towards Russia. For many outside Cuba, the fact that Castro stood up to America was enough to make the Cuban dream inspiring. This David and Goliath confrontation began at the time when United States' foreign policy was entering an uncelebrated phase – the Cold War, Vietnam. There's no doubt that anti-Americanism was part of the appeal for many. But it wasn't only a national emancipation that Castro and the other revolutionaries espoused. They declared that the transformation in Cuban society would sweep away racism and sexual discrimination: Martha Gellhorn, who had lived in Cuba in the 1940s, wrote that she didn't realise Cuba was full of blacks, because the only black people allowed into Havana at that time were housemaids. The Revolution would increase living standards of workers exploited by foreign interests, principally in the sugar industry. And there would be education and health care for all, courtesy of the state.

It was a bold and invigorating pitch. This wasn't a revolution imposed on one of Russia's neighbours by the fearful nearness of Red Army tanks. It apparently came from within, from the heart, although Castro's critics liked to point out that sophisticated *habaneros* greeted the Revolution with their time-honoured indifference to the movement of ideas. What made the Cuban dream more spellbinding to the susceptible was the thought that it wasn't unfolding in a bleak and sooty Potsdam or Tirana but among the laughing-eyed salsa dancers of the tropics. There was a cartoon in *Punch* magazine in the 1970s showing a scowling man with a beard and spectacles outside a travel agent's. In the window were posters for East Germany, Poland and Hungary. A woman was looking at deals to Spain, Greece and South Africa in the adjacent window. She was saying, 'The people's republics are all very well, Adrian, but it's the fascists that get all the sunshine.' Cuba was the glittering exception to this rule.

The end, or failure, of the Cuban dream was widely predicted, or hoped for, almost from the beginning, more so after the fall of the Berlin Wall in 1989, as Communism in Eastern Europe collapsed. Half a decade later, that still hadn't happened, at least not in the satisfyingly public way that Castro's enemies had been anticipating. The disappearance of dollars, Cuba's mini-crash, seemed a good moment to reflect on what had become of the Cuban dream.

Cuba had at last achieved the independence that the events of 1959 had theoretically entrained. And this had happened literally by default – Moscow had welched on aid payments worth $1 million a day. After the decline of Comecon, the last president of the Soviet Union, Mikhail Gorbachev, had cancelled his standing order in favour of Fidel Castro, severing a financial link which had stood for 30 years. There was no doubt that this had had a devastating impact on Cuba. I asked Omar Everleny Perez, a young economist who advised on government policy, if he could give me an idea of what had happened since the withdrawal of Soviet support. He sketched a graph of GDP which might have described the trajectory of a banker during the Wall Street Crash. On the government's own calculations, it had stepped off a window ledge, falling by 40 per cent between 1989 and 1995. 'However, the economy grew by 0.7 per cent last year,' Señor Perez added bravely, looking up from his grim scribble. It was estimated that 80 per cent of Cuba's industrial capacity had been stripped out, as a result of a lack of fuel and raw materials. By 1996, the regime was predicting a much healthier 5 per cent growth for the year, albeit from a very low base.

At 35, Señor Everleny Perez was one of the new thinkers in Cuban economic planning. 'To stop inflation, we have to use the words "demand" and "offer",' he told me in a confident manner. You might never have guessed that what he was saying had been unsayable almost immediately hitherto. 'The way to encourage production is with incentives. There must be a close relationship between property and management.' Without the cushion of state sponsorship, Cubans were coming to terms with competing in the international marketplace – some more readily than others. I was surprised at the candour with which senior apparatchiks were willing to discuss the decisions facing the country. Raul Taladrid, a foreign investment minister, who wore an expensive-looking leisure shirt and rhapsodized about the strawberries and cream he had sampled during a trip to Wimbledon, admitted that there was substantial hidden unemployment in the Cuban economy. This was no more than stating the obvious – every diplostore was overstaffed, and heads nodded behind the counters of unvisited shops and idle offices – but it was nonetheless quite something to have it stated, since jobs-for-all was one of the dearest myths of the Revolution. 'Unfortunately, we cannot provide full employment now,' said Señor Taladrid. His ministry had set the pace, slashing its work-force from 800 to 150. Officials let it be known in 1996 that as many as 800,000 workers were performing at 40 or 50 per cent capacity, perhaps softening up public opinion for lay-offs of 100,000 'surplus' workers from the state sector.

To the extent of balancing budgets and eliminating waste, the minister was prepared to utter the language of Western-style market economics, though he maintained that the Cuban model remained Socialist. 'We wish to be very serious and professional about making progress, but without losing our political tint,' he said. 'We believe in Socialism and we want to save what we've done.' This echoed the view of Carlos Lage, Cuba's foremost economic strategist, who insisted in 1996 that the state remained central to the economy. However, foreigners could take a stake of up to 100 per cent in Cuban businesses – even Cubans living in Miami. They could nominate the boards themselves, and repatriate their profits. People from overseas could buy property in Cuba. The land of revolution increasingly sold itself as a peaceful and well-appointed home for foreign capital, with a healthy, bright labour force. Señor Taladrid stubbed his cigarette out. 'If you want to have a joint venture to produce ashtrays, we will produce ashtrays,' he said matter-of-factly.

There were always at least two questions about Cuba's apparent conversion to market economics. One was whether the Cubans could pull it off. In this respect, they were greatly hampered by the Helms-Burton bill. Named after its sponsors on Capitol Hill, this was a tightening of the American embargo, which also extended its sanctions to any of America's trading partners who dared to treat with Castro.

The measures had seemed unlikely to receive the presidential assent until February 1996, when the Cuban air force shot down two light aircraft belonging to a Cuban exile organisation called Brothers to the Rescue. Four people died, amid controversy over where exactly the shooting took place. Seeking re-election, President Clinton initialled the legislation. The other question about the entry of the Cubans to the international marketplace was: were their hearts in it? When Señor Taladrid told me that Cuba's investment reforms had been set in motion in 1989, I said – innocently as I supposed – 'We know why that happened,' meaning the dwindling of aid from Moscow. But I was treated to a reheated Cold War polemic about Ronald Reagan's efforts to purge Communism from Latin America. After a while, I put my pen down and wondered whether visiting businessmen had to sit through this too, and what they might make of it. If even the urbane Señor Taladrid indulged in monologues about the impact on the economy of constructing tunnels in which to hide from the *Yanquis*, how far did Cuba still have to go before she became the obliging offshore residence for capital that she imagined herself?

A litmus test was Cuba's efforts to overhaul the tourist industry. Government strategists had abandoned the Communist habit of five-year plans – itself a significant development – in favour of annual programmes, but they were committed to the long-term goal of developing tourism as Cuba's principal industry. It was to be more important even than sugar. There had been a sugar crop of more than 10 million tons as long ago as 1893, but a much publicised effort to match this feat under revolutionary circumstances failed in 1970. The 1995 harvest was less than 3.5 million tons; a year later, the regime was taking comfort from a predicted yield of less than 5 million tons. By contrast, tourism officials were estimating that Cuba would attract a million visitors in 1996, the first time the island had done so. After decades in which most holiday-makers were on fraternal visits from Comecon countries, no hard currency changing hands at any point, the Cubans recognised that their tourism amenities and know-how fell some way short of the international benchmark. 'The hotels don't have the comfort that we want in the future,' said Orlando Rangel Delgado of the Ministry of Tourism. 'We're working to develop new resorts.' The Press Centre lost no time in arranging an interview for me with Señor Rangel, who entertained me in his sumptuously chilled library. After what sounded like a ritual reference to the obstacle of the American embargo, Señor Rangel stressed the tax breaks and goodies which Cuba offered overseas hoteliers: the more a foreign company ploughed its profits back into its Cuban operation, the more favourable its tax position. But for the lack of blood on the walls, it could almost have been Kiki plugging the Hotel Via Coco in the East Beaches.

What about remarks Fidel had been making, saying contacts with foreign entrepreneurs bred corruption? Señor Rangel said he didn't think Fidel had had hoteliers in mind.

I asked Señor Rangel what he thought foreigners liked about Cuba. The hospitality of the people, he said, the climate and the beaches. 'And some people come to see what we're doing.'

'Does it concern you that Cuba is a destination for sex tourism?'

'I've had the opportunity of going to different countries, and prostitution is there too.'

'A cynic would say that it's not in Cuba's interests to curb sex tourism; it brings in so much money.'

'Sex tourism is not part of our plans,' said Señor Rangel.

Before I left, I offered a kind of modest proposal for improving tourism. Big hotels like the Habana Libre should be ready to cash travellers' cheques at more convenient hours, I said. Señor Rangel made a note to himself on a pad. I also suggested that the artwork designed for cigar boxes could be marketed on postcards and T-shirts. 'Thank you very much for these ideas,' he said, still writing.

Julietta and her friends at the Foreign Languages Institute aspired to careers in Señor Rangel's department. On the day they went back to college to discover which positions they had been given, to collect their job-drafts, Nestor ran me over to the Institute, which was on the other side of Vedado. I looked around for Julietta but couldn't see her. Nestor said, 'She is not here?' I couldn't tell from his tone whether he was concerned or, for some reason, mirthful. Then there she was, *muy bonita* in floral halterneck top and shorts. I could see that she was anxious. She greeted her friends. Younger Cubans made an attractive lip-smacking noise when they kissed each other upon meeting: it was a real embrace, though, not a Western air-kiss.

The faculty was jerry-built, or rather, Ruskie-built. There were hot, cheap, metal strips around the windows, ceilings of raw asbestos, and exposed switch fittings. The railings on the staircase were missing. I joked with Julietta that they had been melted down to make fighter planes – and then, remembering Castro's excursions in Ethiopia and Angola, I wondered if perhaps they hadn't been. From the classroom, there was a good view of the Ministry of Telecoms office. It didn't look like an office: it looked like a two-dimensional film-studio flat of an office, not intended to be seen except in a wide shot. There was a preposterous, matchsticky satellite tower. A sign said *venceremos*, we will win.

The Cuban education system was one of the great achievements of the Revolution. Before 1959, almost half of the rural population was illiterate; one in two Cuban children was going without an education. In 1996, notwithstanding the difficulties of the special period, an adult literacy of 98 per cent was claimed – the best in Latin America: 90 per cent of five-year-olds were on school rolls. Near the restaurant El Conejito, a 1930s Spanish *casa* with an incongruous *ante-bellum* hall-way had been converted into a primary school. Pupils were taught Spanish and maths and science, and about political organisations and the Cuban constitution. However, a teacher said, 'We lack everything: cleaning things, teaching things. We take good care of our textbooks – these ones have lasted for seven years. We repair them with materials the children bring from home.' Around the country, some secondary schools and sixth-form colleges had been closed or turned into offices.

A determination to educate as many Cubans as possible to tertiary level had flooded the economy with more graduates than there were suitable vacancies. Some were being press-ganged into the services – at least, that's how they saw it. Out of Julietta's class of 56 English students, seven were due to be called up for the armed forces; the seven with the poorest marks. The class had already held two meetings to discuss the army placements. Few of the students had attended the meetings. I asked Julietta why this was. 'Because no-one wants to go into the army.' The faculty had tried to get the students to decide among themselves who would enlist. 'No way!' she said.

The course tutor read out the names of the students who were being conscripted. A blonde woman in a denim skirt on my left and the darkest man in the room were among them. They argued with the tutor, whom they called *compañera*, or *profe*, short for *profesora*. The girl had been assigned an office job, monitoring and translating radio signals. She would be getting in on the ground floor of the espionage business. She claimed that she had a note from her doctor ruling out an occupation of this kind, but the tutor told her that this made no difference. A man in a *guayabera* shirt had stopped by the classroom and was smoking menacingly.

'*Profe! Profe!*' Julietta argued doughtily with the tutor on the blonde's behalf. Julietta herself was alloted a job in a food research insititute. 'I don't like it. But at least it's not the army.'

I thought of Roberto, the veteran of the Angola conflict. I said, 'What would your father think if he heard you say that?'

'He knows what I think. His views are old-fashioned. These days, we need money and I won't earn any money at the food institute.'

Graduates who were lucky enough to find positions in tourism could expect to see a lot of Varadero, the centrepiece of the Cuban holiday industry, the fleshpot that was going to rescue the Revolution. It was two hours' drive out of Havana, an isthmus pointing out into the Atlantic Ocean. The resort took off during the Second World War, when well-to-do Americans looked around for somewhere safer than Europe to take a vacation. After the Revolution, it was enjoyed by privileged visitors from Comecon countries. The low-tide mark of European Communism was the point at which Varadero's popularity with a wider world began to take off. It was said to have the best beaches in Cuba. Notwithstanding the charms of Havana, the Cubans understood that a Caribbean destination had to sell itself on the beauty of its beaches.

The architecture was unmistakably from Cuba's post-Soviet period: there were no air-conditioning stains on the hotels, no warped metal shutters. Alighting outside my hotel from the too-small tourist minibus – 'It was made by Japanese for Japanese,' observed the driver tartly – I saw a poster of a thickset-looking man at a microphone. Had the hotel laid on special arrangements for Fidel's traditional speech on 26 July, the anniversary of the Moncada raid? A bank of television monitors at the poolside, perhaps? Happy hour for the first 60 minutes – the mere paper-shuffling and cuff-shooting of his performance? In fact, the sketch advertised karaoke night. Presumably the hotel management did not expect a great demand among patrons to hear the words of *El Comandante*.

The hotel pool was hardly deep enough to paddle in, but it hadn't been designed with anything so strenuous in mind. There were concrete loungers beneath the surface of the water, and beside them little concrete pouffes on which patrons could rest their drinks. The bona fide happy hour was announced by a disc jockey high in his observation post or bunker – 'Take cover!' was his inexplicable catchphrase. He announced that the price of cocktails was reduced by 50 per cent between five o'clock and six. The speciality of the house was something called a Soviet. In view of a widespread belief in Cuba that the country had been ruined by the disintegration of the former USSR, you half expected the barman to bring you an empty glass, or even a broken one, but a Soviet turned out to be a vodka-based aperitif. Swim-suited husbands from South America began padding to the bar, typically returning with what appeared to be a *Cuba Libre*, a rum and coke, in one hand, and a frothier, milkier confection in the other. Wives were handed drinks. The tourists held them clear of the water: it looked as if they were posing with them for photographs. This was particularly true of a formidably large South American lady in a black bathing costume. When she finally got out of the pool, she stood with her arms at her sides and flicked water off her wrists like a weightlifter shaking off excess chalk.

At Varadero, there were parades of tourists whose children were no longer young but whose wardrobe suddenly was: loganberry Fred Perrys; his 'n' hers Bermudas. Prosperous foreigners came to Cuba for what Cubans took for granted – and it was virtually all they could take for granted – the sun, sea and sex. And the Cubans were desperate for, or at least deprived of, what the tourists took for granted:

consumerism; freedom to travel (which the tourists demonstrated by the very act of coming to Cuba. Many Cubans had braved their seas in order to attempt the act of going away).

The hotel day was organised so that almost every minute was planned – like on a cruise-liner, or at an old-fashioned British holiday camp. Perhaps this helped to explain the growing popularity of Varadero among Britons. I met a rep called Yvonne from the West Midlands. She said, 'It's mostly families here now, with the school holidays on, but generally we see a lot of couples, in their late twenties and older. Many have read up a lot. They understand that there are problems here, they're expecting them. But they all come here with books and say, "I've read about that, and I want to go there."' Yvonne had been in Cuba for a year. 'Ninety-nine per cent of British clients are very happy. A lot come back, or refer the place to their friends. Their biggest worry? How much rum to have.'

Desite Yvonne's help, I spent days failing to sight a single confirmed Brit. There were none on the excursion I made in Varadero's glass-bottomed boat, tourists from Chile and Germany admiring undersea fungi which looked like burnt milk, and tropical fish in their soccer strip. The Chileans said they had come to Cuba 'for a change'. A German couple said they were there because they remembered 1959, the Bay of Pigs. 'And the hijackers,' the woman said, 'they always used to say—'

'Fly me to Havana!' we said together.

I went onto the beach. A woman was settling herself behind a paperback. Could I tiptoe across and steal a glimpse of the cover without disturbing her? Damn; it was in French. A lifeguard tipped me off about a couple whose effects were laid out in the shade of a man-made palm. They were English, he thought. I sat down to wait for them. Varadero lived up to its billing: the water was very clear, hardly a rock or a weed beneath the surface. A German tourist was frolicking in the breakwater with a Cuban girl. Another holiday-maker went in to the sea to bathe and was approached by a woman with a backside so pert it looked like a small shelf. Varadero was the only place I have ever been where the prostitutes solicited in the surf. At length, the couple whom I had been waiting for emerged from the sea to reveal tanned, oily skin.

As they hobbled over the sand to their palm, I thought: she's not British, not with that complexion, that slightly busy swimsuit. Sure enough, the couple were Italian. Finally, at a hotel cabaret, I tracked down Linda and Barry from Buckingham. He worked in a factory; she was a hairdresser. Barry had a receding carroty perm. 'He doesn't tan,' said Linda. 'He just goes bright red and then starts peeling.' Barry seemed to have reached the first stage of this process, for he glowed pinkly. Linda was a sun-worshipper, she said. 'Poor Barry hates it. But he's happy with his book and people-watching.' They were staying in a self-catering chalet attached to the hotel. Their daughter was staying in another one with her friend, but the girls had gone out to a disco with a hotel barman who had the night off.

Linda and Barry were disappointed by a lack of fresh fruit and vegetables. 'We usually lunch on bread, cheese and tomatoes,' said Linda, 'but there only seems to be one bread shop in Varadero, and that's a mile and a half away.'

Linda told me, 'We wanted to come to Cuba before the Americans did.' Barry said he and Linda had been to Jamaica 'and the Americans have ruined that'.

Most Cubans didn't see the fleshpots of Varadero. If Señor Almeida of the Press Centre was to be believed, their equability in the face of such plenty was proof that they understood the country's need for a Varadero. Cubans came face to face with the economic reforms that the Revolution had sanctioned in their own *barrios*. The farmers' markets, to use the nursery-rhyme name favoured by the Cuban state, represented an experiment in private enterprise. The *campesinos* were allowed to sell whatever they grew or raised over and above their output norms, and pocket the profits.

I went shopping with Hilda at a farmers' market in Vedado. Inside a mesh enclosure, stalls were set out beneath a corrugated tin roof. In the meat section, a row of joints on hooks, showing their ribs, looked like eighteenth-century military tunics. Also hanging from hooks was pork dripping, a candelabra of fat. Cuts of *jamon* were going for 65 Cuban pesos, roughly $2 at the prevailing exchange rate. A butcher, Eduardo Fornaris, told me that he was doing well. He was 35 and lived at Quivican, 50 kilometres away. He came to the market every other day. He could make up to 700 pesos on a pig, he said. 'These markets are a good idea. They're the future for Cuba, they're salvation.' Another farmer, Victor Jimenez, was barking his wares. He was selling rice for eight pesos a pound. 'People buy it from me because they don't get enough on the ration.' He got up at four in the morning to come to market. He did this twice a week. He had packed in his old job as a technician in a paper factory.

A woman in a pink and black top, Berta Ramos, was buying rice. She said, 'I also want bananas and brown beans. I cycle down here when I need something.'

I said, 'What do you think of the market?'

'Well, the food's good but it's too expensive. Luckily, I can afford it because my daughter is an artist and she charges in dollars. She gives me money for food.'

Hilda and I bought doughnuts from a woman who also made corn tamales, maize balls and potato wheels ('two for a peso'). A lemon seller had chalked his prices on a scrap of metal. A perspiring black man was wheeling a barrow of avocados, his T-shirt rolled up to his armpits. Because of his sweat, he was glossier than the fruit. A white-haired birdman, Pedro, was slumped on a chair, his flies undone. Doves and cocks were in cages beside the chair. His ducks, he said, were going for 80 pesos each '*más o menos*'. He broke off to attend to a woman with big earrings. The birds pecked at his feet.

For those who could afford what was on sale, the farmers' markets offered a supplement to the diet provided by the state *bodegas*. The special period was accompanied by a downturn in a number of health indicators, which was contrary to the trend in Cuba's post-1959 history as a whole. According to the National Association of Independent Cuban Economists, life-expectancy increased from 62.3 years to 75.5 years between 1950 and 1995; infant mortality fell from 40 per 1,000 live births to 9.4. But the percentage of babies with low birthweight rose from seven per cent in 1989 to nine per cent four years later. And shortly before the first farmers' markets opened in 1994, more than 25,000 Cubans were diagnosed with optic neuritis, an illness which causes progressive loss of sight and has been linked to malnutrition: the regime began importing B-complex vitamins. It was reported that the average Cuban male lost up to 20lb in weight in the first three years of the special period.

The health system as a whole was straining. Its grass-roots was a network of family doctors: the target was one for every 200 households. That ratio compared favourably with anything other countries could boast, though a number of Cuban friends muttered that the quality of GPs was highly variable: people with no particular vocation for medicine drifted into it because there were always vacancies. Cuba had a system of polyclinics and hospitals. The Press Centre arranged for me to visit the William Soler Children's Hospital in Havana province – it was named after a teenage martyr of the Revolution. It was a model hospital, to which any seriously ill child was liable to be referred from anywhere in Cuba. It was clean and apparently well maintained; the staff and parents whom I met in the cardiac unit, into which I had wandered on a whim, seemed sincere in their enthusiasm for the place. The doctors said that their biggest problem was a lack of medicines. Señora Susana Pedroso, a hospital manager, told me that Cuba had begun subsidising the hospitals by taking in patients from overseas and charging for their operations. 'Simple surgery is about $10,000. Cardiology is between $30,000 and $40,000,' she said. Most of the overseas patients were the children of well-heeled families in South America. The private health arrangement was known as Ser Med: like Club Med, I thought. Fidel was very proud of the health service. Cuba could still manage a set-piece like sending meningitis vaccine to Nigeria; providing doctors to treat the victims of the Chernobyl disaster; in 1996, the World Health Authority declared that Cuba was one of only two countries in the world to have eliminated measles. So much Cuban medical know-how, so little medicine for Cubans.

Julietta told me that there was a shopping mall in Havana with columns of household appliances and air-conditioning and piped music. It was in Miramar. We drove through the broad, leafy streets. There were gardens with banana palms, shady verandahs, garages, pavements with trees. We passed a square with what looked incongruously like a bandstand. Nearby, under some trees, there were piles of brownish earth and chalk, and sweating men with shovels who were taking a breather. Julietta said they were building a shelter.

'From the sun?' I said, thinking of the unfortunate *habaneros* who could wait for hours in the hot months of summer in the hope of catching the *camello*. I imagined a cool bus-stop.

'An underground shelter,' she said. 'For the war—'

'That will never come?' I said. I remembered Señor Taladrid and his leisure shirt and his lectures about tunnels and the *Yanqui* threat. I thought about a retired general in the Cuban army who had told me that Cuba had embarked on 'option zero'. Option zero, a cribbing from nuclear thinking, had been predicated on similarly doomy assumptions: invasion, or an escalation of the economic embargo to include Cuba's neighbours. 'Suppose there was zero food, zero fuel, zero transport,' said the general. Anticipating such a disaster, the regime had created local stockpiles of emergency rations and supplies. The invasion hadn't materialised, the embargo wasn't watertight, but Cuban officials had broken out the stores anyway, to mitigate the austerity of the special period. It seemed as though the Cubans had not only plumped for option zero but were also readying themselves for a year zero, when a few hardy or fortunate *compañeros* would emerge from the foxholes of their capital to pick up the pieces of the Revolution. There was a bleak irony in watching shelters go up in impoverished Havana, a city which already looked as though a bomb had dropped on it. But were the authorities seriously thinking of a nuclear attack, I wondered, or did they fear insurrection?

On Avenida 5 y 42, in the heart of diplomatic Havana, we found the shopping mall, the Centro Comercial – unrecognised, so far as I could see, by the small library of guidebooks on Cuba. The shops were all arranged around one street. There was a bakery, where I bought a bag of rolls. Sealed in polythene, they felt fresh to the pinch. Across the road was an Italian restaurant. Like the smarter kind of New York apartment building, its front door was gained at the end of a long, puffy awning. There was no menu to inspect outside – a further sign of *ton*, perhaps. But the revelation was the department store. There were supermarkets in Havana, but they rarely had anything in them, or rather, no-one cared for what they had. One or two of the bigger dollar shops, patronised by foreigners, approximated to the smaller order of Western supermarket. But the department store at Miramar was on two floors, well lit and well laid out. There was a line of checkouts, the tills full of dollars.

I made a note of a Kelvinator No-Frost, which had an American-style chilled-drink dispenser mounted in its door. It was marked up at $2,780.40 (all prices were in US dollars). Given the prevailing exchange rate – 35 Cuban pesos to the $1 – and the fact that 500 pesos a month was considered a very respectable wage, I calculated that it would take a comfortably-off Cuban household little more than sixteen years to take home a Kelvinator No-Frost. A more compact refrigerator was going for $924. I saw a CD-playing ghetto-blaster, a respected Japanese name, for $353. A self-employed decorator called Rafael, who was 33, was eyeing a large-screen Toshiba television. He made about 120 pesos a week. I asked him how long it would take him to earn enough for the television. He pulled a face, and pointed straight ahead of him – towards infinity.

Pedro Ross, President of *Central de Trabajadores Cubanos*, the labour union, claimed in 1996 that more than a million of Cuba's 4.6 million workers received some form of productivity incentive in the form of hard currency, or vouchers redeemable for imported goods. But it was obvious that the showroom products were aimed at the ex-pats and the minority of *habaneros* with access to a lot of dollars. I suggested to Julietta that even if most Cubans couldn't afford what was on sale, at least they could come up to the store and dream. She said, 'No, don't think that. Coming up here and dreaming, it makes you feel worse.'

I met two girls, aged 14 and 24. They said they were looking for perfume but they hadn't been able to find the fragrance they wanted. They said that they often came to look around the store. They had purchased a ceiling-mounted electric fan, for $48. It had taken the family three months to save for it. I asked them if they enjoyed browsing or if it made them feel frustrated. 'Frustrated,' they replied. Upstairs were *la ropa*, the clothes. People were trying things on in wooden cubicles which looked like bathing huts. Closed-circuit television kept tabs on them.

*

There was a bar near my *edificio* called El Cortijo. The flyers outside the premises promised a heavy-handed-looking comedy bill: three guys in you've-got-to-laugh expressions and mime-act black. I thought I would see what insight a comedian could offer on the Cuban dream and what had become of it. El Cortijo was decorated in a would-be Spanish style, presumably in the hope of establishing a link to the matador of its title. A bull's head looked on biliously from its plaque as a tourist shared a knickerbocker glory with two Cuban women. The floorshow was a pale-skinned blonde wearing a kitchen-foil bikini in which one might comfortably have roasted a quail, say, or a wren. She shimmied rather nervously, never taking her eyes off the bruiser of an MC – dark double-breasted suit; Bugs Bunny tie; expensive-looking cheap watch. He orchestrated the revue with a baton-like mike: now cueing the chorus-line (of one), aluminium-wrapped and samba-ing, to enter through the same swing-doors used by waiters for bringing dishes from the kitchen; now summoning the disc jockeys to fade up a rasp of disco music as a kind of punctuation between his gags. I decided that the disc jockeys were probably the two who appeared with the MC in the club's posters. The MC went round the room, asking where everyone was from. I said I was English.

'*Inglaterra*?' he said.

'*Si.*'

I didn't catch the punchline but the gist was that he named the *province* of Cuba he claimed to hail from. He evidently knew his crowd because it got a laugh. His name was Juan Carlos. Stag gags and jokes about gays also went down well. Juan Carlos poured a glass of rum into a folded copy of *Granma*, making the drink disappear, and there was a piece of business with a Cuban soap opera star, Danny Cortez, who happened to be in the audience. Danny Cortez was very drunk and corpsing badly, but he was so inebriated that he didn't realise it. When he went off stage, he fell up a flight of stairs.

Juan Carlos' material touched on the travails of life in Cuba. Cubans enjoy puns, and the audience at El Cortijo appreciated the story of the drunk who thinks he's reading a newspaper headline: '*Cuba Sin Manteca*', Cuba without lard. In fact, the paper was upside down, and the real headline, '*Cinemateca de Cuba*', was about films. After his act, I asked Juan Carlos about this joke. He said, 'You say the tricky thing, the thing you want to say, then you deny it, make a pun, but everyone remembers it anyway.' Juan Carlos had also recited a little verse about the last President of the Soviet Union:

> Gorbachinski, Gorbachinski,
> You screw our petrolinski,
> And now we have to eat soyinski.

This last was a reference to an indifferent soya-based meat-substitute on the ration. But Juan Carlos denied that his was political comedy. 'I wouldn't do political jokes. My humour doesn't have to go directly into politics. It's not necessary.' He claimed that there was more scope for comedy now. 'We're doing jokes about topics that weren't permitted before. We can make criticisms of some of the problems we have. The trick of being a comedian in Cuba is to know what to do and what not to do. José Martí once said that criticism is like a whip with little bells on it. Comedy is the same.'

Making light of the Cuban condition put the resourcefulness of comedians to the test. Freedom of speech was a yardstick that the Revolution had not measured up to: Amnesty International estimated in 1995 that 600 people were behind bars for their political beliefs. Human rights campaigners on the island claimed that as many as 5,000 Cubans were detained on questionable grounds: they were political prisoners, military refuseniks, the 'socially dangerous'. The latter offence was *peligrosidad*: individuals could be imprisoned because the police *feared* that they might break the law. It was also possible to lose your liberty for 'disrespect': slighting the Maximum Leader could get you up to three years in prison.

In 1996, leading members of Concilio Cubano, a loose association of reform-minded citizens, including lawyers, doctors and journalists, were arrested prior to their first proposed public meeting, which was effectively prevented. Cuba's new 'independent journalists', many of whom filed stories for the American-backed Radio Marti in Florida, received special attention. *Granma*, the revolutionary paper, called them 'instruments trying to destroy Cuba's social and political gains and snatch away the island's independence'.

I went round the offices of *Granma* where handfuls of dun-coloured copy, marked up by the subs in blue ballpoint lay beside old Olivettis – the newspaper was in the process of switching to new technology. I asked Señor Lino Oramos, the foreign page editor, if Cuba had an objective media. 'In this difficult situation we cannot forget that we have to be objective but this cannot lead you to betray your principles,' said Señor Oramos, a balding man and accomplished smoker. 'The enemy spends thousands of hours placing propaganda against Cuba inside the country. There has to be a counterpoint. '

'Do you supply propaganda?'

'That's the *role* of a revolutionary press,' said Señor Oramos patiently. 'Of course, that's not to say that we don't look at our problems.' Readers' letters were encouraged. 'Sometimes they might criticise the way the sugar harvest operates in their province. We might ring up those in charge and get their view.'

'Could you criticise the leadership?'

'The role of this newspaper is not to criticise the Revolution,' said Señor Oramos. We had an exchange of views about the ethics of reporting. The *Granma* man complained that the Western media had covered the rafters fleeing Cuba but ignored those who stayed behind to make the Revolution work. I said that the Cuban press had reported unrest in Northern Ireland some nights earlier – neglecting other stories from Britain – and quite right too. News was what made today different from yesterday. Señor Oramos said, 'That depends on your point of view.'

Señor Almeida at the Press Centre had encouraged me to talk to dissidents. Diplomats were more wary. One said, 'If you're going to meet them, you may find that the film is taken out of your camera and your notebooks are confiscated.' I came by telephone numbers and addresses readily enough. But I didn't like to call from Hilda's apartment, in case that caused problems for her; and when I did call – from hotel lobbies – I invariably got an engaged tone or an unanswered ringing. I sounded Julietta out and established that she didn't wish to accompany me to the homes of dissidents. 'You can't trust what these people say,' she said. I had the address of the activist, Elizardo Sanchez, who had been the subject of campaigning by Amnesty International. Having failed to get through to him by telephone, I caught a taxi to his house one afternoon. It was in a relatively comfortable part of Havana. Señor Sanchez himself, who came to the door at my unannounced knock, had the look of a distinguished Spanish *caballero*: neat, wavy grey hair, slacks, a short-sleeved shirt. He was 51 and had spent eight of the preceding 14 years in Cuban cells. In a sitting-room, he showed me a tracing-paper map of the prisons and labour camps which he said the regime was operating: there were 300 in all. The chart represented years of work by dozens of people, he said. Red markers denoted *prisiónes de mayor severidad*; blue, *prisiónes de menor severidad*; green, *centros de corrección*. Señor Sanchez said that the prison on Isla de la Juventud where Castro had been incarcerated after Moncada was the only 'high severity' institution functioning before the Revolution; now there were more than 40. 'This map shows our own gulag, an archipelago within our own island,' he said.

Campaigners complained at the summary nature of the legal process. I asked Señor Sanchez whether political prisoners had had access to lawyers.

'Yes, but most of these people don't have time to have a lawyer to represent them. Sometimes they are sentenced and imprisoned within a week.'

'What is the size of the opposition in Cuba?'

'At the beginning, we were not many. Until eight years ago, we were no more than a dozen. Today we count thousands all over the country, structured in little organisations. As to the quality of such groups, I can say that we are like Vaclav Havel and his friends in Czechoslovakia, or Professor Sakharov and his collaborators. The most important thing is not our number but what we represent. We represent the majority of the population. These movements under such regimes are like the visible part of an iceberg.'

'But Cuba's a very different case to Eastern Europe?'

'Yes, in Cuba, the Revolution was very popular. Political scientists who are dissidents say that the government would still have 20 to 30 per cent of votes in a free election. The difference between the Cuban and European experience has to do with traits of the totalitarian model in Cuba. It's a hybrid between the model in Europe – Romania, say, or the USSR – and a phenomenon of Latin America, the *caudillo*, the strongman. Here we've had a completely new and strong model. Cuba hasn't changed because the model is stronger.'

'How are things for you?'

'We live like Havel and his comrades used to, two years before the change in Prague. We're surrounded by an atmosphere of intimidation and repression. I could go to prison at any time and nothing can help me or protect me. The government doesn't take into account international opinion.' Señor Sanchez was last in prison in 1992. His longest spell of confinement was six years, in the 1980s. 'In 1988, I was free, I went abroad. I came back to Cuba and the following year I went to prison again for two years. I was hit – I remember it was International Human Rights Day. I lost consciousness. This beating was organised by the secret police, our own Securitate. I was taken to a military hospital, for 18 days. They were waiting for my scars to disappear.'

I said, 'Why did you return to Cuba?'

'The destiny of Cubans is not to leave our country. I have the right to live in my own country. I have to pay a very high price for this. But a sign of the level of maturity of the Cuban dissident movement lies in the fact that during the last year, a great number of dissidents have decided *not* to leave. And besides, I love the weather.'

A television camera mounted across the street from the Sanchez *casa* kept the place under observation. 'The neighbours have told us so. The house has been attacked nine times by the secret police. Fourteen people used to live here, now there are only five: myself, my mother and my brothers. People have thrown stones at the house. They were organised by the secret police, by the brigades for rapid response. The last time, the house was surrounded for two weeks. No-one could come in or go out. It's a method of intimidation. Mussolini did the same thing in the twenties.'

When I asked Señor Sanchez how he managed for material wants, he said, 'The government has given me free food, clothing and soap in prison. It's a very generous government! I learnt to live on a little. There was always someone giving me cigarettes – the most expensive habit I have. As to surviving outside, I'm part of that 10 to 15 per cent of the population who rely on relations abroad. I receive donations from foreign non-government organisations, sometimes foreign newspapers pay for articles. My family still has a small coffee plantation in the western provinces.'

Señor Sanchez said the opposition did not anticipate an imminent uprising. 'After 36 years of repression on the part of the military regime, we're an exhausted people, hopeless and depressed by the daily struggle for subsistence. The propaganda says that we are brave, that we were particularly brave in the struggle in Africa, but I'm very doubtful. I believe that we're peaceful – more prepared for receiving tourists than making war. Don't forget that we were the last colony to be free of the Spanish. But in spite of our apparent lack of concern, a certain frivolity, anguish and sadness have been hidden for many years, and much hatred accumulated.'

'Do you agree with Fidel that history will absolve him?'

'It's clear that his government has done a lot. It has turned our country into a country of prisons and it used to be a country of carnivals. The President's point of view is completely ideological. In a sense, he doesn't know what's going on, because of his ideological vision. He's ruling the country in the middle of loneliness, as Gabriel García Márquez called it "the absolute loneliness of absolute power".'

If Fidel took the path of democratic reform, as world leaders had often urged him, it would enhance his legend, apart from anything else, Señor Sanchez commented. Instead, he was permitting modest changes in order to win time, while allowing the world to think the reforms were more substantial than they were. 'In my view, transition doesn't have to mean the end of Castroism. Castroism can exist in Cuba like Sandinism in Nicaragua. But Fidel Castro doesn't see it that way.'

Señor Sanchez apologised for talking too much: 'I used to be a lecturer in Marxist philosophy'. I asked him about the Cuban solidarity groups in Europe. 'I think they are well intentioned but they're supporting something that no longer exists. The Cuban Revolution ended years ago. If these people could come and live like Cuban people for a couple of weeks – not beaches and hotels but *barrios* – then their perspectives would change.'

As I was going, I said, 'Is your phone always out of order?'

He said, 'You'll have to ask Fidel. He's Minister of Communications. He's also Minister of Agriculture, of Tourism, Minister of the Armed Forces. He's our Super Minister.'

7

The House of Tango

ANYTHING CAN HAPPEN in Cuba, Cubans told me. What kind of an outlook on life was that? It sounded devil-may-care, and in a way it was. There was resignation in it too. Anything can happen in Cuba, the land of miracles: the fertile, hungry, land; the land of dazzling, forbidden hotels; of tropical bureaucracy. Anything can happen; there's nothing you can do about it, so you might as well enjoy it. That's where the devil-may-care philosophy came in. Life was difficult but what was the use in fretting? It was like the old saw about serious and solemn: life in Cuba was serious but there was no point being solemn about it. Don't worry, be unhappy – that's how Cubans seemed to get by.

On the streets of Havana, you began to see what they meant: after a while, you noticed that things were not quite as they seemed. There was something deceptive in the everyday scene of flaking stasis – the leaning *casas*, the balconies like sooty fireguards, the creepers of exposed wiring. Was it my imagination, or wasn't that place a boarded-up ruin yesterday – number 960 Neptuno, where salsa was now blaring brassily from a downstairs room, the musicians rehearsing with their shirts off because of the heat? And what about the bookshop at 1061 San Lazaro, where Señor Merayo took my arm and guided me from the shelves to a hidden backroom with the tables set for lunch, so that I felt less a patron of a *paladar,* and more a member of an underground resistance welcomed into a safe house?

There were unexpected changes. Things could and did happen. Businesses seemed to spring up and disappear just as quickly. The men who sold sunflowers simply came and went, understandably: they set up their pitches on street corners with their three-wheeled bicycles, the kind butchers' boys once rode in England, and when they had sold all their blooms, they pedalled away again. And then there were the *bodegas,* selling Cubans their ration for pesos. You soon learnt that they didn't bother to open on days when there were no deliveries of beans or rice or chicken. But how to explain the fly-by-night barber shops, or the printers with their thirties lithograph machines, who were running off hotel tariff cards and bills of fare one day, and were nowhere to be found the next, though you swore you had retraced your steps to the same spot?

Things could happen, if you were lucky enough or patient enough. I can't remember how many times I walked past the empty Roseland supermarket between Calle Aguila and Calle Galiano before the House of Tango materialised on the opposite side of the street. It wasn't the sort of place you would think you could miss, with its pictures of brilliantined men, and the cry of a balladeer hanging in the air. Yet I had never seen it before, and could find no reference to *la casa del tango* in four guidebooks. In the parlour of the House of Tango, a small elderly man was sitting on a stool beside a gramophone-player. He was resting his head on a speckled hand. Two highly made-up old ladies were sharing a couch with a younger, bearded man who was reading *Granma*. The four of them were listening companionably to a tango tune as though they were sitting out a number at a *thé dansant*. They were surrounded by images of glamorous women and matinée idols. Publicity stills and record sleeves decorated all four walls and the ceiling. There was a portrait of a diva, Libertad Lamarque. Her diamanté necklace, earrings and hairband were all real, or at least 3-D: her jewellery included solid nuggets of paste and her hairband was whiskery with feathers. Another canvas was of Benny More, the Cuban musician whose name recurs like a theme in David Rieff's book about Cubans in Miami, *The Exile*. But the star who had the best showing was a man with slick-backed hair and a horsey mouth – a swarthy George Formby. He was Carlos Gardel, the elderly man told me. He was an Argentinian singer, the master of the tango. Everywhere you looked, you saw his face. There was even a likeness of Gardel behind the dial in the middle of the telephone. 'He was born in France and raised in Buenos Aires,' said the man. 'That is his scarf and that is his hat.' A length of white silk and what looked like a shiny chimney pot were composed on top of an upright piano. The old man was a musician himself, he said. His name was Edmundo – like Edmundo Ross, the bandleader, you thought. You pictured him on stage in younger days, dapperly captured in a single spotlight, the music-stands behind him hung with tabards on which his monogram was picked out in lamé.

I had always thought of tango as an Argentinian invention, but Borges called Havana 'the mother of tango'. The Cuban writer G. Cabrera Infante claimed that a faithful biography of the dance would document spells in Cadiz and Montevideo; but its birthplace had been Cuba, he said. I asked Edmundo about tango. 'It's poetry, it's kindness, it's tragedy,' he said all at once. 'It is the Bible of life. In turn, Gardel is the God, he's my God. He's also *Christo*.' Edmundo lifted his eyes to the glossy ceiling.

There was one particular picture of Gardel, said Edmundo. It was a large damp-eyed study which Edmundo had had framed. It hung above chests of drawers which were full of mugshots and biographical details of famous tango artists, arranged in alphabetical order. Edmundo often spoke to this picture of Gardel, he confided. The 24th of the month would be the anniversary of the singer's death. He had perished in an aircrash in Colombia in 1935, on his way to concert dates in Cuba. I thought of Glenn Miller, Buddy Holly – the faint-making Gardel had been the original rock 'n' roll air fatality.

'*El tango es Gardel*!' declared Edmundo with sudden heat. The Argentinian singer sung to women, to love. In a quavering voice, Edmundo started to sing, 'The day you love me ...' He was 70 years old. He had spent 50 years in showbusiness, a humble servant of the tango, but also a comedian. He had been collecting tango records and memorabilia for 50 years, and had founded the House of Tango 30 years ago. His life was made up of these formidable round numbers. Edmundo told me that he had been married for 50 years. Proudly, he indicated one of the painted grandmothers on the couch. 'Claribelle,' he said. 'She is my sweetheart. *Mi novia! Mi novia eterna!*' The woman simpered demurely.

I asked Edmundo if there was anything unique about the Cuban way of love.

'*El secreto del amor aqui?* It has been somewhat misunderstood.' He looked out at the street, at the Roseland supermarket with its bare, unvisited aisles. In a corner of the tango parlour was an accordion behind glass, a stuffed squeezebox. The once deft but now brittle fingers of Eugenio Zelaya, 1909–77, had run up and down its mottled keys. Edmundo put on another record. It hesitated and stuck, like memory. I tried again: 'I've heard that there is something special about the bottoms of Cuban women.' I smiled self-consciously at the ladies on the couch.

Edmundo said, 'It's part of our idiosyncrasy.'

'Maybe it's because of our African and Spanish roots,' volunteered the young man with the beard. 'And Portuguese and British roots – maybe this mix is the reason.' He put down his copy of *Granma*. 'Today many Cubans, me included, criticise the leaders we had in those times who sent the English away. I would have liked English ancestry.' In memory of a few months in the 1760s when Cuba, or at least Havana, was the property of an English monarch, a gun was nightly fired at the Morro Castle overlooking the city by enlisted men who wore tricorn hats, periwigs, red tunics covered with gold frogging and criss-crossed by yellow straps.

Edmundo said, 'One of the characteristics of the Cuban women is to have a great development in the bottom but it doesn't have anything to do with the tango. The tango has rhythm, it has cadency, it is a sexy dance. It is erotic, sensual. It is also very romantic. If you want to understand *el secreto del amor aqui*, you should know the tango.'

Perhaps he was right. After all, the tango was a euphemistic coinage for romantic entanglements where I came from. 'It takes two to tango,' we said, when what we really meant was that one person wasn't likely to have got another into bed unless that other had been willing. 'Could you teach me?' I asked Edmundo.

'Ha! I'm too old. Anyway, it is better for you to learn from a woman.' He got to his feet, and fell into a little shuffle. It was as if he was determined to disprove his own claim about his age. He soft-shoed the distance to his chests of drawers and looked through his files for the address of Purita. I should go and see her, he said. She was the best dancer in Cuba. She was young, she danced on television. 'When Purita has turned you into a tango dancer, come back here and you can be a member of *la casa del tango*.'

You couldn't call on the best dancer in Cuba in dirty shoes. On the afternoon of my first class, mine were filthy. Fortunately, there was a shoeshine-stand on the way to Purita's apartment. It was on Infanta, almost opposite the Carmen church. Unusually, it was off the street, in a cramped front room the size of a confessional. Most of the boot-blacks in Havana worked the shaded pavements of the old city. They were even harder to pin down than the hairdressers and printers. Their clients sat at the top of squat wooden staircases. On a slack morning, or at the first sign of trouble from a policeman (whose attentions could lead to a tax demand), the polishers snatched up their splintered winners' rostrums and tried their luck elsewhere.

The place I went to was run by a tall, thin, white-haired man, Rolando Darias. He was 72, a retired ambulance-driver. You sat on his high leather chair, which was broad and sturdily made. In cannibal Havana, it might have been cut out of a fifties Cadillac. Rolando worked with his transistor radio on, and surrounded by pairs of old shoes. I assumed that they were in to be repaired, though I wondered if he wasn't holding onto them pending settlement of outstanding black-ing bills. On a shelf was a worn volume like a prayerbook. It was Lenin's political thought. 'I keep my papers in it,' Rolando confessed. He had hung onto some leather tongues which had fallen out of old shoes, and he slid these into your pair to keep your ankles or trousers clean. He used brushes and a pot of ink to repair scores or abrasions in the leather. There was a top-coat of polish. The finish that Rolando aimed for was an even matt. He was a steady, painstaking craftsman like a furniture-restorer – quite different from the duster-wielding bootblacks of Habana Vieja with their matador flourish. He had been shining shoes for ten years, but he didn't really care for the work. He had been happier on the ambulances, he said.

Purita lived on St Rafael in central Havana. A tense-looking young man in a moustache was waiting for me in the lobby of her *edificio*. He led me up three flights of steps in the half-light. There was a grille in front of an open doorway, and a smiling woman in her late twenties in a halter-neck top and shorts: Purita herself. Her apartment was as dim as the stairwell. Light filtered thinly through a dusty window in Purita's kitchenette, and just about crossed the yard or two to her sitting-room before it failed altogether. Pushed up against the walls of the sitting-room was her furniture – a green sofa, two armchairs with black and red cushions, a dining-table with four chairs, a rocking-chair, two old, upright refrigerators, and a push-bike. The walls were covered by pictures of Purita: Purita on her wedding day, testing the strength of a courting-grille – a professional photographer's set-piece in Cuba; Purita seen in medal-clinching attitudes on the dancefloors and tango oches of Latin America. Several of the pictures had been mounted on crushed paper got up to look like velvet. Purita's mother came into the room, a white-haired woman with a business-like handshake. I suspected that she was the curator of the Purita museum. There were also several images of a younger version of the mother. In one, a formal but glamorous head-and-shoulders, the straps of her evening gown had been substituted for brightly coloured feathers, like Libertad Lamarque's plumed headdress at the House of Tango.

On the phone, I had explained to Purita that I wanted to learn the tango. I hadn't mentioned Edmundo's promise that this would initiate me in the ways of Cuban *amor*. This was probably just as well, for the young moustachioed man was Purita's husband, and he looked on unhappily enough as things were, dropping the needle on an LP of tango melodies as his wife directed him.

From the start, I sensed that the tango was the dance for me. 'You must be like a block of wood,' Purita said, little knowing that my entire ballroom career thus far had been based upon mimicking timber. We began with 'the basic step'. I had to crook my left arm at the elbow, and brace my right arm in order to hold my partner around the waist. 'Tighter, tighter,' said Purita. I was to stamp my right foot, and lead off with it, sliding the left up to meet it. 'Not too far,' said Purita. 'Imagine you're painting the floor.' With these moves under my belt, I was allowed an early breather. I had to hold myself perfectly still, all except for my right forearm. This was called upon to give Purita a pretty blatant goosing in the small of her back, in the name of guiding and propelling her. She sold dummies this way and that, like a rugby three-quarter. She was a foot shorter than me, but very quick on her toes. She reminded me of Mick Jagger. It wasn't just the way she made her lower lip stick out sometimes, or a kind of ugly-beautiful look about her, but her toned ruthlessness – though of course she was, at 28, young enough to be a Rolling Stones granddaughter, or date.

I had to wait until she had completed five shimmies before striking out again. This time, it was with the left foot, in a flat-footed action recalling an ice-hockey stick. I swung my right shoe into the same neighbourhood as the left, though leaving a distance of a country yard between the two. I brought my feet together, at the same time turning on my right heel so that I was at right angles to the direction from which I had come, ready to repeat the sequence.

Purita said I was lunging too far with my initial step. At least, I consoled myself, I was punctuating my movements with just the right amount of arrogant Latin heel. But no: 'You must slide,' she corrected me. 'You are painting the floor.' I had been trying to think what this expression reminded me of; of course – it was 'wiping the floor'. Nor was Purita satisfied with my deportment. I was insufficiently wooden, something my previous dancing partners would have found difficult to credit. 'What about his shoulders, Braulio?' she asked her husband. 'They are not square, no?' Braulio agreed with his wife about the roundness of my shoulders: he brightened just to have been asked. Purita said to me, 'You must be like a blockie.'

She showed me more moves: 'the eight steps', she called them. I had suspected that I was having it too easy while Purita was selling her dummies. Now it emerged that I was expected to match her virtually swerve for swerve. First, I swivelled 45 degrees on my right foot, dragging my left round to join it; then vice versa. One more time, the same as the first; and I was supposed to finish with both toecaps pointing at Purita. This exercise also proved ticklish. She told me to think of my feet as snakes, but I couldn't make them wriggle over her tiles in a convincingly serpentine manner.

I wanted to know when Purita was going to teach me how to hurl her away from me, and save her in the nick of time from dashing her brains out against a refrigerator with a languid and yet utterly masculine catch. 'Ah, the *tombe*,' said Purita. 'Not yet.' First I had to learn a gesture which might have come from a Tudor court. From the upright position, I had to slide my left leg behind my right, in a flat-footed style, while at the same time pointing a pretty ankle with the right. This was the *quebrada*. Looking over my shoulder, Purita watched a reflection of my feet in her television screen.

The heat brought back memories of awkward dance classes at school, and of not being able to tell whether it was your palms or your partner's which were perspiring. It was so hot on the tiny dancefloor in the concrete *edificio* in the narrow street that I had to keep wiping the sweat out of my eyes in order to see where I was going, the way you have to sleeve the condensation from a car window on a cold night. Purita being so supple, and so damp, my hand kept slipping under the waistband at the back of her shorts. I was too hot to appreciate the eroticism which Edmundo had talked about, and too exhausted. Another inhibiting factor was the lack of room. With my longish stride – made longer by my over-eagerness at striding – we were forever barking our shins against the furniture.

Purita told her husband to play 'Jealousy'. It seemed the right choice for that temperamental dance, in that hot, cramped room, with Purita's husband watching unhappily from the dining-table. If he was jealous, it wasn't of me, I felt, but of all the men who had held his wife so tightly and intimately, and above all of Amado, Purita's long-time partner. Amado appeared in many of the pictures on the walls, haughty and pony-tailed. Purita had been dancing with him since they had met at a party when she was a girl of 13. They were spotted by a professor of dance who got them their break on Cuban television –

'Purita y Amado' was now a fixture of the winter schedules. They had recently made their third movie; they had performed in Brazil and Venezuela; they had appeared before Fidel himself – he had asked them how long they had been practising, and told them how much he had enjoyed their routine. Purita and Amado were stopped in the street and rung up on radio phone-in programmes by people who told them that they loved their dancing. They were the Fred and Ginger, the Torville and Dean, of Cuba. When I had told Julietta about my classes with Purita, she said that she thought Amado might be gay – it was the way he talked, she said, the pitch of his voice. Be that as it may, Amado was once married to Purita for seven years.

And so we went on in Calle St Rafael: the throbbing chords of 'Jealousy'; me storking or craning between the chairs; Purita saying 'Be careful!' when she meant that I shouldn't overreach myself, and 'Be a block!' when she meant that I shouldn't let my shoulders drop; and my fingertips sliding in and out of her shorts.

Purita's husband put on a smart shirt. He was going to work. Braulio was in charge of lighting at the Nacional, the grandest hotel in Havana. He was cheered by the rather deliberate kiss that Purita fed him at the door – it might have been from her repertoire of dance moves. She asked me at the end if I had enjoyed the lesson, and I answered truthfully that I had. I had felt the effects of the heat and humidity, that was all. I thought of footballers buckled by cramp in South American World Cup ties, and wondered if I shouldn't be calling for salts: the sweat was cold-compressing out of me.

Over the next few weeks, I went for classes at Purita's two or three times a week, Purita fitting the lessons around rehearsals for her cabaret appearances. Each time it was the same ritual: the devoted Braulio waiting stiffly in the lobby; the climb up the double-backing flights of stairs, which was like a tango routine in itself; and, in the cluttered sitting-room, the scraping and rearranging – practically the redecorating and *moving* – to make space for dancing. Sometimes Purita would call her husband out from behind the dining-table to help her demonstrate a step. Poor man, he so enjoyed this stooging. Once, Purita told me about the break-up of her marriage to Amado.

'We had couple problems, nothing to do with work,' she said. 'It's not a problem now.' Like her, Amado had since remarried, she said.

During another class, I had a moment alone with Braulio. The lights in the apartment had suddenly dimmed – a power outage, or could it have been the people in the next apartment making lunch? Braulio was in his element, the head of lighting at the Hotel Nacional. I asked him if being Purita's husband ever made him jealous.

'Sometimes: it's difficult being married to a star. I'm not jealous of other men, but she is so busy I hardly see her.' It sounded like the voice of a man talking in the dark to keep his spirits up.

One day, Purita and I had a little audience: Braulio, of course, but also Purita's mother, who stayed for the whole session (instead of retreating in a somewhat martyred way, as was her custom) and a genial old boy who was an admirer of the mother. I had arrived early. Purita and the others were talking in the gloom – it had turned five o'clock, and though the sun wasn't setting in Havana until around eight then, the apartment didn't admit much light at the best of times. They didn't seem fazed that I was early, though in general the Cuban trend was towards lateness. (When I called at the Press Centre one morning and asked to see Almeida, I was told that he'd be appearing soon. 'A Cuban soon,' the receptionist advised me drolly.)

We shifted the furniture and Braulio put the bike away – pulling a wheelie, he steered it out of harm's way into the kitchenette on its rear tyre. In our last lesson, Purita and I had attempted 'eight in the round' – a mincing, side-on scissors-kick manoeuvre. We had also essayed backward dips with *ganchos*, which involved locking our knees in a wrestling hold. Now we moved on to a kind of pairs zigzag. I had visited Rolando's stand on Infanta before my lesson, and had to take care not to frank the treads of my newly sweated shoes across the toes of the old party who was squiring Purita's mother.

When I finally encountered Amado at Calle St Rafael, he was wearing what appeared to be a knitted singlet, and a pair of footballer's shorts in make-believe satin. He had let his ponytail down. It fell into the type of long, would-be feminine cut favoured by men who appear on daytime television saying they are really women trapped in male bodies. He was just leaving, Purita said, and I sparringly suggested that he was afraid of the competition from me. At this, the great Amado snorted and pulled up a chair, insofar as the cramped dance-floor would allow. I could feel his disdainful eye on me as Purita and I went through our paces. 'No, no, no,' he said. He got up. 'You must push her – excuse me.' I stood aside and Amado took Purita's arms as though he was gripping a longbow. He nodded in the direction of her husband, her second husband; his successor. Braulio put 'Jealousy' on again.

Amado strongarmed Purita between the sofa and the refrigerators with a look that suggested he was deliberating whether to ravish her on the rocking-chair or set her to work down a nickel mine. 'Do you see?' he asked me. He cast Purita aside and turned his attention to me. 'Hold me,' commanded Amado, 'I will be the woman.' He was one of the hairiest men I had ever seen, never mind danced with. We executed 'the eight steps', my size elevens threatening to overwhelm his unexpectedly petite pumps. 'Your shoulders must be square,' he said. Grimly, he reached under my armpits and tickled me.

'It's so that your shoulders will be level,' said Purita.

Amado and I danced on. We went into a *quebrada*. He grunted that my *ganchos* were 'okay', and I knew a moment of hot-making pride.

Purita and Amado danced a complete tango number for me – it was a small miracle in the land of miracles. They had a rippling fluidity. They made even the risible business of entwining their knees look both menacing and erotic at the same time, like a cross between a martial art and a courtship ritual. Edmundo had been right: the tango was the sexiest of dances. When Amado span Purita around, her skirt became a bell-jar. What was so stirring was the sight of a supremely accomplished tango, with all of its diving catches and pantomime swoons, in the confines of the little Calle St Rafael apartment. It was the sort of triumph that Cubans achieved over their circumstances every day. It reminded me of a Spanish ballet I had seen in the ruined palace of the Gran Teatro, three or four generations of Havana womenfolk fanning themselves in the stalls, the teenage ballerinas flourishing their dresses like bullfighters' capes, and slamming their heels on the wooden stage so hard that you feared for what remained of the frescoes. Again, the transcendent things had stood out – the extra steps that the girls had performed unaccompanied at the end of each dance, the equivalent of grace notes, when all you could hear was their parade-ground drilling and a whisper of fans; the flawless faces of the dancers, sexily contrasted with their sweat-pricked costumes.

Purita taught me how to turn through 360 degrees while making *quebradas*. She taught me the *tombe*, and I learnt to catch her on my knee. She showed me the *mariposa en circulo*, the butterfly in a circle. Braulio chalked a circle out on the tiles, but the step eluded me. It was as though I had a faulty gyroscope. After half a revolution, I became a Frankenstein's creature of shorting ganglia. Stalling for time, I told Purita the winsome story of the domino-marked butterfly which had alighted on my bare heel as I was riding a bus in the countryside. Maybe this was a sign, I said, that given time, and sympathy on the part of my professor, I would one day master the— but Purita was cross with me. 'You are not practising enough,' she interrupted me. 'The *mariposa en circulo* is your special task for the next class.' She could be critical, especially of my shoulder action, which she said spoilt otherwise encouraging work by my legs. But in what turned out to be our last class, as we were tacking up and down the sitting-room with less than the usual amount of drag and resistance from me, she exclaimed, 'You're a dancer of tango!'

I didn't believe her. On the other hand, I have a card in my wallet from the *Asociación Cubana Amigos del Tango* which has my name on it, and '*Asociado de honor*' written in Edmundo's hand.

8

Treasure
Island

WHEN I SET OFF FOR TREASURE ISLAND, it was off
the map – rather stirringly, I couldn't help feeling. Of course, it was
only in Robert Louis Stevenson's novel that it had ever enjoyed a
compass bearing at all. But legend had it that he had modelled his
fictional isle on a patch of Cuban territory, the Isle of Pines, perhaps
half remembered from a Caribbean voyage he had once made.
Admittedly, the writer's own account was more ambiguous. In an
essay entitled 'My First Book', Stevenson recalled looking over a
schoolboy's shoulder at the easel on which the child was daubing. This
apparently inspired the writer to sit down before an adjacent canvas
and rough out the Toby Jug profile of what became literature's most
famous non-continent, later inked in by his father for the end-papers
of the book. What was not in doubt was that there was a piece of land
off Cuba's southern coast which corresponded in several particulars to
the home of the marooned Ben Gunn, and the happy hunting grounds
of the sly ship's cook, Long John Silver. But this real-life island seemed
almost as swathed in cartographical fog as its supposed literary copy,
which, according to Stevenson, had only been surveyed on a scrap of

map held by Blind Pew. Had I set sail for the place equipped with an up-to-date gazetteer, for example, I should have searched in vain for a single reference to it. It had been struck from the atlas. La Isla del Pinos was renamed by Castro in 1978, in honour of the contribution made by the young to the Revolution. It now went by the less euphonious title of the Isle of Youth, Isla de la Juventud. You suspected that Castro's decision had also owed something to his memories of the 22 months he had spent on the island as a young man, incarcerated after the botched assault on the Moncada Barracks. One benefit of the new name was that it presumably made the place easy to remember for the young people, most of them from Africa, who came to Cuba to attend college on the island. (Though Kenneth Kaunda of Zambia, moved by this largesse, had confused matters still further by asserting that the territory was truly 'the island of Africa'.) Barely a generation ago, the population had been just 7,000, but it had since swelled to 80,000, with overseas students accounting for a good 20,000 of the total. Castro had inaugurated this tertiary education scheme, at considerable if undisclosed cost to the Cuban exchequer, as part of his design to see Cuba at the vanguard of the developing world. By the mid-nineties, however, the withdrawal of Soviet funds had put a stop to this philanthropy. Engineers from Angola and doctors from Ethiopia and bureaucrats from Zambia were finishing their degrees, but after they graduated, there would be no more foreign students on Isla de la Juventud. The only other people who seemed to be drawn to the place were divers, who had found out about its clear waters and deep coves. No-one else appeared to bother about it. One or two of the guidebooks tried to interest you in it, but you sensed that their hearts weren't in it. The authors knew that visitors who were willing to venture away from the mainland were more tempted by the beaches of Cayo Largo and Cayo Coco, or, at least, that the Cuban tourist industry was better geared up to sending them there. The island was an important military base and its period as a penal colony was by no means over – perhaps here were explanations for its unchartedness. At all events, it seemed as though, after the last African visitor was capped and gowned, the Isla de la Juventud would revert to the desert island of Stevenson's fiction.

*

I was pleased by the lack of traffic to Treasure Island. Discovering a
mould-speckled 1915 edition of Stevenson's novel in the Bookshop of
the Centenary of the Apostle beneath my apartment felt, in the
absence of any general circulation of people to the island, like stum-
bling across Pew's jealously guarded chart itself. Of course, to do the
thing properly, you really ought to go to the island by sea, I thought.
There was a ferry on the southern shore of Havana province which
could take you to Nueva Gerona, the only place approaching the
status of a city on the island. But it was difficult to argue with the
contrasting charms of a flight which lasted only 15 or 20 minutes, and
which was free (*Cubana*'s inaugural direct service between Britain and
Cuba included a complimentary domestic flight). All the same, I put
my name down for an air ticket to the Isla de la Juventud with a guilty
conscience about the comfy anachronism of it all. It was like
embarking on the journey to the centre of the earth on the Channel
Tunnel rail-link. However, when I saw that my fellow passengers
included, if not a peg-leg pirate, then at least a man on a pair of
crutches, I nursed the hope that Stevenson's shade would not rush to
judgement. Perhaps it was possible to recreate some of the mood of
the voyage of the *Hispaniola*, after all. I became more confident in this
respect after the passenger nearest the emergency exit crossed himself.
True, this wasn't an altogether unusual sight in Latin America – hadn't
the entire aft section of the *Cubana* flight from London cheered an
unremarkable landing? – but it presently became clear that the man
had had a point when he enlisted divine protection. The interior of the
plane, a Russian AN-24, didn't inspire confidence. Screws warped and
bulged out of true in their panels, and there was something
uneasy-making about realising that the door to the cockpit was made
of plywood. Hardly had we become airborne than the aircraft began to
leak like a ship. At first, the upper bulkheads of the cabin merely
glistened like briny timbers. Then you realised with a start that the
plane was taking on cloud: condensation frothed all around us. It was
like an explosion in an Italian café. I became aware that none of the
Cubans aboard was laughing at this; the only people who were, were a
French couple. I say 'became aware' because I couldn't see my fellow

passengers by this time, whereas I could make out that titters were coming from the seats in front of me, hitherto filled in plain view by two Francophones.

At length, the old *Cubana* brig cleared her aeronautical bilges, and it was possible to see out of the window. The sea had the texture of snakeskin. We flew over several apparently uninhabited, swampy-looking islands, which seemed to be floating – or rather, water-logged as they were, to be sinking. I was watching the shimmering horizon as keenly as Jim Hawkins. I saw an atoll which I thought might be our destination. It was completely covered in vegetation, like Treasure Island itself. But as we drew nearer, the lush crops transformed themselves into mud – or was it quicksand?

My first sight of Treasure Island proper, after 25 minutes, was of a peak – reminiscent of Stevenson's Spyglass Mountain – and, beneath it, a thin, green strip of land curved to form the mouth of a bay. Stretching away from this inlet were lines of water, suggesting irrigated fields. There were palm trees on a cleared beach; a pair of houses – or were they huts? – a road – no, two; but no sign of any traffic. The corrugated roof of a farmstead, a boggy lagoon. The plane, yawing like the *Hispaniola* herself, set down on a runway bordered by grass, which changed colour from verdigris to Lincoln green the further it grew from the ashphalt. I got off the plane into a fine rain shower – in the Cuban summer, a discovery almost as rare and enchanting as buried treasure (though, again like buried treasure, more trouble than it was worth: it swiftly hiked the humidity quotient). Inside the airport building, the baggage carousel was scarcely bigger than the guinea-pig roulette wheel on which Mario had sprinted groggily into hutch six in the Zapata peninsula. Rather to my surprise, it wasn't manual, and when the porters began pushing bags through a window of the building onto the carousel, it revolved to the plausible whirring of an engine.

I caught the bus into Nueva Gerona, a farmer budging up for me on the long rear seat. The ticket cost a peso. We passed a sign extolling the Revolution, featuring a – surprisingly rare – full-length likeness of Fidel, who was looking cheesed-off for some reason. Cubans told me that his image didn't feature much in the official iconography for the simple reason that he wasn't dead yet, though this didn't stop his *name* appearing on more than a few hoardings.

There was a Cuban hotel in the town but they didn't take foreigners, and anyway, they were full. My suspicion concerning the Cuban apartheid over accommodation was that it had less to do with isolating Cubans from seditious foreign influences than with keeping tourists in places where they could only spend dollars, and which were consequently beyond the means of locals. There was one hotel for visitors in Nueva Gerona, the Gaviota. There were only two on the whole island, though it was the size of Greater London.

By a little after six, the mosquito hour on the Isla de la Juventud – like the sun-over-the-yardarm hour, or its contemporary equivalent, happy hour, elsewhere – I was sitting on the balcony outside my room at the Gaviota with a neat grouping of bites on my right wrist. They were tightly clustered, like a marksman's shots. The humidity stood in invisible sheets. It was like other types of weather – rain, snow – it came in tangible formations, only you couldn't see it. The only noise came from the thrashed speaker by the bar, which was playing house music. A European tourist was smoking on a nearby balcony, wearing a dark thong. He was reddish-brown, the hue not suggesting sunburn but accomplished familiarity with the climate. He eyed my balcony with a look of unembarrassed appraisal – did he linger on my perspiring form, I wondered, simply because there was nothing else to do, except suffer the humidity, try to block out the racket from the bar, wonder when the island's one taxi might call again?

The pool was empty, save for a brackish puddle. At the *carpeta*, they were frank enough to say that it would be 'two days minimum' before the process of cleaning and refilling was complete. They had brochures for trips: $24 per head for three hours, to see the 'model prison' where Castro had been held, a house where José Martí had once lived, a ceramics craft centre. 'What time does the tour leave?' I asked.

'When would you like?' replied the man behind the desk, unimprovably, though he should strictly speaking have qualified his answer by saying that it all depended on when Mundo could bring the taxi around. The receptionist said that the advertised boat trip was off, as the boat was broken. It was the 'wrong season' for the slated crocodile expedition, he added.

Nueva Gerona was a one-horse town – I saw the horse, in fact. Mundo took me for a drive down the main street. He pointed out the school, the old Spanish church, the post office, the hair salon, the small nightclub, El Patio.

'What's it like?' I asked him.

'It's small,' said Mundo.

People were out on the streets in very few clothes. The hour was late but it was too hot to sleep, at least it was for those of us with sweltering, metal accommodation. Mundo had studied in Florida before the Revolution. Did he miss it?

'Sometimes you miss a big city,' he said, making Miami sound like a comfortably proportioned mistress.

Picking up my key at the *carpeta*, I noticed a pistol on the counter, and another handgun poking out of a raffia bag. I thought of the holster of oiled sheepskin that Harry Morgan kept below decks in *To Have and Have Not*. 'They are just in case,' said the laconic receptionist. You hoped that the hotel staff knew their way around firearms better than they did swimming-pools and boats. The air-conditioning unit in my room claimed to need a warm-up or cool-down period of three minutes. There was no sign of it firing or freezing up long after this time had elapsed. Eventually, it groaned into operation, but it failed to put out any cold draught, or even anything you could have recognised as air. You could only tell it was on because of a faint vibration discernible if you pressed your hand hard against it. It issued what I now know to have been its death rattle – a fugue for sclerotic ducting and thrashed parts that no amount of tinkering with its controls could interrupt.

I lay all night in hot, damp bedding, woken from time to time by my sweat. The experience reminded me of a line I'd heard about the old whorehouses of Havana. They were said to be so hot you could feel the sweat rolling *onto* you. The tin shutters were ajar, to compensate for the winded air-conditioning, and I was bitten, or dreamt I was bitten, many times. I had the impression of waking to find something dining bloodily off my stomach. There was an old refrigerator in the middle of the room. I hadn't put anything in it but it wasn't empty. Every hour or

so during the night, the impossibly avant-garde composer who was
renting the icebox essayed a free-form solo on the jew's harp.

At breakfast, an electric-lime lizard scaled the walls of the dining-
room. He had a tumescent pink chest, and tiny crampons on his
splayed hind limbs. His eyes were like a stuffed toy's. You imagined
that if you could pick up the lizard and shake him, his pupils would
rattle like pulses. A tourist who looked something like Woody Allen
was cuddling his Cuban girlfriend. He was bald on top and grey
around the ears. He had smooth, small, hands; a child's hands. He was
still embracing the woman when I ran into them at the *carpeta* half an
hour later. Woody's date was massively – and hirsutely – hewed,
big-busted, big-butted, and very dark. Woody had her in a necklock.
He was wearing a yellow sunstopper, shorts in Baden-Powell brown,
and sandals. He was part of a group from France. I wondered whether
Woody's companions were pleased for him, yet worried among themselves that he might get hurt.

Although there was only one taxi on La Isla de la Juventud, that
wasn't the same thing at all as saying there was only one taxi-driver.
There were at least three of them. Mundo sent Wilfredo to the motel
for me at ten o'clock, in the island's Toyota. Wilfredo was younger than
Mundo. He had already been into Nuevo Gerona to collect the
mysterious – but by now very familiar – brown, bog-paper docket that
gave us permission; in this case, to travel across the island to Punta del
Este, to see its famed white sands and caves housing daubs by Cuba's
first inhabitants. It wasn't entirely clear why a permit was required.
The Cubans claimed that they were entering responsibly into
'eco-tourism' and didn't want just anybody poking about in the Isle of
Youth's conservation areas. I suspected the real reason had more to do
with military activity in the swamp.

Wilfredo took the motorway – really just a wide, metalled
carriageway, as on the mainland, with next to nothing moving on it.
The place was like a hot Romney Marshes. There were butterflies like
scraps of brightly coloured tissue paper, and, after a few miles, a
hoarding of Che Guevara with solid beams of light radiating from his
face, recalling the poster for *Godspell*. A horse and cart in the country,

a woman riding in the cart: when she looked round at the taxi, you saw that she was yet another beauty queen.

We came to a military checkpoint. It consisted of a sentry hut and a well-kept bungalow. The checkpoint was at the entrance to Lanier swamp, the frontier of the territory which you were not allowed to enter without one of the government's Izal-paper chitties. A guard collected our documentation and went off with it to the bungalow. A minibus full of men in uniform, which Wilfredo and I had overtaken some miles back, drew up alongside us. A bald officer carrying a brief-case stepped out. There was a man in Ministry of Interior fatigues, and then perhaps a dozen more officers. They all went into the bungalow. It was like finding the British Chiefs of Staff on a brainstorming session in the Lake District. The guard reappeared and waved us through. We drove down an unmetalled road, vultures rising from it as we approached, lizards quicksilvering into the roadside grass. Snails were moving across the road, but they weren't slithering so much as hobbling. It was a jerky, clunky action, suggesting prosthetics. I asked Wilfredo to stop so that I could look at the snails. They weren't snails at all, I found; or rather, they were ex-snails: red crabs were now cuckooing in their vacated black shells. Further on, there was an abandoned-looking house, and a man in camouflage trousers weeding the lawn in a cloud of butterflies.

Wilfredo pulled off the road. We left the car and walked into the overhanging entrance of a cave. A bat glimmered, and there was a loud, familiar drone which I couldn't immediately place. On the wall of the cave were drawings of concentric circles, made thousands of years ago by Cuba's indians. They looked like RAF wing-markings circa 1939–45. I realised that the drone I half recognised was the noise made by mosquitoes. Having taken a moment to find us, they were now biting. I retreated to the car, finding several of them sucking tensely from both forearms, as poised as tango dancers attempting a movement with *ganchos*.

Wilfredo drove on until the road ran into sand. It was the shore of a limpid estuary: Punta del Este at last. Toothpaste-capped breakers were turning a mile out to sea on the otherwise empty horizon. There was a pair of deserted flip-flops in the sand and, I saw as we parked, the

stockade of a wooden house. Brownish palm fronds brushed its
corrugated roof. Flowers of yellow and purple grew in a sandy garden
inside the ramparts. Under the eaves of the house was a little wooden
table, wooden dominoes set out on it like fingers of stale flapjack.
Wilfredo told me that this was a frontier guard-post, which doubled as
a government courtesy residence, but I didn't need anyone to tell me
what it was. I had recognised it immediately as Ben Gunn's cabin.

Inside the stockade was a man in a frontier guard's uniform and
another wearing only boxer shorts. They were in the kitchen, preparing
rice. I glimpsed their stores: bottles of rum, and egg-trays. Would they
mind if I went for a swim? They wouldn't, they said.

I changed in a guest room. The furniture was wooden and rudi-
mentary. The towels, though, had been folded into origami shapes: a
swan, a heart. The water of the estuary picked up the colour of the
blond sand on its bed. I waded into the middle of the current and felt
a prickle on my ankle. A jellyfish wobbled by, looking like a rubber
plate.

It seems Nueva Gerona Taxis – or Nueva Gerona Taxi, to be strictly
accurate – had tipped off the frontier post about my visit, and the rice
the men had been cooking was for my lunch. There was also freshly
caught fish from the estuary, glasses of beer, and a thimble of Cuban
coffee, hot and bitter like gunpowder. A kitten played with a leaf. She
was the guardhouse pet, explained Elizardo Argote, the man in boxer
shorts.

The polythene rustle of wind through the fronds was interrupted
only once that afternoon, by the ringing of a telephone. It was as
incongruous as finding a telephone in Ben Gunn's redoubt. You
wondered, all the same, if it might not be the balloon going up – would
Elizardo and his companion, Daniel, abandon the griddle, look out
their tin helmets from among the half-empty rum bottles in the
storeroom, put out sandbags by the pink-lipped conch shells which
bordered their door? The invasion of Cuba not having been declared,
it transpired after a bit, I asked Elizardo who tended to put up at their
idyllic retreat.

'Mainly senior people from the party or the military. Sometimes foreign guests,' he said.

I said, 'Has *El Comandante* stayed here?'

'Sure,' said Elizardo. 'He was sitting where you are two days ago.'

Two days ago? That damned elusive Fidel!

That night, Mundo dropped me at the nightclub, El Patio. There was a thunderstorm and it was raining heavily. There was a creeper-covered awning outside the club, and a polite young man beneath it in a wringing wet shirt and bow-tie who was operating a bolt-action gate. Entry was eight pesos. I asked him if I might have a look inside the club for free, and he quietly assented. All was dark but for the stage, where card backlots of an Arcadian arbour suggested a village hall *Romeo and Juliet*. The turn gave me a start: a black man in a too-tight, blue acrylic top and khaki slacks, what he was wearing most eye-catchingly was a lank fright wig. He was vamping it up to something which sounded like an old Supremes hit dubbed into Spanish. But he was so chunkily masculine, the nods to femininity in his wardrobe so unconvincing, that instead of appearing titter-makingly camp, he was frankly weird. He looked like the Mummy in drag.

The mainly Cuban clientèle sipped glasses of rum on hard wooden chairs. The drag act stepped among his public. They laughed, half-terrified in the approved way, and shrunk back in their seats. The turn sat on a man's knee. As with Juan Carlos' act at the El Cortijo club in Havana, you expected to see the star picked out by a spotlight, but the sparks budget didn't run to one.

The turn, I suggested to one of the management, was '*loco*'. The manager replied solemnly that in fact he was a comedian. The comedian was by now working the crowd on the far side of the room, puckering a terrible moue in the direction of a man sitting with several of his friends. Suddenly, the comedian flung himself at their table. I thought, 'That's something. You don't often see the act attacking the audience.' The comedian lay full-length on top of his victim, and then the pair of them toppled over. I half expected a riot. But the next moment, the comedian was up on his hobnails again, not a false hair out of place, and returning to the stage carrying his prize: the man's shoe.

As I left, the rain pouring through the creeper, the dark plates of the sky jarring and shifting to expose a chink of lightning, the doorman made his under-the-breath pitch. There would be *bailarinas* later, he whispered. '*Sin ropa.*' He performed a diffident mime, intended to illustrate just how little the dancers would be wearing.

Though I had stumbled across a working replica of Ben Gunn's cabin in Playa del Este, I had yet to come face to face with an English maroon, that most disquieting and memorable of Stevenson's creations. However, I had read that the inhabitants of the Isle of Youth included English-speakers whose ancestors were fishermen from the Cayman Islands. They had settled in what was then the Isle of Pines during the nineteenth century. Cuban history had slyly recreated Cuban literature: authentic displaced Anglophones were lashing their flotsam cabins together at much the same time as Stevenson was winning golden opinions for making up the same kind of thing. The avuncular Mundo came in handy during these researches. He believed that most of the Cayman Island Cubans lived in the south of the island, which made sense considering where their great-grandparents had set sail from. Calling on these citizens would entail more government red tape, however, since their homes lay on the far side of Lanier swamp from Nueva Gerona. However, Mundo considered, he knew of a couple of families who lived nearer the city and whom he thought spoke English. They lived at the hamlet of La Demajagua, and were farmers. Perhaps it would be worth visiting them?

In a blue-painted wooden farmstead, which looked like a toy farm brought to life – cows beneath a tree, chickens placed as if for effect: all it lacked was a shard of mirror for a duckpond – Mrs Florence Powery, who was born in 1926, repined over an England she had never seen. The whole family shared in her dream, which centred on a land entirely unlike the England I knew. Mrs Powery had kept a picture of the Queen on her wall until it had grown tatty, and she had taken it down for shame. She said, 'When we go to the British *embajada*, I always looks at the Queen. I don't know why but I think she is my Queen. She's so nice, oh my. Someone told me she and I are the same age.' Mrs Powery had a length of blue ribbon in her hair, and tortoiseshell grips. Her dark skin, and the Spanish which flavoured her English – *embajada* instead of embassy, for instance – Mrs Powery owed to her Cuban father. Or 'Cubian', as she called him. Her mother, on the other hand, had been a Cayman Islander or, as Mrs Powery saw it, English, and so for that matter was she. 'They say where you're born is your country so we have to say we are Cubians but I feel more English,' she said. The way she said 'Cubian' reminded me of a London minicab driver who had once taken me to the airport before a flight to Cuba. 'You'll be landing at Cubic City?' he had wanted me to confirm.

Mrs Powery was a widow. Her husband had died four years earlier, of a cerebral haemorrhage, or 'thinking too much', as Mrs Powery defined it. From a Tupperware box, she produced a photograph of a boggle-eyed man in specs. This was the late Mr Powery. The Powerys had raised ten children: Julian, Susan, Allan, Elsie, David (who was living in Grand Cayman), Tom, Delia, Alfred, Armando and Rene. I remarked that the younger children had been given Spanish names and Mrs Powery said, 'I don't know why – maybe because we ran out of English names.'

One of her sons, Tom, said, 'My mother raised us with an education. We used to live well, far apart from Cuban people, among Jamaicans.'

'Some Americans too,' said Florence.

'Some Americans too,' agreed Tom. 'I don't feel Caymanian because I was not born over there, but I can't say I feel Cuban. They have a different way of thinking and acting. They don't think about whether they are doing good or bad. They don't analyse what they are doing at the time. Afterwards, they think, 'Well, I did bad.' Tom, who was 37, had been a shipping agent before coming home to work on the farm. He said, 'I was reading about England in a school book which a Jamaican gave me. It talked about the Tower of London, Buckingham Palace. It was very interesting.' This volume proved to be Nelson's *West Indian Readers*, published in 1946. The Powerys still had it. It read, 'London is the capital of empire ... the largest and wealthiest city in the world.'

Mrs Powery said, 'I always read, but now we can't get any English magazines. Oh my, I would so like to get magazines from England! I used to like to read novels, and my brothers also. My mother used to fuss with us because we would read so late at night. Sometimes, for her not to see us, we would use a flashlight. Oh my, it was so good!' Mrs Powery said her parents had always favoured what she called 'British ways'. 'They had British ways of going to church, of cooking. They used to cook potatoes, fish and meat. Not rice. We are behind the Iron Curtain here,' Mrs Powery said sadly. Nevertheless, she had been keeping tabs on the English scene. 'They always criticise her a lot in Cuba. It's because she's very powerful, though of course she's not in power now.'

'Who?' I said.

'The Queen's sister, ' said Mrs Powery, 'Margaret Thatcher.'

A sky-blue gravy boat occupied pride of place in a glass cabinet. It was made in England. 'I prize it because it is something from the olden days. I thought that when I passed away, I want it to keep going down the family,' Mrs Powery said. 'I'm a Lutheran but I don't exactly go to church – we don't have a church. The government took it away in the sixties. It was in Gerona. Now the building is used for something else. The minister used to come out here.' The family went to the funeral home at Gerona for her husband's last rites. 'I had a funny dream about him the night before last,' said Mrs Powery. 'He used to work on a ship, and I was thinking, where could he be? He never writes me any letter. I got angry. I thought he had another woman. Then it just came to me about the letter – it was because he was dead.'

A black man was on the stoop smoking a pipe. The Powerys were of one mind that life was getting harder in Cuba. Farmers like themselves, with animals and an orchard, might be able to sell their surpluses for hard currency now. But they still had to accept prices determined by the government, they said. Most of the family wanted to leave Cuba. Mrs Powery said, 'We have to wait four or five years to take up the remains of my husband from the cemetery. I don't want to leave no part of him behind now.' They hoped to go to the Cayman Islands.

For some reason, this prompted me to say, 'How do you imagine England?'

Mrs Powery said, 'I think it must be very beautiful, according to the pictures they have at the *embajada*, some of the old books you used to see. It's very beautiful.'

The family insisted that I took some *guavas*. I got into Mundo's taxi. Then I got out again and went back into the farmhouse and gave Mrs Powery, who was short of English books and magazines, my copy of *Treasure Island*.

People who knew that I was writing about Cuba made me flinch by assuming I was working on a guidebook. The requirements of objectivity, thoroughness, of catholicness, felt beyond me. But on the Isle of Youth, I decided it wasn't asking too much to sample all the accommodation available to foreigners, and after a couple of nights at one hotel, I dextrously slotted in a stay at the other. This was the Colony, a haunt of divers. Looking out from the hotel's raked beach at the almost motionless ocean, the water so clear that it was the colour of the sand beneath it, the impression was of a strata of sand tones – blond, grey, shading (further out) to black – of the kind you might find in a cross-section of cliff on the Isle of Wight. A finger of jetty extended out to sea for 200 yards before becoming a bar. The jetty's bulwarks were clustered with mussels which looked like coins long ago dropped in a wishing-well. The scene was like an advertisement for rum, which in a sense it was. Turning around, what you saw was an old American car in the shade of a palm, satellite dishes on the hotel roof, and, inland, wheeling vultures, for all the world circling the spot where a cutlassed pirate was decomposing.

A column of Cubans – men, women and children – was wading out to the jetty. The hotel beach appeared to be off limits to them. This was implied by a mesh fence. The only things that went through this were the hotel's horses, hosed-down, at dusk, to reappear in the morning. Some of the boys were playing frisbee in the water. The frisbee, *la plata*, travelled across the smooth surface – which, confusingly, the Cubans would also have called *la plata*, the plate – as hard and flat as an ice-hockey puck. The Lolita-like girls – or was I ascribing that to them? – naturally ignored the boys. The girls had long eyelashes, brilliant teeth, glistening demerera skin. One propped herself on her elbow. Only her head and upper chest were out of the water. Another was on her belly, feet pointing up in the air.

In the most subtle instance of apartheid I had yet come across, the Cubans were allowed onto the pontoon, almost to the very edge of the bar itself, but were not expected to take advantage of its chairs and tables. Sandy was an actress, rehearsing Boccaccio in Gerona. She was 22, and had studied English in Havana. She was pretty, slim, wearing a navy swimming costume over her flat stomach. What did I think of her country, Sandy asked me. I said I thought that it was very beautiful but had many problems – how many times had I said or heard that? What about her?

'Terrible,' said Sandy.

Her friend, a young bald man who said he worked as a computer programmer on the IBM series 4, seemed to have a different view of things, or at least, wished to express a different view. 'It's not all so bad – our country is very beautiful,' he said, exposing an ingot of what looked like solder in a rear tooth.

As I was returning to the hotel, a party of tourists let me pass them on the jetty. They were clearly European, though not Spanish, so my reflexive *gracias* didn't seem right. I added a *danke*, then qualified or excused it by saying in English, 'Of course, you *are* German.' One of them asked where I was from. I said, 'Can't you guess? You must be German because you're all properly dressed.' By this I meant their state-of-the-art swimwear and bandbox fresh T-shirts. 'Whereas I—' and here I indicated my raiment: midnight-blue long-sleeved silk shirt with nightclub-MC highlight or weave; demob shorts; an unmatched pair of socks in contrasting shades of dun; desert boots which had never really recovered from the runny tarmacadam of Mogadishu; and a hat reeking powerfully of the guavas from Mrs Powery's farm. It seemed superfluous to *say* where I was from.

'Ha-ha-ha!' said a strawberry-blond man sporting a Lycra thong. He clasped me on the shoulder. 'No, no, no – *simpático*!'

'How are you enjoying your holiday?' I said, retreating into civilities, a near neighbour of hostilities.

'Very good. Our first day,' said a tall grey man with a beard.

'Have you come from Havana?'

'No, Luxembourg,' said the thonged man. 'Ha-ha-ha!' He kneaded my shoulder afresh, and with that the Luxembourgers were on their way down the jetty towards the bar. I heard the strawberry-blond say 'Simpático !' again and laugh his machine-like laugh.

There were sprats in the water the colour of tarnished copper. Half an hour before sundown, the heat went out of the day, and the first 20 yards of breakwater were as pale gold as the sky.

There was a cabaret at the hotel in the evening. It included a percussion act, Alberto, dark-skinned and perspiring. He wore grey camouflage fatigues and a coronet of shells over dreadlocks which had more shells attached to the end of them. His instruments consisted of chests and gourds, suspended from or lashed to a metal A-frame like a loveseat. We watched Alberto bang the chests with his fingers. He also used his elbows, but mostly it was his fingertips and a little palm. I was sitting by the footlights and he called me up to join him. A stout Colombian was also fetched out of the audience. The first thing we had to do was listen to Alberto naming the drums, and then repeat what he said. The Colombian and I were given gourds decked with beads, shikeras. We had to mimic Alberto. I had to shake the gourd twice, and chant. This produced an indulgent hand from the audience. The Colombian went next. His was a slightly more complex routine, but he also earnt an appreciative ripple. The Colombian was older than me, and wearing shorts to my trousers. I guessed that this was all leading up to a contest between us. It was going to be a knockout contest over Alberto's instruments: dead man's chests.

Alberto went into a complicated series of chants and shakes which, I deduced, I would be called upon to reproduce. At the end of his routine, I feigned walking off stage: Alberto gave me a different routine to do instead. It consisted of a shake or two of the gourd and a certain amount of camping it up to the audience. I can do that, I thought. It brought the house down. Alberto asked if I was Alemán. When I said English, this also went down well, not least among the Luxembourgers whom I now recognised at the bar.

I had to settle myself at Alberto's chests and recreate still more complex routines. The first involved a run over all the chests; the second, a gentle finger-snapping on the left-hand chest, building to volleys on all three; finally, the climax, a big clatter through the chests and a shake of the shakers. I extemporised a flourish on a pair of upturned frying pans. I stepped back and bowed, to cheers. The Colombian made something of a meal of his routine, I couldn't help thinking. It featured a great deal of spinning around. Alberto put our performances to the test of audience reaction. Mine got a rave review. My rival, however, was only applauded by his own party, and desultorily at that. I had anticipated a stronger show of support for him from his fellow South Americans, who included Brazilians, Mexicans and Argentinians. There was an interesting United Nations aspect to this, I felt. Did Europeans in the end stick together, even at the cost of backing notoriously secessionist Brits? Did Latins rat on their own, as myth insisted, or were the people of drug-crazy Colombia simply beyond the pale?

Alberto mimed kissing me, his tongue out. A waiter appeared at my elbow with a complimentary viscous drink, a 'pirate'. Among the first to congratulate me were the Luxembourgers. Perhaps moved by the same kind of internationalist thoughts that I had been having, the bearded one started to explain that he and his countrymen spoke several languages, Luxembourgese apparently being a distillation of many tongues. 'We can understand most people. Unfortunately, few of them can understand us,' he said.

When the show was over, Alberto was effusive: what a good percussionist I was, and did I want to take it further through private tuition? José, the deadly earnest compère, explained to me that he wanted to visit Austria. He had received an invitation. I was on a some-what different tack, giving José advice about wearing a bright jacket, telling jokes about the crowd, e.g. 'Anyone in from Colombia tonight? At least we'll be all right for drugs, then.' Start the show later, I said, have a disco. Maybe put the girls in pirate garb for a number. 'All you'd need is eye-patches,' I said.

José, who looked as if he would rather have talked about something else, said it was difficult to get resources for the show. I asked when the coach was coming to take the troupe back to Gerona. 'Eleven thirty,' he said, 'twelve, one, one thirty,' and shrugged his shoulders.

'Hi, you speak English!' In the lobby of the Colony, it was the voice of a small, grizzled-looking man, floral shirt, shorts, salt-and-pepper stubble, a *Popular* cigarette. 'You're German,' he claimed, rising from a vinyl banquette and approaching.

'English,' I said.

'I wonder if you can help me,' and out rolled his story. He had put in to harbour in his sailboat the night before; run up a bill of $68 for meals at the hotel; all told had expenses of about $200, including harbour fees. But his American-issued Visa card wasn't accepted here because of the embargo, and nor were his stateside travellers' cheques. Could I give him about $200, and take the equivalent in travellers' cheques in exchange? He listed the banks and hotels in Havana which he said would accept them.

'Are you on your own?' I asked him.

'With my son. We came down from Key West. We're going to Grand Cayman, then Costa Rica. I have property there.'

It wasn't a fishing trip. They were surfing some of the time. 'You know surfing?'

'Of course, it nearly killed me,' I said, recalling a first and last spill.

'My motorcycle nearly killed *me*,' said the grizzled sailor. He told me his name was Jeff. I had thought he looked Cuban. He said a girl in Florida had thought the same thing. He produced his driving licence, just as he had done for the sceptical girl, he said. There in his wallet was a laminated card which had the word 'Florida' printed on it, and a photograph of Jeff. 'Yes,' said Jeff, returning to the subject of his motorcycle crash, 'I was on my Harley and a guy pulled out of a turning. I hit him doing 40 miles an hour. They split me open like a peanut, spilt my guts out on the table. That was in December, two weeks before Christmas. The doctors said I'd never walk again.' He pulled up the floral shirt to reveal a scar as formidable as that distinguishing any of Stevenson's pirates. Perhaps a pirate was what he was. I said I would see if I had the spare dollars to help him out. A German diver who was staying at the hotel was also considering what he could afford to lend him, said Jeff. Later, it struck me that the hotel would never have allowed him to run up a restaurant tab unless he was a resident. If not Long John then this was surely Little Jeff, the dubious sea captain, if not the sea cook of R.L.S.'s original title: the unshaven chin; the plausible, subtly ingratiating manner; the almost-convincing volume of detail ('there's a bank to the side of the Havana Libre hotel …'); the pursuit of illicit treasure: tourist doubloons.

Jeff was gone by the time I returned to the lobby. The receptionist said she didn't know whether a German guest had helped him. In fact, she didn't know anything about a little sea captain called Jeff. A yacht with white sails was making for the horizon. I like to think that Jeff was at the helm, an ill-gotten float in the pocket of his shorts.

Noting my interest in the descendants of Cayman Islanders, Mundo had drily let slip that there was a flesh-and-blood Englishman living on Isla de la Juventud.

'A Cayman Islander?'

'No, an Englishman,' said Mundo.

'One?' I said, hearing something in my voice.

'One. An old man.'

On my last day on the island, Mundo took me to meet Mr Waterton. He made a right-turn by a shady pond where cattle avoided the sun. Had I been driving, I would probably have gone straight past the Waterton spread without noticing it: a crude barbed-wire gate that you had to untie from the gatepost and drag out of the way; a track running between patches of yucca and pineapple to a farmhouse; two or three mixed-breed dogs, a pair of torn-looking canvas breeches drying on a line.

Arthur Waterton and his family came out to meet me. He had deep-set blue eyes and huge farmer's arms. They were spotty and sack-like. His hands were the colour of corn. He had a full head of hair, swept back: it wasn't white, in fact, it was scarcely grey. His wife looked like a doughty and unforgiving Yorkshire matron, but she was Cuban. Their grown-up sons went about the place in boots and shorts.

Mr Waterton was born in 1922. His parents sailed to Cuba after the First World War, so that his father, who had been wounded, could convalesce in a hot climate. 'Even here, he found it difficult in the winter,' Mr Waterton said. He himself hadn't set foot in England since 1938, when he had accompanied his parents on a visit. 'I remember it vividly, going into shelters for bomb practice.' Mr Waterton had spent most of his working life overseeing the supply of electricity for the island. He was now retired, living on a pension and the proceeds of the farm.

I had brought bottles of Cuban beer, but we drank iced lemonade, with water from the farm well. Mr Waterton's parents were strict Methodists, he said, 'and I have more or less followed'. He had thought of leaving after his parents died, 'but this is my home'.

He built the farmhouse in 1958, a year before the Revolution. There were wooden shelves lined with books, most of them in Spanish, an old record-player and a neat stack of LPs. There were oil lamps with black sumps in them on a sideboard. They were still used, Mr Waterton assured me. 'The power goes out Saturday morning, from six o'clock until one o'clock, and on Tuesday nights. We have to make sure we pump the water up on Friday night, or very early on Saturday.' I felt sorry for the Watertons until I remembered that he used to be number two in the power operation for the whole island. He said he had problems getting fertiliser and fuel. They always kept a few dollars by, in case the opportunity of buying something – soap or clothes – presented itself.

His mother's 'people' came from Oxfordshire. 'We used to exchange letters but there was an interruption in the correspondence.' I imagined a mix-up at the sorting office, a postcard going astray. 'We didn't hear from them for five or six years,' he said.

There had been a burglary at the farm at about the same time. Mr Waterton's notebooks were stolen but money and good clothes were overlooked. He was always being mistaken for an American: perhaps that had had something to do with it. 'There were many more foreigners around – including Americans – when I was growing up. People get the wrong idea.'

'But you're the only Englishman on the island?'

'I've never met another.' The British embassy in Havana had a note of him and his family. He mostly spoke Spanish. He had been brought up speaking Spanish and English.

I said, 'Do you think in Spanish?'

'Yes. When I'm talking to Cubans, talking in Spanish, I think in Spanish. Sometimes I dream in Spanish.' He went for weeks without uttering a word of English. His boys spoke some English. Mr Waterton and his wife were trying to get them off the island, out of Cuba. 'They're graduates and have no future here. The country's more or less bankrupt.'

We talked about attempts to turn parts of Cuba into tourist attractions. 'It hasn't worked,' said Mr Waterton derisively, his mouth creased into a scowl. It was hard to say whether he was just a typical farmer – always doleful – or if he had been ground down by his experiences. When I asked a question about Cuba, on the subject of investment, say, or the interest of foreign firms in coming there, he always replied in terms of a person rather than a country. He spoke of 'he': it could only be one man. 'He's got a reputation for not paying his bills,' said Mr Waterton. It was as if he were talking about a neighbouring farmer failing to settle his seed account.

What did he enjoy? Listening to the BBC World Service, he said. 'Every day, at seven o'clock, though we're not supposed to.' He went to meetings of the local farmers' union. 'I know all these people. I've spent my life here.' But not happily, you felt. He wasn't half-mad, like Ben Gunn, but he was an English maroon all the same.

His wife gathered some guevas for me. Mr Waterton gave me a bag of pineapples. There was a cool breeze. I said, 'This place must be peaceful.'

'It is,' he said, 'but it can be lonely sometimes.'

9

Headhunters
of Havana

As Nestor was driving me through central Havana one day, I spotted a funeral procession. I had seen my first one a week or so earlier and been intrigued: the utilitarian hearse with wreaths resting on an unstable-looking roofrack; the cheap coffin, apparently draped in blue serge or sailcloth; the motorcade of Ladas and flatbed lorries full of mourners. We were at a point in the city where the way to Hilda's *edificio* lay down a right-hand turn. The Columbus or Colon cemetery, where the cortège was bound, was straight on. I said to Nestor, 'Follow that coffin,' but he didn't believe me and turned right instead, as he normally would have done.

I said, 'I mean it.' I had been intending to take a closer look at the cemetery – the one place in Cuba of which my mother had distinct girlhood impressions: cherubim, and tombs that might have come from the Nile delta, glimpsed from a horse-drawn buggy. A funeral was as good an excuse as any. Nestor said, 'I think you are perhaps a little bit *loco*.'

We cut through side-streets in an attempt to catch the procession. We went too fast, and came out ahead of the hearse, and had to fall behind and take our place between a flatbed and a motorbike-combination which was so noisy that the motorcyclist was wearing earplugs. The column of vehicles entered the distempered-looking main gates of Colon, and drew up inside. It was uncomfortable sitting in Nestor's idling car: 38 degrees, according to the radio. At least we could assume that the undertakers wouldn't leave a body lying around for long in such heat. 'The Catholics go to the church,' said Nestor, pointing out the distant chapel roof, beyond the lines of shabby angels and smocked saints, the rockery of icons. Non-believers were still entitled to a plot in Colon, even though there was no priest to attend them at the graveside. Perhaps this was an innovation of Castro, granting every *habanero* access to what had been the rich man's cemetery in colonial days, a gratifyingly literal confirmation of the Revolution's cradle-to-grave welfare, or so you could perhaps be forgiven for thinking after a morning coincidentally spent hearing about Cuban research into a cheap, universal childhood vaccine. Presently the cortège moved off, avoiding the chapel and cleaving to the shade of the Colon's main wall, on which the tangerine paint was cracked; a cross appeared at intervals – it looked less like a crucifix than the 'X' of noughts and crosses. There was no room to pass, and in any case it might have given offence. In order to get to the grave without missing the proceedings, therefore, Nestor again slipped ahead of the mourners, making a detour along the avenues of the dead.

He sat in the car with his book, Dale Carnegie's classic self-help manual *Como Ganar Amigos e Influir Sobre Las Personas, How to Win Friends and Influence People*. 'It's about marketing,' said Nestor. I insinuated myself into the interment scene: the youthful-looking widow; the flowers from the morning's burials, already wilted in the heat; the perspiring grave-diggers in their uniform of grey trousers. One was a black man missing several front teeth. Another approached me with a piece of brown card. I knew at once that this was the death certificate or the burial warrant – it was unmistakeably bureaucratic, like the official, blotting-paper letters Julietta and her fellow graduates had received, advising them where they were to report at the start of their careers. The grave-digger waved the card in front of me and said,

'*Como se llama?*' At least I think that's what he said, though the dead man's name was plainly typed on the card: Bernardo García, aged 63. Perhaps the man couldn't read. He couldn't have been asking me *my* name, could he, wondering if it might be García too, and hoping that the late Bernardo's *extranjero* relative who had come so far to pay his respects would not forget the sextons toiling in 38 degrees? I made a modest contribution to the cemetery fighting fund.

Colon was so vast that not even an outpouring of grief could disturb its peace. Stealing away from the García observances, I found that they had become a dumb show before I was a fraction of the way across the grounds. In their crowded and noisy city, there was a particular attraction for *habaneros* in the proverbial quiet of this place. You could visit Colon to reflect, or to keep a discreet rendezvous. In Pico Iyer's novel *Cuba and the Night*, the silent cemetery was a place of secrets. A beautiful Cuban tells her Western lover, 'No one is making a deal here, no one whispers from the corner, no one tries to hear what we are saying. I could say anything to you here – about Fidel, about my hopes, about Martí, anything.' It was in Colon in 1952 that the young Fidel Castro distributed a call to arms he had penned in my *edificio*.

One of the secrets that the cemetery guarded was faith. In the days when it had been imprudent to admit to religious belief, people had still visited Colon for an audience with *La Milagrosa*, the miracle-working mother. Señora Amelia Goyra died in childbirth on 3 May 1901. Her child had also perished. Mother and child were buried side by side, but when the coffin was subsequently opened, they found the baby's body in its mother's arms. Ever since, Señora Goyra had been an object of supplication to *habaneros* worried about problems such as illness and infertility. A mason had rendered a likeness of *La Milagrosa* holding her baby. The first time I saw the statue, I noticed that the infant bulged troublingly over the maternal forearm. But on other visits I found it swaddled in a set of baby clothes, which concealed the craftsman's questionable eye for form. Petitioners approached the statue and rapped one of the brass links on the lid of the tomb, as though knocking at a door. This was in order to attract *La Milagrosa*'s attention before a request for intercession. A groove was worn in the lid of the sagging tomb, where the ring had been tapped against the marble day after day.

Bees plied between the creamy tributes which grateful petitioners had left at the foot of the statue. There were more baby clothes with the flowers, and marble tablets on which messages of appreciation had been chipped. One thanked *La Milagrosa* for 'the operation on my brother'. Another, in English, said 'Save Us. In You We Trust.' At an adjacent plot were rows of chiselled marble lozenges, all attesting to the powers of the shrine. They reminded me of the slate nameplates you saw in the gardens of British bungalows. From those who had successfully appealed to *La Milagrosa* on a housing matter, there were model wooden houses, not unlike the one Mario the guinea pig had bolted from during my game of *ruleta criolla* near the Bay of Pigs.

Lourdes Izaguirre, who lived on Calle Santa Fe in Havana, had come to see the statue on behalf of her 15-year-old daughter, who had pains in her bones. Lourdes, who was in a T-shirt and jeans, looked as if she needed intercession herself. A botched-looking ear-piercing was clearly infected and angry. She told me a story about meeting a woman from the provincial city of Spiritu Sanctu, who had made the long journey to Havana and walked up from the bus station in order to make her appeal at the shrine. Some supplicants asked that their unborn babies went to term. Lourdes told me that she believed completely in the power of the statue. Had it always been possible to visit *La Milagrosa*, I asked her.

'Yes, but before it was not so easy. I would always come when I needed to, but now I don't worry about coming.'

'What happens when people's requests aren't fulfilled?'

'They don't bring flowers or gifts,' Lourdes replied. It was an eye-for-an-eye with *La Milagrosa*. But it didn't mean that people couldn't, or wouldn't, try again another time. An older woman, Lourdes' friend, finished her observances – touching the foot of the stone infant, taking care not to turn her back on the statue when leaving the graveside – and added that in any case, it could take years for a request to come true, as in the case of a woman wanting children.

Faith wasn't the only mystery of Colon. It was in the cemetery that I stumbled on one of Cuba's strangest secrets, a secret of the grave. A week or so after Señor García's burial, I returned to Colon on a day when I had more leisure. I wanted to see the Revolution's sepulchres, the monuments to modern Cuba's most revered sons and daughters. There was an irony about the fact that these romantically remembered freedom-fighters had found their last rest beside the scions of sugar dynasties. I visited the Armed Forces monument. There was a Cuban flag flying outside it. The monument itself was a bunker. It looked like a larger version of the dovetail-joint rendered in granite which commemorated the IRA's dead in Milltown cemetery, Belfast. The bunker was under repair, but a workman waved me on when I asked if I could look inside it. On the first level below ground was what looked like a morgue cabinet, a chest of stacked slabs. Instead of steel doors, it had a marble fascia, and there were pegs to prevent the slabs from being disturbed. A certain amount of time and expense had clearly been spent on statuary and marble. On the second floor down, where less daylight penetrated, and it was dusty, and loose wiring lay underfoot as knotty and treacherous as tree roots, there were only concrete boxes. They had been named and dated freehand: 'Jacimto Santirez, 9.4.70', someone had scrawled on one. On a few of the boxes was the patriotic addendum '*Venceremos!*' We will win! On others was an abbreviating '*V*', and on others nothing at all.

I asked Nestor to drive to the far wall of the cemetery. I was curious to see whether the man whose burial I had inadvertently authenticated now had a headstone. Nestor was taking a corner when I saw over the heads of the statues, rows and rows of concrete casks like the ones in the soldiers' vaults. They were piled like shoe-boxes in a two-storey, open-sided building. They were exposed to the elements, but partially hidden from sight because the building was in a hollow, behind a grassy bank.

The caskets were arranged in stacks of eight. The lids were crudely fastened with bolts. Each casket bore a name and date. 'Ramona Diaz R, 15.12.76'; 'Jose Concepcion Puentes, 25.2.76'; 'Daniel Fernandez Smith, 12.8.90'. At first I thought that the boxes held ashes, but they were much too big. They were bigger than urns; they were the size of small coffins. A casket labelled 'Manuel Gonzalez Perez, 1.1.82' was cracked. Part of the lid was missing. I realised that many of the caskets were cracked. They contained bones, and the decrepit remnants of what might have been burial clothes or winding sheets. It was like being in the crypt of Moonfleet church.

At first, I thought that I was among unacknowledged casualties of Cuban wars. Perhaps there had been too many of them to be admitted. The fact that women's names were on some of the caskets didn't rule this theory out. Women had also served in Angola and Ethiopia. When I saw the boxes of those who had died in the nineties, I thought it wasn't impossible that they had been veterans. The military mausoleum had held more than one set of remains of a *veterano*. But then I spotted a photo of an old lady affixed to one casket. She didn't look like a retired Africa campaigner to me. There were flowers on top of some boxes: dried bunches of real flowers, and withered plastic wreaths – the sun had done no favours to their man-made bloom.

Having walked the length of the tomb – what was it like? The unvisited basement of a library? The stockroom of a vast Clarks? I was reminded both of the appalling exhibits of Cambodia and of the Egyptian pyramids. Unmentioned in any guidebook, despite or more likely because of the celebrated status of Colon cemetery, these remains had the quality of a find. I stuck a hand under a broken lid and tapped a fingernail against a mossy femur. Some old bones had spilled onto the floor. They were vertebrae. If I hadn't known, I would have taken them for chicken bones, or even for something not resembling bone at all, but fungi.

When I finally retraced my steps to the plot where I'd seen Bernardo García buried – the stretch of freshly turned dirt which awaited Havana's newly deceased – a grave-digger was standing in the shade of a tree.

I wanted to know about the caskets? No, they weren't for the war-dead, said the grave-digger. They were for the poor. The cheaply interred were allowed to lie in Colon's earth for two years, after which they were dug up and repotted in the unvisited tomb. I realised with a little stab of regret, on Señor García's behalf, that his remains were destined for the stacks. His grave of a week was unmarked. It had a number, the sexton assured me, but he couldn't tell me what it was. He couldn't remember exactly where the bodies had been buried as recently as last Wednesday (or was it Thursday? Like the grave-digger,

I was already beginning to forget Señor García, and I was supposed to
be his posthumous benefactor; the angel, so to speak, of his funeral).
Near us stood one of the pretty, red-roofed, make-believe chapels
that the Spanish had bequeathed the *habaneros*. They were actually
entrances to a basement: you could move around under the burial
earth just as you could in the subterranean storeys of the Armed
Forces monument. Planted in the ground reserved for new arrivals
was what looked like a well. It was a *dry* well, a ventilation shaft. Look–
ing down it, I saw more concrete caskets. The dry smell on the air was
probably of dead bodies.

The grave-digger had been employed at Colon for 20 years. Did he
care for the work? '*Mas o menos.*' He had never seen a ghost; he didn't
believe in them. But he did believe in *La Milagrosa*. I left him twitching
out the long straps, like reins, with which the coffins were lowered into
place, helping *habaneros* on their last journey – or last but one, as it
turned out.

You could understand that the mortal remains of the likes of Señor
García might be disturbed when they were exhumed and transferred
to Havana's open-plan paupers' grave. You would expect a few cracks
in the caskets, the odd bolt working free. But entire lids smashed in,
or indecently ajar? Bones scattered like spoor? You didn't require a
morbid imagination to suspect that there was more to it than careless
handling, damage in transit.

In the land of miracles, it was scant cause for surprise that the solution
to the mystery of the Colon caskets was to be found in an alley where
a mechanic was rearing a pig. It was no more unlikely than anything
else. The alley was in central Havana, off San Lazaro, where the rather
proper beggars hustled for alms beside figurines of the eponymous
saint: Saint Lazarus propped himself up on tiny crutches and wore a
leopardskin, like a lame circus strongman. At the mechanic's, three
men were sweatily applying themselves to the engine of a Lada.
Pancho the porker, I was glad to find, had been washed down since I
had last seen him. His colour was now plainly revealed as welcome-
mat brown. Flies doodlebugged the humming slop in his pail.
Mesmerising as this was, it looked as if Julietta and I had made a

wasted journey: what I'd really wanted to see were repairs to American cars. Nothing going on in the garage that morning was going to add to my knowledge.

In the alley, a woman put a couple of planks on a trestle and began covering them with plants. One, which looked like the top of a pineapple, was called *curejeg*, she said. 'If you are lost in a forest and you find this you will never die of thirst because it has water inside.' Her stall also carried sacred Mexican sugar cane, which was good for the kidneys, and paradise plant. If you boiled paradise plant and had a good soak in it, it cured your itching. The deceptively winnowed-looking *vence batallas* was another tonic. A tubful of it brought health and good fortune. By contrast, the little fruits of the *caimito* were to be taken internally. They kept away people who had 'double intentions'. The apothecary stand, with magical remedies by the bushel, was almost the only concern in Havana which didn't appear to be short of anything, which still seemed to be a *going* concern.

A handsome, bearded man was choosing plants beside me. He filled a plastic washbasin with bright red and orange flowers as well as medicinal herbs. His name was Salvador Gonzalez. This was 'Salvador', an artist of some renown according to Julietta. He was responsible for decorating the alley until it resembled a trendy yard or passage in Islington or Greenwich Village. There was a rocking-horse with a cattle-skull masthead; a metal fish suspended from a pole like a prize catch; a mural of Salvador himself on the gable end, wearing a splendid cloak, holding a trident which formed the 'v' in the artist's signature. In a metal cage as tall as a man was a collection of charred relics like those of a *Santería* shrine.

Salvador said he was shopping in preparation for a *fiesta* that evening. It was a party dedicated to *Palo Monte*. *Palo Monte* was a Cuban religion. *Santería* was the greatest cult in Cuba, but it wasn't the only one. There was also *Abakua*, originally from Nigeria and Benin, which was exclusively for men. *Babalaos* like Kiki and Billy were unimpressed by the followers of *Abakua*. They emphasised their junior status. 'Why go to kindergarten when you can go to university?' was how Kiki put it. But *Palo Monte*, like *Santería*, mingled elements of European faith with African creeds: as with *Santería*, you couldn't be of the faith unless you had first been baptised a Christian. *Palo Monte* was a second-rate religion like *Abakua*, in the *babalaos'* admittedly partisan view, but they were far less sniffy about it. On the subject of *Palo Monte*'s devotees, Kiki and Billy might have been cardinals speaking of high church Anglicans.

Palo meant stick, *Monte* was generally translated as hill – to some extent, *Palo Monte* was a feelgood name, intended to express how close the religion was to nature. But it also recorded the antecedents of the faith among the Bantu people and early Cuban followers who had been forced to live wild after fleeing slavery.

I told Salvador that I had some experience of *Santería*. '*Santería* is a Cuban cultural phenomenon derived from Yoruba, *Palo Monte* comes from the Congo,' he said. 'You are invited to my party tonight. You will see.'

Julietta chose this moment to tell me in an aside that *Palo Monte* was a 'very strong religion'. Followers not only sought favours for themselves and their loved ones, she said, but also brought down curses on their enemies. Devotees were apt to practise *rayarse en balo*: branding themselves on the torso with blades; not quite drawing blood but scoring nicks or grooves in their flesh. And their rites included the use of human bones, which they obtained for the purpose from the cemetery. This term, ostensibly generic, could refer to only one place in Havana: Colon.

Sooner than burst out shouting at Julietta, I vented my spleen through sarcasm, saying that I was sure her parting words to me at José Martí airport would be, 'By the way, I'm Fidel's mistress.' Why hadn't she told me about *Palo Monte* while Kiki was inducting me into the ranks of the *santeros*? Surely she could see that I might be interested in this related subject? Why had she kept silent about *Palo Monte*'s blood-curdling practices when we were discussing the damaged caskets in Colon, which the rites very possibly explained? 'Well,' she said, 'you never asked.'

Salvador's *fiesta* wasn't entirely convincing. It took place in the alley he had turned into an installation. A group of French tourists had wandered into the proceedings: some had been unresistingly press-ganged into participating. A white-robed Salvador was spitting rum over their heads, and genially flagellating the delighted foreigners with the plants he had purchased at the stall that morning. There was a musical group with peso notes tucked under their caps. One was keeping time on the head of a garden hoe. He had a gold coin in his right ear.

Smoke issued from a bowl in front of the caged shrine. People were holding red and gold flowers and drinking rum. Salvador thrashed a tottering fat *cubana* on the shoulder with a spray of herbs. Was the woman drunk, possessed, or showing off? It was the same question you had asked yourself about the men in a trance at the *Santería* ritual; at least, you had asked the question *to begin with*. Soon enough, you had found other things to occupy you.

At the end of a number, I approached the man with the coin in his ear and asked him if it was true about *Palo Monte* and human bones. Yes, they were part of the ritual, he said. They were made into pots.

'Where do you get the bones?' I asked him.

'We go looking for them at the cemetery,' he said, and gave me his business card.

Pedro Manuel Osamendi, a 63-year-old musician and former bus inspector, lived in a *solar*, a slum, near the main railway terminal in Havana. It was more like a stable than a house. A tall, dark girl led me through the yard to a room where I found him looking as though he'd had too much rum. He was wearing a pair of trousers and holding an extinguished cigar. There was a tin Christ on a cross and, on top of a cupboard, statues of a black couple in rocking-chairs, and an earthenware dish with an effigy of a chicken by way of a handle. I told Pedro about my initiation into *Santería*. How did *Palo Monte* differ from the cult of the saints?

'*Santería* is more widely practised than *Palo Monte*,' he said. 'If you are a follower of *Palo* and you change to *Santería*, which is a step up, it can put an end to some of the things that you used to do.' Pedro himself had taken this course. 'After I devoted myself to a saint, I kept the pot simply to adore it.' His eyes were cloudy. I wondered if he was what Hemingway would have called a rummy. Did a rummy's eyes look like *that*?

I had heard, I said, that whereas *Santería* stressed the primacy of saints, *Palo Monte* venerated the dead.

'We believe in the same saints as *Santería*,' said Pedro. 'These two religions are similar. If you have a problem, whether you're a believer or not, you can consult *Santería* or *Palo*.'

He got out of his chair and opened the cupboard. If he was trying to make the point that the two cults had otherworldly knick-knacks in common, it was a point well made. The cupboard contained: three glasses of water; a corn-cob fork; a pepper pot; a matchbox containing a magnet; a medicine bottle full of mercury – Pedro poured some into the lid of the bottle, then tipped it onto the floor, where it rolled itself up into balls; a pot of foul-looking green goo ('That's what the pot drinks'); and a papery, embalmed toad which was squatting on a coaster. The largest item was the pot itself, a sealed and blackened cauldron. It was a *prenda*, said Pedro, 'the fundament you use to know the things you want.' There was a human bone in the pot, he said, a bone from a head. 'It's an old bone. The pot is 50 years old.'

'Can I have a look inside?'

Pedro shook his head. 'No-one can look in the *prenda*.'

I decided to work my way round to the contents of the *prenda* again later. Perhaps I could butter Pedro up. I wondered aloud whether any *Palo Monte* believer could qualify for a pot. It emerged that you had to be very experienced, 'at the third level'. But Pedro didn't want me to think that the brethren of *Palo* were treasure hunters, only interested in the sacred ironmongery at the end of their spiritual journey. 'You go into this religion because of tradition, or maybe if you need strength. For me it was tradition. It was done in the same way our ancestors practised. I was 15 years old when I was initiated. It was like a party. There was a cock to be sacrificed, money to pay for the rites, and rum. You don't receive blood in a *Palo Monte* initiation, you receive marks on your stomach. It can be with a razor or a knife or a cock's talons: in my case, it was a razor. The cuts are cured so they don't become infected.' I could see the old scars on Pedro's chest. He was lean, but when he moved, his torso looked like folds of chocolate.

'Why do you have these marks?' I asked, thinking that they were almost like stigmata.

'It's a rule. It came from the slave times.'

'Would it be possible for me to join the religion?'

'But you are a *santero*! You can't go back.'

I regretted having told Pedro about being received into *Santería*: later, I would find that I felt better about it.

Pedro was explaining how gunpowder fitted into *Palo Monte* observances. 'You must be careful. You can easily damage yourself, or the saint.'

'Gunpowder is used?'

'If you have a very tough problem, or someone wishes you bad luck, you make a trail of gunpowder and light it—' Pedro clapped his palms together. 'That will blow your problem up! You don't find this in *Santería*,' he added. He might have been indulging in one-upmanship about gentlemen's clubs, and in a sense he was.

'Can you wish bad things as well as good things—?'

'And *do* bad things,' interrupted Pedro. 'You can for instance wish someone bad luck, that he is sick or has obstacles in his life, or even dies. Of course, this person can then go to another religious man and say, "I've been wished bad luck, can you help me?" '

'What happens?'

Hacer daño, to make a spell, said Pedro, a believer came to him with his problem and Pedro consulted the pot. I said, 'Have you put curses on people?'

'I've never been allowed to create any danger for anybody.' Perhaps Pedro sensed my disappointment because he continued, 'There's an exception. If someone wants to damage me and I suffer that damage, I can consult the pot and return the damage. Yes, I've done that. It's like a war. In any battle you have to defend yourself.'

I asked for an example of this reciprocal damage. He said, 'Someone might leave some powder at my door. Now, I could put my foot in it and it could make me sick or crazy. I might start feeling that I had problems.' The powder contained a secret ingredient. It could be the waste of 'dangerous ants', or part of a beehive, or crushed human bones. Before this mixture became a spell, it was presented to a *prenda*. It was then sprinkled over the threshold of the intended victim, where the spell-maker blew on it. Pedro checked his own doorstep every day.

'Of course, it's not always possible to tell if someone wants to bring danger to you. Some people put this powder inside an egg and then throw it on your roof, where you can't see it.'

'Have you received this powder from an enemy?'

'Yes. I knew because I started having problems at home and at work. I knew somebody was trying to stop me.' Pedro's *prenda* was able to point him in the direction of the culprit.

'The pot can actually tell you who's responsible?'

'Not necessarily, but it's extremely clever. It can suggest who was responsible. I usually know who I'm in battle with. If for some reason I don't, I can use my two religions, my old religion and my new religion, to find out. If I suffered some damage, and I didn't know who was responsible, I would gather three spiritualist people together. It's like doctors gathering over a sick person in hospital.' The retired bus inspector scratched his Mephistopheles goatee. 'We might not be able to say the name of who was doing this but we would be able to recognise the person from his characteristics.'

'And you took revenge on the person who used powder against you?'

'If I've been sent an evil spirit, I just work on it and send it back,' he said.

'What do you mean – "send it back"?'

'There are people who have the power to go to the cemetery and take the spirit of a dead person. They have the power of that spirit over the person who has been giving them problems and they can damage him in return.'

'And you have this power.'

'*Sí*. Not only for bad things, though,' he added quickly. 'I acquired this knowledge through papers from my ancestors, which were written in Bantu. There are other people who don't have this knowledge even though they belong to the religion.'

'Can you describe the process?'

'I can't go into details. It can only happen at certain times of the day – after all, it has to be inside the cemetery and the cemetery closes at given times. You can go with someone you trust, but generally you go alone. I don't damage anything. I make certain rituals, perform my rites.' He received *la acción del muerto*, he said, the action of the dead. 'I don't touch the grave itself. This is a ceremony you perform to attract the spirit. You offer something to the spirit so that it comes.'

'What? A sacrifice?'

'I can't tell you.'

'Well, how long does it take?'

'It takes half an hour, maybe an hour.'

'Aren't you worried about grave-diggers or mourners?'

'People don't pay attention to other people in a cemetery,' said Pedro, and I remembered that Colon had been undisturbed by the burial of Bernardo García, the secrets of Pico Iyer's Cuban beauty, my rummagings in the paupers' plot. I asked Pedro where he had found the bone for his pot.

'The bone was already inside the pot when I received it.' He had seen it since, though. He removed it from time to time, to shave slivers off it for the pots of new believers. Suddenly he got out of his chair and acted out a mime of walking briskly, and bending to lift something heavy, something that required the strength of both outstretched arms. Was he pretending to visit Colon and raise the lid of a tomb? Was he drunk? He said, 'Before the Revolution, there was a pile of bones in the cemetery where they were put to be incinerated. People got bones from there. Since the Revolution, they've regulated that.'

I told him about the damaged caskets I had seen in the stacks at Colon. Had they been opened deliberately, for the sake of the bones? Pedro said, 'Not everybody has a chapel for their family, and these caskets are called municipal boxes. The family pays a certain amount of money for having their relative's bones in this place. If there's one missing, it's a big problem. But yes, it can happen that people steal bones. It's a risk you take if you take one of these bones but it's possible.' People buried in the ground were also apt to become posthumous bone-donors. Grave-diggers could be bought off, for 50 pesos or so. I felt another pang on behalf of Señor García. I thought of a painting in the Museum of Art in Havana, *Un Novato en La Otra Vida*, A Novice in Another Life, by Rafael Blanco, a worm's eye view of a coffin being lowered into a plot, watched by a devil and a skeleton in a white cap.

'I have to limit some of my comments,' said Pedro. 'Some people could hear the details and make trouble. What we do could be considered profane.'

He was adamant that he couldn't demonstrate any of the *Palo Monte* rites practised at Colon. He reminded me that he was now a *Santero*; he held onto *Palo Monte* for purely sentimental reasons. The man who requisitioned spirits had a strict sense of propriety: no levitations outside cemetery hours; no manhandling of tombs; no showing off to outsiders.

Over the next six months or so, I made occasional visits to the *solar* near the railway station with bottles of rum, but otherwise I left Pedro alone. His reservations slowly dissolved in the alcohol. One cool, dry day in January, he came with me to Colon. He was wearing large brown shoes with square toecaps, and mustard socks. He was carrying a bag and smoking a cigar. He was going to show me how to raise the dead.

Nine cents in Cuban money were left by the gates, the price of admission for a *Palo* man. 'The gates are guarded by the dead. We have to give them money so that we can come inside.' The gates were guarded by the dead but the graves were guarded by the armed cemetery police, a militia I'd not come across in Colon before. A man on a bicycle approached us wearing an armband. His main concern appeared to be charging me a dollar for visiting the cemetery, but the pistol in his waistband was a strong argument against ransacking caskets for skull bones. Fortunately, Pedro was going to instruct me in a more discreet method of grave-robbing.

His brown shoes picked their way through Colon's boulevards, through fallen leaves and plums and berries. We reached a tomb undistinguished in any way from its neighbours. It was made of granite and surmounted by a cross and metal links. I could only make out 'José' from the faded inscription, though the incumbent couldn't have been dead for very many years since fresher chiselling recorded the passing of a wife in 1960. In that great city of the dead, the couple occupied a plot a block away from the military mausoleum. Only the spirits of people who had been of the religion in life were suitable for rehabilitating. The lore of *Palo Monte* was particular on the point. 'And we know who believed,' said Pedro.

I wondered whether there was any time limit on reclaiming souls. I was thinking of the period after death which the Catholic church says is spent in purgatory. But Pedro said the only rule was that the funeral must have been held. 'It can be the same day.'

The *Palo* man chalked symbols on the tomb, a religious 'signature' from the language of the Bantu people. He produced a phial of gunpowder and deposited grains of explosive on the chalky graffiti. A handful of change and an empty, unstoppered rum bottle completed the incongruous tributes on the tomb of the late *Palo* follower. Pedro removed the cigar from his lips, turned it back to front, and put it back into his mouth, smouldering tip first. Gripping it between his teeth, he blew smoke over the granite. The idea was that he and the spirit shared the cigar, one end each. 'I call to the spirit three times,' said Pedro. '*Fulano, vamos; fulano, vamos; fulano, vamos.*' He muttered the invocation under his breath.

The *Palo* priest took the cigar from his mouth a second time and placed the glowing leaf to the gunpowder. In the flashing moment of detonation, he snatched up the cap of the rum bottle and twisted it home. The spirit had sprung from the tomb in the explosion and was now captive in the bottle like a genie. What awaited it was a kind of posthumous cannibalism: it was intended for the pot. Pedro said, 'You make him understand that he will live in your *prenda* like a slave and work anytime you need him.'

'Does a spirit ever refuse to get in the bottle?'

'No.'

'Don't you worry that you might spend eternity in someone's pot?'

Pedro laughed. 'No, I'll be dead. And my spirit will become stronger and stronger in the pot, because it's fed with the blood of animals.' The spirit was the secret ingredient that brought out the best in a blend of 70 other elements. Armed with a batch of this eerie ratatouille, the *Palo Monte* seer could tackle any problem that a petitioner brought him.

'That is how you take *la acción del muerto*,' said Pedro, savouring the cigar and the look on my face. This was worth the price of a little rum,

I felt. The geegaws and mementoes at his *solar* were all very well – the pellets of mercury, the toad on its coaster – but what I had been waiting for, it struck me, was a display, a miracle. I had been a doubter. My attitude was show me, prove it. Pedro's display had worked. *Palo monte* was real after his feat in a way that it hadn't been before. I'm not saying that there was anything in the bottle which Pedro and I took away from the cemetery. Perhaps the puff of smoke and the flash of gunpowder, like a conjuror's sleight of hand, were intended to prevent the gullible from rumbling an illusion. But the rituals and ceremonies – unassumingly demonstrated by Pedro, with no demands for payment – persuaded me to suspend disbelief. God – or whoever he was – was in the details, in the solemn Bantu doodle on the tomb as in the words of the Mass or the cool of a country church.

10

The Love Hotel

I COULDN'T TAKE MY EYES OFF the Cuban woman in the airline office. She had good English and good legs, but most of all she was buying a ticket for an international flight. Her name was Dorcas and she was booking a seat to Nigeria. She was leaving Cuba for the second and final time, she told me as we stood in line: I was reconfirming a flight. Visiting her mother in her home town, Camaguey, she had been stopped on a corner by someone she knew, punched in the face and robbed. 'The next thing, I was in the hospital.' She was wearing sunglasses indoors. When I knew her a little better, she let me see her eye, the trick-telescope ring around it, and I understood about the sunglasses. Or at least, I understood the *principle* of them. The pair she wore looked like a diamanté diving-mask. Had the word 'confidence' suggested itself to me at the time, I might have understood much more besides about Dorcas. As it was, I dully registered the approximate age – late twenties – of the woman who was going to enlighten me in the Cuban way of sex.

She had left Cuba to study in West Africa. Now she was working in a malarial swamp which had its own king, an elderly gentleman who numbered Dorcas among his friends. The king lived in an 'ugly, modern palace', built for him by the Germans. He always recognised Dorcas' car when she called. She was an assistant to an accountant in the oil business, but spent most of her time liaising between her company and local tribespeople. The queen, or at least one of the queens, was the real power in the place, Dorcas confided. International travel was beyond the pocket of most Cubans. The trustworthy Roberto, CDR chief, had been allowed to attend an all-expenses-paid geology conference in the United Kingdom. He once showed me a yellowed paragraph he had clipped from *The Independent*. It described how a group of potholers had gone to the aid of people trapped in a cave in Wales. 'I helped rescue them,' he said shyly.

Dorcas was keeping a *turistaxi* ticking over outside the airline office. Her sister was in it. Sila, the sister, was 35 but looked older. She looked *beat*. She had a sallow complexion and sunken eyes. The taxi took us to a pharmacy in Miramar. It was air-conditioned and soothingly lit: it was like a duty free of drugs. Dorcas bought capsules, lotions, cough medicine, 'nerve tablets' which looked like the pill, and an inhaler. They were for her sister and her sister's family. Her sister waited in the taxi. Dorcas said, 'Cuban doctors are good but they don't have the stuff they need. Cubans say, "I'm okay" but they're not. They say "okay" but really they're dying.' She spent $70 at the pharmacy checkout. 'In Cuba, it is a crime to be Cuban,' she said.

The three of us went for lunch at the Neptuno Hotel in Miramar, where Dorcas had taken a room. She told me that she had been see-ing an Arabian businessman in Nigeria but he had suffered a fatal heart attack. I told her about my girlfriend in Rome. Dorcas said, 'There is a saying, "You always have a woman in the Caribbean."' She went to her room while Sila and I sat in the lobby. Dorcas was expecting a call from a gentleman friend in Holland. She loved Holland and had fled there during recent disturbances in Nigeria. ('It wasn't safe to go out after seven at night. They were running around, looking for a head, looking for a heart.') Sila's role, where her sister was concerned, was to wait: waiting outside the airline office, waiting outside the pharmacy, waiting now. I established that she lived in Havana with her 11-year-old son, and that her husband only saw them once a month because he worked away from home. More than this Sila did not care to tell me. Two prostitutes were sitting opposite us. One had a blonde perm and a split skirt. The other, who was more hard-faced, unabashedly checked out the bulge in my wallet pocket. When Dorcas reappeared, I asked her in an aside whether her sister would be prepared to tell me more about herself. Dorcas said, 'Who is around?' and shot a glance around the lobby – not nervously, for Nigeria had cured her of nerves. 'Nothing frightens me,' she said, though perhaps the muggers of Camaguey did a little.

On the way to her house, Sila asked whether I wanted to see the worst part of the city. I wondered how much sarcasm she had meant to get into the question. Her look suggested she had rumbled me as a slum-crawler. Her house was by no means in the worst part of Havana, but it was poorly appointed for all that. The walls looked dirty but what they needed was repainting. The possessions in the house were so few that they looked like still-lives: a cluster of brown mugs, an empty tin of Quality Street, a jar of Bearnaise sauce holding an almost sentimental last drop. Dorcas' great-grandmother was sitting in the kitchen: they lived a long time in Cuba, you had to give Fidel that. On the other hand, the old woman looked like a tortoise.

I met Sila's son and asked him how his day at school had been. He said, 'Good,' and retired to a bedroom – it was the best room in the house – to eat some sweets I had bought for him. He was just bashful but his mother positively refused to talk. Dorcas said, 'She has no opinion,' and she may have been right. Resignation had overwhelmed Sila.

There were several photographs of the family. Those of Sila showed her much as she was now: blankly vexed. But Dorcas looked better than her picture. Her lips were fuller – that was the difference, I decided. In the flesh, Dorcas was the colour of a good cigar.

That evening she telephoned me. What was on her mind was Havana's best-known nightspot. 'We are going to the Tropicana. I will be your guest?' she asked – or said. The money was neither here nor there as far as Dorcas was concerned, she explained, but Cuban etiquette required me, as the man, to pay for everything. It seemed that my failure to buy lunch for Dorcas and her sister was what had upset Sila earlier.

At the Tropicana, you could see dancers wearing the same amount of material that tennis pros use for dabbing their hands on between services. Girls came on dressed as chandeliers, in suspender belts hung with baubles and Duraglit-tinted G-strings. They were linked by a cable, like goods in a hi-fi shop. There was a faint but not unalluring whiff of sweat as girls went among the crowd, trailing their ruffed sleeves over men's heads. A pair of stalls near the band cost in excess of $100, I knew. I didn't begrudge it exactly, but there was something I didn't care for in Dorcas' tone, something proprietory. I heard myself hold out the rather ungallant solution of accepting the price of Dorcas' ticket from her out of the public gaze, so apparently paying for both of us at the door.

'Stephen,' said Dorcas, a new edge in her voice, 'This is the Caribbean. You must enjoy yourself today because nobody knows about tomorrow. You must have a girl. You are not in London now; you are not in Rome.' This was a reference to my girlfriend, I assumed. Dorcas was warming to her theme. 'Like they say, when in Rome, be like the Romans,' she said. 'I am a free woman. That is why many men like me. I am independent. Who knows about tomorrow? Tonight we dance, maybe we make love.'

The implication appeared to be that Dorcas would be mine – picking up the tab was merely a chivalrous fig-leaf. I said, 'Look, I like you very much, but we're friends. I don't wish to sleep with you.'

Dorcas wasn't listening. She liked the sound of the *Galleon*, she said. A fibreglass tea-cutter which set sail nightly from Havana harbour, the *Galleon* condensed the experience of an 18–30 holiday into a few hours of darkness. It would be much more fun than the cheesy old Tropicana, Dorcas felt. 'You can pick me up at my hotel. We'll have some drinks. My sister isn't here, she's at home. I have a big room, a double bed, if you are sleepy.'

I thought, *I* should be saying this to *you*.

Dorcas said, 'Are you afraid I will rape you?'

I thought about this for a moment. 'Yes,' I said. 'Well, no, obviously not, I don't mean – look you're very nice, but you know what it's like when you're a stranger somewhere. You meet someone, they're kind to you, it doesn't mean, it doesn't mean—'

'Look, come over here. I'll be in my room. We'll have a drink. We'll go to the *Galleon*,' said Dorcas, 'or,' she added more softly, 'the Tropicana.'

I said, 'I'll call you back.' I sat on my bed. I felt like one of the subjects of the king of the malarial swamp in West Africa, afraid to go out after seven o'clock at night. 'They were running around, looking for a head, looking for a heart.' Eventually I rang Dorcas' hotel. But I didn't discover what I would have said to her if she had still been in her room.

From the distance of a draughty hearth in the Northern hemisphere – where they were presumably calculated to warm the cockles, to put it no stronger – pullulating legends of Caribbean sexuality had always struck me as unconvincing. The shy glance from beneath the banana palm; the fast-ripening adolescence; the sense that here, at least, men were men and women were grateful: all this smacked too much of male wish-fulfilment. What was asserted or nudgingly implied about the region as a whole was held to be particularly true of Cuba. Why, didn't dusky Cuban maidens roll cigars on their thighs, that kind of thing? A man had only to state his physical preference in a mate, it was said, and thanks to a happy chance of history, she was on the stocks in Cuba. The island's skin-tones were an interior designer's wall-chart on the theme of brown, from cream woodchip to stained mahogany. There were even Indian and Asian colourings. Provided your taste wasn't confined to wintry redheads, you couldn't fail. This was true not only in the sense of your finding a woman who took your fancy but of the woman uncomplicatedly reciprocating. This state of affairs was celebrated in the enthusiastic tribute of tourist Scott Kennah of Dillingham, 'Alaska, USA', recorded in the visitors' book of the Coral Hotel, Varadero: 'Outstanding females, always willing to give 'extra'. Viala Cuba! (*sic*).' I used to see foreign men accompanied by Cuban girls and wonder what they told themselves – she likes me for my sense of humour? – until it struck me that perhaps they believed in the myth of tirelessly uncomplaining Caribbean women: it wasn't sex they wanted; it was to be understood. (It might have been touching if it weren't so corny.) A myth was what it was, though. The aphrodisiac of the thigh-rolled cigar turned out to be a placebo: the Cubans hadn't made smokes that way for generations. And when it came to the tourists and their girlfriends, money completed an eternal triangle. For foreigners at least, what Greene said in *Our Man in Havana,* that sex was a matter of selling or buying, still held true. The girls who turned bedroom eyes upon their European lovers were thinking of the dollars that they would be making. The special period was encouraging women to go into prostitution. There was no argument that the girls were head-turningly attractive (a gay friend who visited Cuba said they were almost enough to make him straight) but if you believed that it was love, you had allowed your head to be turned in a different way. Your wealth conferred seigneurial status.

I pitied the Western men: they looked so ridiculous. But the moral high ground wasn't comfortable. I felt a hypocrite. I wasn't indifferent to the attractions of the women I met in Havana. I flirted with them, I flirted with Julietta – that was just it, I flirted. I was involved with someone to whom I had willingly promised to be faithful. But I felt divided. Here I was in one of the sexiest countries on earth, surrounded by beautiful women who were available to me, in one way or another. Was it foolish to keep my promise? Who was I kidding when I sorrowingly shook my head at the sight of Westerners with Cuban girls? So what if convertible legal tender conferred a *droit de seigneur.* That was the way things were and I might as well get used to it.

Take the case of the exquisite 'Lady' sisters. I sometimes ate at Café Paris on Calle Obispo, a former 'people's cafeteria' reopened as a dollar joint. The old wooden Westinghouse freezers, which looked like animal stalls, had happily been retained. So had the neon sign of a steaming bowl of *café au lait,* and a kind of electric stained-glass window showing the Eiffel Tower. One night I had a ride home in a 38-year-old Mercury, with interior light and original finish. I was driven by Hector and the 'Lady' siblings: 21-year-old Milady and her 19-year-old sister, Lady, a student of the piano. Hector began by turning up the en suite salsa and passing me a can of Lagarto beer, the one bearing an image of a lizard in a *campesino* hat playing the maracas. He finished – after a ride down the hot, drizzly Malecón – by offering me both sisters, at very reasonable rates. They were slim, with long dark hair. Lady was darker skinned than her sister and wore a short black skirt. Milady was wearing a cream miniskirt. As Hector outlined his proposition, both girls eyed me as though my assent or participation were the very thing they had been hoping for. I felt that it was the right thing – that they would *respect* me more – if I went home alone, but Cuban women were getting harder to resist.

I lay in bed at night and thought of them – *negras* and *mulatas*. My window practically opened onto the bedroom of the young couple in the next *edificio*. He was lying on their bed, naked but for a towel over his crotch. She wore a white cotton nightdress with a short hem, and when she rocked back on the mattress, showed a pair of white knickers. He sat astride her, massaging her legs. He bent down over her, and she stroked his back.

I got up, dressed, and went out. Three young men sat beneath a streetlamp and watched me walk onto Infanta. A short way down, an upright fan was revolving in a room where men were playing chess. Half a dozen games were going on, beneath poor strip-lighting. On the wall was a photo or daub of Fidel at the chessboard. He was wearing a quizzical expression. As far as I could make out, Fidel was *white*.

I reached El Malecón and began walking toward the old city, on the side of the promenade away from the sea wall. It was a hot night, the tang of ozone scarcely carrying on the air. El Malecón was filling up: courting couples; mumbling old drunks who had mislaid their shirts and looked unlikely ever to recover them; groups of friends or family with a liquid picnic of a rum bottle and Tropicola mixers; likely lads and *prostitutas*. I was hailed a few times. The favourite ruse was to ask the time. Others used the well-tried: 'My fren, where you from?' or launched straight in with 'Italiano? Alemán?'

A *casa* was propped up on wooden struts – some of the struts weren't long enough, and were themselves braced on a small wooden groyne or block no bigger than a bootblack's steps. Two policemen were talking to a pair of prostitutes who were sitting on the wall. As I watched, one officer took off his hat and steered a questing buttock onto the wall. A dark woman – pert but big-bottomed, attractively-featured but not pretty – was sitting between myself and the officers, talking to a boy on a bicycle.

Presently, the dark woman and the cyclist moved off, towards the old city. But they hadn't been gone a minute when the girl wandered back alone. She was Doroteca. She was 22 and she worked in a nursery. Did I want to go *paseo*? She smiled. There was no sense in her of the furtive, sick-making thrill that I was feeling. But what about the man I had seen her with, her husband? She wasn't married, she said. A boyfriend then? No. She had a place all to herself – well, she had a room.

I said, '*Tu eres muy bonita pero tengo una novia.*' (You're very pretty but I have a girlfriend.) This didn't faze Doroteca, who established – do I tell her, I thought – that my girlfriend lived far away. I insisted that we go our separate ways, and was glad I had, when I saw the boy with the bike (her pimp? her shaker-down?) waiting for her on the other side of the street.

At the turn from Malecón into the Prado, a stall selling fast-food was playing perhaps the loudest music in Havana and prostitutes were plying for hire by the light of passing cars. There hadn't been so much touting and soliciting five years earlier, during Carnival on the Malecón – a parade of homemade floats, as crudely satisfying and effective as DIY shrines and effigies; waxed cartons of beer cooled on blocks of ice, a Havana tradition unchanged since Hemingway described it in *To Have and Have Not*; one clattering salsa band after another, and wave after wave of *bailarinas* in nothing-to-the-imagination costumes, gyrating to 'found' percussion instruments. It was the last Carnival in Havana, the one before Moscow stopped the money.

On Prado, I was propositioned by two black girls. One, a 19-year-old in stringy dreadlocks, was wearing a sundress which brimmed over her hips. I would only have to pay $30, and the friend – a wary older girl in a denim dress – might be thrown in too. The first girl tugged my wrist and patted me on the fly.

I talked to other girls, or they talked to me. I didn't know if my growing confidence was a sign that I was coming to my senses or losing them. I wandered up to the Inglaterra, crossed Parque Centrale, and passed the Floridita. On Calle Obispo, women were sitting in the street fanning themselves. I saw a pretty girl in a short skirt and followed her. (I had just been propositioned by a woman of an uncertain age who had walked off taking the only other available route.) I thought I was lost but eventually I came upon a nightspot I half recognised called the Aquarium Club. A man and a woman were talking at the door. The club seemed promising, late-night. Half a dozen faces looked round wearily from the bar as I entered. The lighting was low and blue. It was as if the drinkers were undergoing low-dosage radiotherapy en masse, and had given up hope of anyone coming by to let them out.

A few more turns – dark roads, men in doorways, music and lights behind upstairs shutters – led me back onto the square in front of the Inglaterra. I had decided to have a drink at one of the places near the Floridita when I ran into the girl with ratty dreadlocks again. A young man who was with her began negotiating a fee on her behalf.

Julietta affected shock at any mention of sex – perhaps it did shock her. In one sense, she had had a sheltered upbringing, living at home into her twenties, raised on the stern certainties of *la Revolución*. But she wasn't a child. She was sleeping with someone who had been in her faculty at university. It was a casual thing, she said. He wasn't her boyfriend. She hadn't given up hope where her Norwegian was concerned. I outlined my argument about the seigneurial effect of being a foreigner in Cuba, but she said, 'Why do you talk about money all the time?' I wondered if her faith in romance was a Cuban trait – as opposed to something she would grow out of – because there *was* a Cuban way of looking at sex. To say that Cuban attitudes were the same as those I was used to would be as misleading as the myth of primal Caribbean sexuality. In Cuba, the contours of the *mulata* backside were discussed in the lowest dives; they were also a subject to which Cuban masters had devoted the best years of their lives, an obsession to compare with European strivings to capture grace on canvas. Cuba was a country where men hailed each other on the street with a cry of '*Macho!*' A senior politician might conclude an interview by asking the journalist, 'Tell me, have you had sex in Cuba?'

I had been pestering Nico for weeks to find me a whorehouse. I was interested because Cuba claimed to have closed down its brothels. It would be the first country in the world to do so if it had. Unbecomingly, I raised the subject when Julietta was visiting, knowing that it never failed to produce a frown of displeasure. There was the friend of Nico's who knew a place at Miramar. I said, 'I only want to go and see what it's like.' But Julietta said, 'You cannot be so naive. You will have to choose a woman.' Nico finally made contact with his friend, who reported that the whorehouse had been closed down: Nico mimed popping a letter into the mouth of a mailbox and hitting it with the heel of his hand – a gesture of finality. I said, 'Don't you know of any other places?'

'The government has shut them,' said Nico. Now the trade was all in the street and hotel lobbies. 'I know some *jiniteras*, if you want to meet them, friends of mine from the *barrio*.'

I went to an address he had given me, an apartment block not far from the Press Centre. The only doorway which was lit was number 406, the number Nico had mentioned. The door was opened by a middle-aged woman wearing a waistcoat over a massive bust. She also wore lycra shorts, flip-flops and loads of eye-shadow. She was like Alice Cooper, only brawnier. The woman's name was Olga. On a wall was a rug depicting the Last Supper, in which Jesus was looking very cheerful and the disciples were all square-jawed and wearing capes, as if they were comic book superheroes. There were *Santería* dolls on a table and fresh flowers in a vase, which was in the shape of swordfish rampant.

A young woman, a *mulata,* walked into the room in a polka-dot miniskirt and an off-the-shoulder top. She was wearing boots and a choker. She had dyed blonde hair. Olga introduced me to Jani. Jani was 18 years old and came from the provincial town of Holguin, she told me. Jani sat on a couch facing me and smoothed down her skirt. Any man might have been attracted to her. I wondered if Olga was her landlady, or madam. There were four bedrooms in the apartment. Olga told me that she had been living in it for 19 years. 'When I first came here, this was a nice building. Decent people lived here,' she said without apparent irony. The three of us drank the beer I had brought.

I asked the women how hard it was to make a living. Olga said she had problems with her son. 'He has a different way of thinking.' I gathered that he didn't approve of what his mother and her tenants did for a living. Olga had been a hairdresser. She had retired from that, she said, and lived on a pension of 80 pesos a month. 'In the beauty shops, there were no products,' she explained. Conditioner was $2.65 a bottle in the dollar shops, but she had only been allowed to spend two cents per head on her Cuban customers.

'What do you do now?'

'I buy a diet product and work from home. I drive people around. I also rent out my rooms to girls.'

She had three girls staying with her at the moment, she said. They were aged between 15 and 20. They paid her a couple of dollars each for rent, more for meals. 'They go with tourists, never with Cubans. The tourists are the ones with the dollars.'

Jani had been in Havana for six months: 'When I was growing up I wanted to be a nurse, but everything was so difficult. I went to technical school but I didn't like it. I couldn't find a job through the school. When I came here, my plan was to make some money and go back to my home town to help my parents.' Her parents knew what she did for a living, she said.

'Do they mind?'

'So-so.' She didn't look as though she was convincing herself. She worked the Riviera hotel. 'The men call me over if they like the way I look. I walk around the lobby and they call me. Sometimes, we go into the disco, sometimes I hitch a lift on the Malecón and men pick me up. The tourists know that there are girls standing on the Malecón. They come here with the idea that Cuban women are sexy – it's in all the magazines. They've heard that Cuban women are very sensual.' They had also heard that Cuban women were very reasonable. In Jani's earshot, men had said, 'The cheapest bitches are Cuban.' She had slept with men from Italy, Spain, Germany, Puerto Rico and Britain. 'At the moment, I'm going around with a Puerto Rican.'

'How old is he?'

'Fifty-four. Most of them are over 40.'

'Are they married?'

'Sometimes.' Sometimes, the men fell in love with the girls. Sometimes they even married them. 'I know a couple of girls who married Spanish men. But they didn't stay with the men long once they got to Spain. The girls threw them away.' You might have expected Jani to take a certain vengeful pleasure in this but she looked rather wistful, as though mourning love's young dream.

She told me about a friend of hers who met an Italian and married him. As if in a classical tragedy, the Italian asked his friends to proposition her, to test her fidelity. 'Finally, she slept with them,' said Jani. 'The husband was furious. The girl was deported, sent back to Cuba. But one of her husband's friends came here and found her and took her back to Italy again.' I thought that I was going to hear a happy ending, but it seemed that the woman was last heard of working in an Italian whorehouse. 'I don't like the idea of working in a whorehouse,' said Jani. 'That would be dirty.'

'Have you fallen in love with anyone?'

'Yes, a German. It didn't work out.' She lit a cigarette.

Sometimes, Jani spent two weeks with a single trick, his entire holiday. It might be at his hotel or in a private house. At a hotel, the man had to pay $60 in bribes to the porters in order to keep her in his room.

I said, 'How much do you charge?'

'It depends on the man, how much money he has. If he's a wealthy man, I can smell it,' she laughed. 'Suppose he's staying at the new hotel, the Cohiba: people who stay there are supposed to be wealthy, they are people with $900 in their pockets. If I'm with a man for two weeks, he takes me out every night, there's privacy and intimacy every night. I get very close,' she said. It was as though she were justifying her fees.

'Do they ever talk about their wives?'

'Sometimes.'

'What do you do?'

'Sometimes I listen. Other times, I tell them I don't like it.' She said that the majority of the men came to Cuba on business, or to receive medical treatment. 'The doctors in their countries send them here because they're not very strong, but when they see the Cuban girls, they try to find the energy.'

Jani had had no problems with the police so far. 'But they do catch girls. To begin with, they send them warning letters. The third time, the girls go to prison for three years. But if they go to bed with the police or give them money, the situation changes.' I thought of the officer I had seen sidling up to a prostitute on the wall of El Malecón. Jani said, 'Many policemen come from the eastern provinces and they've never seen beautiful girls like you find in Havana. In the first years of the Revolution, the police came from the city, many of them were educated. But no-one from Havana wants to be a policeman now because the pay is bad.'

'I've heard that prostitutes are used to supply information to the state.'

'That's right. We know a lot of people.' I remembered telling Doroteca, the prostitute from the Malecón, that I was English, a *periodista*. I thought, 'I've said too much. If it gets back to my press handlers that I've been with prostitutes, it'll wreck my chances of seeing Fidel.' Prostitution was so shameful that Fidel was still refusing to acknowledge that it went on. On the other hand, if it had got around that I'd been enjoying the company of pretty *habaneras*, it would probably have counted in my favour with those lower down the hierarchy. Almeida at the Press Centre would have approved, I felt sure. When I told Nestor about taking the air on El Malecón at night, he said, 'You're half-Cuban.' My confession that I had failed to get up to anything made no difference. 'You are in the water,' he insisted. 'You are like a fish. You are still English, but you are swimming.'

Olga the madam confirmed that prostitution was tied up with the regime. She knew of a group of Spaniards who had entertained rent boys at a house belonging to a member of the provincial government.

I asked if prostitutes were aware of Aids. 'Yes. We carry condoms,' said Jani. 'I was with a Bulgarian and his hotel room was full of lots of equipment. He had this gadget that looked like a pen. You put it on your skin and it told you if you had Aids or not. It was a like a pen with invisible ink.'

Some men asked for unprotected sex and were willing to pay more for it. Jani had had unusual requests, she said. 'Sometimes they've been rough and asked for strange things. For example, I was offered a lot of money to have sex with another woman. But I didn't because I like men. Another day, there was a Spaniard who was a little bit crazy. He had a friend. He asked me to sleep with the friend so he could watch. Besides that, he had a vibrator.' Jani had declined his requests.

I told her I was surprised to hear that she still liked men.

'Some of the girls only do it for the money, but I'm not tired of men yet,' she said.

Olga went and fetched more beer for the three of us. She told me, 'My house is your house. You can come any time. We would be pleased to see you.'

One Saturday afternoon, when Nestor was putting in a few hours at his legal practice – it was difficult not to soften to a regime which made the lawyers work weekends – Julietta and I flagged down a Lada to take us to the beach. In the summer months, *habaneros* got in the car, or on their push-bikes, or waited for buses, and made for the East Beaches. They were a few miles out of the city, a little way beyond the white elephant of the athletes' village which Cuba had built for the Pan-American Games. I sat in the back of the Lada. There was no interior panel on my door. The window didn't open. Nor, come to that, did the door.

Our first port of call was Julietta's apartment: she had to pick up her bathing things. We went a few blocks and pulled up at a red light. The lights changed but the Lada wouldn't budge. The driver got out, threw up the bonnet, removed the carburettor, and placed it tenderly against the windscreen.

Julietta lived on the top floor – the 25th – of a tower block which overlooked La Plaza de la Revolución. We boarded the Russian-made elevator. 'So small!' snorted Julietta. We found her father busy at the dining-room table with a set square and charts. He was gnawing a cigar which had gone out. Julietta's mother offered me coffee. There was basketball on the television. In the middle of the game, the screen flickered suddenly and went blank.

I turned to Roberto. Without looking at me, he said, 'It's the electricity.'

The offer of coffee was now suspended. And the lift was out. If the power cut had struck five minutes earlier, Julietta and I would have been trapped in it. There were two or three power cuts a week, Julietta said. She had spent 30 minutes or so in the lift on several occasions but the record was five hours. 'A man was stuck by himself. He was shouting but no-one came because they couldn't hear him.' The building was less than three years old but it already had a decrepit, Soviet look. There were six apartments to a floor, 150 in all. If each held five people, like Julietta's – which didn't seem unlikely – that was 750: 750 people trudging up and down stairs in a blackout. Roberto said the paper usually published details of forthcoming outages. 'Four till nine or nine till one or one till seven,' he said. The orderliness made it easier to bear. The paper also printed warnings to boil water after heavy rain. 'But we have no malaria, because the pipes run underground,' Roberto added dutifully. He showed me over his library, which he had fashioned himself out of what looked like packing-case wood. 'Here are the science fictions ... here are Russian books – my wife's: you know she was a translator? These are war books—'

'Second World War?'

'Yes.'

'What's that one?' I pointed at a green volume which had inexplicably caught my eye.

Roberto withdrew the book from its orange-box shelf and handed it to me. He said, 'It's about great war heroes of the Soviet Union.'

As Julietta and I were leaving the apartment, he said to me, 'Take good care of my little girl.'

'Was he joking?' I asked her.

'Half and half,' she said. We took the stairs and walked down 25 flights to the street. The Lada got us as far as the brow of the hill overlooking the East Beaches and broke down again, apparently finally. On the beach, a couple were cuddling enthusiastically beneath a palm tree. He was about 30. He had a beard and shorts. His girl-friend – say 25 – was wearing denim shorts and a black bikini top. Julietta said, 'They make love wherever there's shade. Some people make love in the sands.' When I looked at the couple again, he was squatting between her thighs, planting decorous kisses on the waist-band of her bikini briefs, her shorts by this stage having been peeled down her thighs. They shared a beaker of *ron*. Another girl in shorts which were already epidermically tight waded out into the sea in them.

Julietta and I had been talking about *jiniteras*, whether or not you could spot them. 'She's a *jinitera*,' said Julietta, meaning the girl in the too-tight shorts.

'How can you tell?'

'Most of them are very dark-skinned, as she is, and they have long hair which is not their hair.' Apart from hair extensions, they wore high-cut bathing suits and lots of jewellery. Julietta said that some women sold themselves for the price of a pair of shoes – say $30 – or less. In order to secure a lucrative pitch in a hotel lobby, the more ambitious among them were prepared to sleep with doormen or bell-boys. The john (always a tourist – Cubans with *pesos* couldn't afford hookers; Cubans with dollars didn't need them) was expected to buy the girl 'lunch'. This was not the getting-to-know-you billing and cooing that it sounded: following the meal, the tourist accompanied the girl to the hotel dollar shop and bought her gifts of her choosing. If she was lucky, she would be fed, dressed and put up in his hotel room for the duration. Julietta confirmed what Jani had said, that some Cuban women ended up married to foreigners. 'A friend of mine married a foreigner. Cubans sometimes get married without thinking too much about it. I know someone who was married for 15 days then filed for divorce. The family said, "Why did you get married?" and the couple said, "Hey, it meant we could have a party, a cake." '

Julietta wore an orange bikini. Her armpits were shaved, I noticed. When she went into the sea, she turned flips in the surf. When she returned, I asked her, 'Have you heard of the love hotels?' They were the solution to the problem of love in an overcrowded city, or so I gathered.

'They are called *posadas*. In Spanish, it means a place where you rest.'

'Let's go to one.'

'Stephen!'

'Just to have a look.'

'My father would kill me. He would kill *you*.'

'We won't tell him.'

We got a ride in an olive-and-cream 1955 Chevrolet, driven by a man in aviator sunglasses. His name was Santiago. He knew a *posada*. 'It's called Motel Las Rosas. It's on the Via Blanca.'

'Is it any good?'

'Sure.'

Santiago wore a wedding band. I supposed that he knew the *posada* from the days before he got married. '*Since* I got married, too,' he said. 'It saves embarrassment.' Whenever we went downhill, he turned the engine off and freewheeled, to conserve petrol.

It was dark by the time we pulled up outside Las Rosas. It looked like an American motel from the fifties. There were 20 cabins or chalets with shuttered windows. Light emerged through a few slats. Santiago said that *Las Rosas* had been built in Batista's day. It was originally known as 'The Monumental' – as in hangover, or erection. It was now run by the state. Las Rosas, like other love hotels, had been allowed to put the red light back in the window because of the tensions created by the shortage of housing. The state also made money on the *posadas*.

Santiago knew the manager. He said he would tell him that he had a Cuban woman and her foreign boyfriend in his car. I should give him a couple of bucks to square the manager. On the back seat of the Chevvy, Julietta took off her beach things. She put on a short denim skirt. We had been talking about the Cuban way of love, whether or not it differed from the way we did things in Britain. One similarity was the fiction that men and women maintained, pretending to each other that they didn't know what was going to happen between them even when it was almost upon them.

I followed Julietta's lead and changed. Santiago returned to the Chevvy with the motel manager while I was still *déshabillé*. I felt as though I was in the touring production of a farce. Julietta said, 'We must look as though we're a couple, very much in love.'

I held her hand. She said, 'I'm sorry. My hand's cold.'

'Yes, I noticed. Are you nervous?'

'Not nervous. It is the unknown. It can have a strange influence on your life.'

The *carpeta* was lit by a single naked bulb. There was a defunct-looking bar, stocked with a single rum bottle. At the desk, a guest's directory or tariff, bound in mock-leather, itemised the *Las Rosas* rates:

> *3 horas: 10 pesos*
> *6 horas: 16 pesos*
> *12 horas: 28 pesos*

The manager led Julietta and me through a door into what looked like a dark corridor. In fact, it was open to the elements on one side. We passed chalets which looked unoccupied but didn't sound as though they were. In one, a lamp which I sentimentally mistook for candlelight was burning wanly.

The manager held a door open. We were in a carport. A pair of chunky sleeping policemen had been concreted into the floor, possibly to tell amorous drivers when to apply the brakes. There was a door in the side of the carport and this led into the sitting-room of a chalet. It had the atmosphere of a waiting-room: two cane chairs were arranged at standoffish angles to each other; between them, a Thermos jug and a pair of upturned tumblers rested on a low wooden table.

A bedroom wall was mounted with what looked like a wipe-clean chopping-board. It had a motif of summer fruit. There was a furred-looking air-conditioning unit over the headboard of a double bed. Like a newlywed, I reluctantly let go of Julietta's hand in order to bounce on the mattress. It gave like a sponge. I peeked beneath the blue coverlet: there were no pillowcases or sheets; though, in the half-light, no sign of stains either. There were little bedside nightstands but no lights that I could see – only a bulb in the sitting-room, and in the bathroom. The chalet had its own vinyl-bound tariff, like the one at the *carpeta*. I thought about pocketing it, but as I was turning it over in my fingers, Julietta hissed at me. She had memorised the rates, she said. I hadn't realised that she knew me so well.

We asked if we could see another cabin. It was identical except for a pot plant in the sitting-room – was it extra? – and a telephone. This only raised reception, said the manager. The only other difference was the design of the chopping-board on the bedroom wall. I told the manager that we preferred this cabin to the last. Could we get something to drink? Perhaps he kept a few *cervezas* in the defunct bar. But the manager said that guests were expected to pick up anything they had forgotten from a nearby garage. Thinking of Roberto – the decorated war hero, the CDR boss – I asked Julietta, 'What will you tell your father?'

'I'll say, "We went for a little tour of Havana, Daddy." '

Writing about two people having sex is notoriously difficult. But writing about two people not having sex is difficult too. And yet that's more often than not what happens – isn't it? Julietta was involved with someone else; so was I. All the specifically Cuban constraints – the seigneurial power of dollars, the well-used room, Julietta's father – might have stood for nothing had it not been for this universal impediment.

11

Writers

IN A LIBRARY ON PRADO IN HAVANA – a single strip light, a stopped clock, a thrashed fan – I asked if they had anything by G. Cabrera Infante. The novelist was expelled from the Cuban writers' union in 1968, by which time he had already spent three years in exile. He vehemently rehearsed exactly how underground his books were in his native land in a collection of vindicatory essays, *Mea Cuba*. I had boldly taken the book into Havana as hand luggage. The librarian said she would go and have a look. Depending from her *balcón* was a pair of red spectacles. One of the lenses was cracked. At her heels was a frizzy-haired poodle.

Cabrera Infante edited *Lunes*, the literary supplement of the newspaper *Revolución*, until it was closed down in 1961. Contributors had signed a letter protesting at the suppression of a documentary film. Writers who were associated with the magazine included some of the most interesting, the most colourful, figures in Cuban letters: the short-story writer Calvert Casey, the poet Heberto Padilla, and Anton Arrufat. Cabrera Infante wrote in *Mea Cuba* that his novel, *Three Trapped Tigers*, was placed on a blacklist, 'the Castroist Index'. Those who championed the book lost their jobs. He conceded that Cubans might be able to find his work, but if they let on that they wanted to read it as well, they might wish they hadn't.

When the librarian returned, she was wearing the spectacles, and carrying four hardbacks. There was something called *Tap Roots* by James Sweet, about the American Civil War, published in 1942; a pair of liver-spotted Somerset Maughams ('the revolver was not there: his heart thumped violently against his ribs') and Dickens' *A Tale of Two Cities*.

The librarian said, 'I'm sorry, we have the books of Cabrera Infante but I'm afraid I cannot give them to you. We're doing a lot of work here. Perhaps you can read these instead?'

'You have his books but I can't see them? Why not exactly?'

'Because they are being reclassified,' said the librarian.

'Will I be able to see them next week?'

'Maybe.'

'Have you read him?'

'No. But I would like to. Many people have asked for his books and recommended them.'

I opened the Dickens, and I was reflecting on *that* introduction, when a scrap of paper appeared on the table by my hand. It was the name and address of the librarian. 'If you come to my house, I have a friend who has Cabrera Infante's books,' she said.

From the unglazed window of her apartment overlooking El Malecón, Lourdes the librarian watched *los balseros* scrambling for Miami in 1994, she told me. I had seen some rafters myself: forlorn-looking figures dangling their legs over the sides of inner tubes off Havana's shimmering beaches. These turned out to be fishermen. Sea-faring men of a sort, then, presumably putting to sea in the best craft their money could buy – and all looking likely to capsize at any moment in the torpid swell. It was a head-clearing thought that *los balseros* were even less well prepared than this. Lourdes, who was in her early forties, was wearing a mildly ribald T-shirt and a short blue skirt. She had procured tea for her English guest. She strained the contents of a saucepan through a cloth into a tin mug and divided it between two smeared glasses, which she topped up from a tap. 'So tell me,' she said lightly, handing me my tea, 'is London really as rainy as they say?'

Her husband slouched downstairs from the family's sleeping quarters overhead. He wore pumps with the laces missing, like a man in police custody. He offered to sell me two foil sheets of tablets for $5. They were labelled PPG and issued by the Cuban government, he claimed. Lourdes said, 'They are good for the heart, they help you after an accident.' Her husband leered at me and cocked a terrible forearm.

'They also make you potent,' added Lourdes. Five bucks seemed a snip for such a panacea, and you wondered that the authorities weren't lacing the drinking water with it. But Cuba's admired health system scarcely ran to that kind of thing. In Havana, in Santiago de Cuba, you might see young interns who were poised to join the ranks of the country's surgeons: there were 1,267 at the last count, according to state radio. There was no lack of talent; what there was a lack of was medicines. I thanked Lourdes' husband for his proposition, but said that I was anxious to meet the person who had Cabrera Infante's books. At this, Lourdes said, 'My friend is a sculptor. He is very good but his place is not so nice.'

She took me to a blackened stew of a building off Parque Central, where an old boy was leaning woozily against a bare wooden prop. A dark-skinned man wheeled his bicycle past two young girls who were playing on a landing. The floor of the landing was covered with tiles in a floral design, except where it had fallen through and the tiles had been replaced by a footbridge of four-by-two. What must once have been a beautiful spiral staircase now finished ten feet off the ground in a whorl of rusty hoops. The balustrade was rotten and looked as if it would give way to a good firm cough. The sculptor who had the Cabrera Infantes was out, it seemed.

That evening, I was eating at the Inglaterra when I was wordlessly joined by Lourdes. I looked up in some alarm. She reminded me of my plans to make a trip out of the city the following day, to visit a young writer. His name had been given to me by *Index on Censorship*. I had letters for him. Lourdes thought that she might be able to help me with my travel arrangements. She was a little tipsy. 'I have just left my husband for a few hours,' she confided. 'He is my second husband. You know, I loved my first husband very much.'

'Oh?' The food had the familiar tang of disinfectant so I didn't begrudge pushing my plate away. 'What happened?'

'It was another woman.' Lourdes helped herself to one of my cigarettes. 'You know, my husband – my new husband – is very jealous,' she said.

Sure enough, next morning I found that Lourdes had organised a pillar-box red 1952 Chevrolet; 'The year I was born!' she exclaimed. Its owner, Rene, had acquired it a month earlier from a man who was last seen making for Florida. Rene said that in the event of the police stopping us, I should pretend to be a hitch-hiker. Lourdes craned over the bench seat of the Chevrolet and asked me what sort of dishes we Britons enjoyed. As I was giving her my recipe for toad-in-the-hole, I asked myself again whether I was doing the right thing by bringing her along. It was bad enough going to meet writers with whom the regime didn't entirely see eye to eye, in a car I wasn't supposed to be in, without risking the wrath of a jealous husband who had access to wonder drugs. On the other hand, perhaps a librarian wasn't a bad companion for an investigation into Cuban books. Cuban books were as much to do with what readers could read as what writers could write.

About an hour out of Havana, we were flagged down by a motorcycle patrolman. Rene took his papers from the dashboard and got out of the car. I turned to Lourdes and she looked at me. 'So you eat a lot of roast meals in England?' she asked me in a dreamy voice.

The writer whom Lourdes and I were going to see wasn't on the telephone, but fortunately we found him at home. The journey – to a small town on Cuba's Atlantic coast – had taken three and a half hours, with two police stops. Our host, who asked not to be identified but whom I might call A——, was sitting in football shorts and singlet, long legs tucked underneath him on a rocking-chair. He was in his early thirties. A short story of his had appeared in a recent anthology of Cuban writing. 'We had help from Spain and the United States to publish it,' he said. A——'s contribution dealt with the dominance of the man of the house, the punishment a father dished out to his child.

'This is an allegory?' I asked him.

'Of course. It's an allegory for a society with a man who wants to rule everyone and doesn't hear anyone, and wants everyone to do what he says because he thinks what he says is the best.'

I was interested to know how hard it was for writers to write in Cuba. Western embassy officials said that while the Cuban media was expected to bang the drum rather than inform, as one put it, criticism was tolerated provided that it promoted efficiency. The radio had been running sceptical pieces on transport policy. A week before meeting A——, I had spent an afternoon in an attic with a theatre troupe. They told me that drama was being used to change things. The play *Manteca* (*Lard*), for example, about a man keeping a pig illegally in Havana – a kind of Cuban *Private Function* – had emphasised food shortages, and contributed to pressure for farm reforms. But the actors and dramaturges were aghast at the idea of satirising the leadership. 'You ask about Fidel,' said one. 'Fidel in Cuba is something like an idol and we are not accustomed to making jokes about him.' I mentioned Boris Yeltsin's weakness for alcohol. The Russian President had failed to disembark from his airliner during a scheduled stopover in Dublin. This had been sent up in Moscow as well as in the West, I said. Could a similar thing happen here? The actor regarded me gravely. 'We are not aware of a situation like this with Fidel,' he said.

A—— said, 'Lately, writers haven't been doing a lot of work because they're worried. Five years ago, they were working harder, but now there are problems with food, electricity, buses. There isn't much time to write. The people are depressed and upset and writers are just the same. If, in England, you had two years of living like we do, I'm sure, a lot of people would die.' He smiled. 'We have to go on but it's not easy. We've seen a lot of changes since the troubles with *los balseros*, including economic changes, and in a general sense they have been for the better. But we haven't had fundamental change. The main, important thing that we need to be changed has not been changed.'

'Are you talking about a thing or a person?'

'It could be a person, yes,' A—— replied. We shared an eggcup-sized ashtray on a low table. We tiddly-winked our ash towards it.

A——'s generation of writers was the first to have grown up since the Revolution. 'Everyone expected something and it hasn't arrived.

We went to school and heard a lot of great things, but what Cubans expected turned out to be dreams. There are a lot of contradictions. For example, many people went to jail for having dollars. Now they say it's up to you if you have dollars or not. When I began to write, there was a lot of dogmatism. There were a lot of matters you couldn't write about, a lot of books that weren't written. Writers were producing their work in a very lonely way. Some writers can breathe again now, even though they have material worries. There's a certain freedom. If somebody tells me to write something I don't believe in, I won't do it.'

It was a certain freedom, I supposed, but it didn't sound like very much of one. I asked A—— if he could understand why some of his compatriots had braved waves and sharks to reach Miami.

He said, 'You would understand if you lived here with us for two or three years. In Miami, they hope to have the choice to make their own lives the way they want.'

'Have you considered it?'

He laughed. 'I'm not crazy. Besides, as we say here, even when I'm being strangled I'm still Cuban. What would our national identity be if all the Cubans leave Cuba?'

'So it's wrong of writers to leave?'

'Yes. Because if everyone leaves the country it will never be a real country.'

Including Cabrera Infante, I asked, remembering the copy of his book *Mea Cuba* in my bag.

A—— nodded. 'He's an excellent writer. Of course, he's banned here.'

I gave Lourdes the librarian a meaningful look, but she just smiled at me good-naturedly.

I met the outlawed Cabrera Infante at his London flat in the autumn of 1995. There was something oriental-looking about him. He wore his beard in a clipped goatee. He sat in an armchair surrounded by the kind of bookshelves for which you need a set of steps. His chinos were twinned with a beige corduroy jacket. I told him that I had just been reading, in his *Infante's Inferno*, about his love of the cinema during his childhood. He said that Cuban cinema had become propaganda. 'In

Havana, they're very keen on using culture for propaganda. In terms
of propaganda, Fidel Castro is a genius.' Castro had used the embargo
for propaganda. 'The Cubans have been living with the embargo for
more than 30 years and all of a sudden they notice it. You know, I went
to the USSR in 1960, I was in the first delegation of Cuban journalists
to go there. There were queues but not ration cards. But in Cuba,
there's been rationing since 1962. They've made procrastination into a
system.'

'Do you think it's incompetent or malicious?'

'Both. What's intriguing is to know what Fidel Castro did with the
money the USSR gave him. Of course, they had their adventures in
Africa but that was also partially financed by the USSR. Cuba didn't
have to buy weapons.'

Cabrera Infante's wife spoke Spanish and made strong coffee. She
kept walking up from the rear of the flat to join our discussion. She
said she was struck by the parallels between now and a hundred years
ago, when Spanish suzerainty over Cuba was in its last throes. 'With
one terrible difference,' added Cabrera Infante. 'They have the
machinery to control people better. There's the pervading presence of
several different groups of police – it's uncanny how many groups
there are. Regimes such as this feed the paranoia of people. If you are
constantly afraid, you won't be able to talk much. It's the same
principle they used in concentration camps. The inmates could have
overwhelmed the guards, there were more of them. Only two things
work in Cuba: police for the interior; propaganda for the exterior. All
the rest is window-dressing.'

I said, 'Would you go back, say after Castro's death?'

'I'll think about it. I won't be on the first plane. Anyway, Castro
won't die. He won't be able to allow himself.' I thought of the story
that Cabrera Infante's old friend Anton Arrufat had told me in
Havana, about Fidel promising to water Japan's trees well into the
twenty-first century.

Cabrera Infante said, 'I made a joke that started most of my headaches. Castro once said, "This revolution will devour its children," and
I said, "No, it will devour its grandchildren." '

'It's come true,' chipped in his wife.

I asked Cabrera Infante, 'Did you ever admire Castro?'

'In the first months of 1959, I had the misfortune of taking a trip with him to Washington, Montreal, and down to South America: it was 21 days. We were all cooped up in this small plane. If you're with somebody with that amount of intimacy, you're bound to know more about him by the end. He was a bully, nasty and egocentric. He had a total disregard for everything he didn't want to see or hear. He's one of the most incredible opportunists ever. Castro quitting cigars is like Hitler becoming a vegetarian – to live longer.'

I mentioned that I was hoping to talk to Harold Pinter about Cuba. Cabrera Infante said, 'Pinter is a very bitter man because he hasn't written a play that's any good for years. He says all kinds of ridiculous things.' He had heard stories that Pinter and his wife had waited up with champagne for a vote concerning Nicaragua in the United Nations. 'What does he know? It's one more instance of radical chic.'

Harold Pinter's name had cropped up from my earliest enquiries into Cuba. His name was breathed at an Islington trattoria by a member of the Cuba Solidarity Group. It was printed on the flyers that the group issued before a demonstration against the American embargo: Pinter was listed among the speakers ('invited'). I pursued him through the publicity department of his publishers. Ironically, the same house printed Cabrera Infante, whose views on Cuba could scarcely have been more different. Six months after my initial enquiry, a new voice at his publishers passed on a telephone number for the playwright. When I dialled it, I discovered at once how good it was – I didn't need to ask to know that the tones which answered were Pinter's. He told me that he was just opening in the West End in a revival of his play *The Hothouse*.

I said, 'I'm planning to go and see it.'

'Yes, give it a go,' said Pinter. We arranged that I would come and see him in London that autumn, when the run was underway.

On the day of our meeting, I woke up late and hungover. More interested in when my Tube would turn up than attuned for Pinter-esque moments, I nonetheless experienced them before I reached our W8 rendezvous. On the Underground carriage, a man was lying face down across four seats. His legs were hooked around an armrest. He was able to sleep without the motion of the train pitching him onto the floor; he had plainly slept like this before. He gave off a hoppy aroma, not of beer so much as body odour. This grew more pungent as the journey wore on and more commuters joined the train. I watched them eyeing our compartment greedily from the platform – four spare seats! – and saw their moues of distaste as they strapper-hung next to the prone, smelly man. Then it occurred to me: what if he wasn't sleeping but dead? No-one showed any impatience to step forward and plumb for a pulse.

I found that I had arrived in West London with half an hour to spare before my appointment with Pinter. I made sure of the address, then found a café. I ordered a coffee. Drinking it, I remembered I'd spent the last of my cash on my Tube ticket. I explained to the French waitress that I would have to pay for my beverage with a cheque, the kind of detail which might have been handy had I been writing up meeting Pinter for, say, the *Daily Mail*: 'The playwright lives in an exclusive postal code, where I had to pay for a cup of coffee by cheque.'

Fumbling over payment, I made myself late. I told myself that Pinter the irascible flayer of human failings was the writer not the man. In the flesh, he'd probably be a spanielly figure in a cardigan, too muddle-headed even to recall our appointment. I ascended his smart road and rang the buzzer outside a modest schloss. The door was opened by a young woman in dogtooth check. The second thing I noticed was a couch. It looked less like the kind of thing on which you might recline with a slim treasury of verse and more like the furniture favoured by psychiatrists. For want of anything intelligent to say – I was late; I was hot – I said, 'I saw the play at the weekend.'

'Oh yes?' replied the chequered assistant.

'Yes; very good. It stands up surprisingly well. I mean, considering its age. Well, sometimes they don't, do they?' I added grimly.

The woman picked up a telephone handset. She announced my name into it. She turned to me. 'If you go up the stairs, Mr Pinter will be there.' Perhaps it was something to do with the couch, but hearing these words was like being told, 'The doctor will see you now.'

Pinter greeted me: no cardigan, but a black jumper-cum-shirt, black slacks, brown suede shoes, and sandy-hued socks of exquisite thinness and, I speculated, lack of warmth. He had a toothbrush moustache, presumably for *The Hothouse*: he was playing the *Cluedo*-ish-sounding part of Colonel Roote. He showed me to a sofa, worried hospitably about whether a carriage lamp was in my way, assumed a rocking-chair on the far side of a cream carpet, and asked me to tell him what my book was about. After he had sweated this out of me, he said, 'I have to say firstly that I have never been to Cuba.'

'I was going to ask you—'

'I have to establish that straight away. At any time. But I was well aware that the Cubans had overthrown a vicious dictatorship which was fully supported by the United States. It was subsidised and embraced by the United States, like all right-wing dictatorships. I thought the Revolution was an admirable thing and I've been keeping quite a close eye on what's happened.'

His hair was perhaps a little wispy, but in other respects he was a poor advertisement for his claim that he was 'getting on' – which he offered as the reason why he didn't anticipate visiting Cuba. 'I can't be everywhere. Only a couple of months ago, I suddenly went to Bulgaria.'

The American embargo was monstrous, said Pinter. It had been comprehensively out-voted at the United Nations. 'It's the United States which is the aggressive force here. I went to the United States embassy and Foreign Office twice, with George Galloway [the Labour MP]. We said to the Foreign Office, "Why not object to the embargo?" and one of the ministers said, "Ah, but it's a bilateral matter." I thought, What the hell can he mean by that? I wrote a letter to the Foreign Office – which I have somewhere. It apparently set the cat among the pigeons because I bumped into a civil servant a few weeks later who said, "Your letter did worry us, I have to tell you." I'd looked up the word "bilateral" in the dictionary and it means a mutual act. An embargo by one country of another is *not* a mutual act. It's an act by the country that's doing the embargoing. There's nothing bilateral about it.

'Undoubtedly, there are repressive elements within the Cuban regime. But this is far outweighed by the solidarity and pride in their achievements in literacy and health, which are so discounted by some people. They say, "Oh well, literacy and health, yes, yes, but what about freedom?" What they don't grant here is that literacy gives freedom, because literacy allows the use of the free mind.' I was interested to see that a gesture which I'd taken at the Comedy Theatre for one of Colonel Roote's belonged to Pinter himself: making a point, he flourished a finger as if it were the tip of an épée.

'I want to say something more about human rights,' he said. One had to look 'quite nakedly' at oppression wherever it happened. The expression human rights had been widely – and wildly – used. In the United States, said Pinter, more than a million people were in prison. They were mostly black. 'The death penalty is legal in 38 states and there are about seven ways to do it, as far as I recall. You know, the gas chamber—'

'The electric chair—'

'The electric chair. And hanging. And firing squad. And all the rest of it.' Our conversation was beginning to sound like pastiche Pinter. 'What gives the United States the right to talk about human rights?' the playwright demanded.

I asked Pinter what he thought of Castro.

'He's a quite remarkable man. I thought what he said at the United Nations was excellent and I supported it. I kept it, actually, because I knew you were coming. I usually keep an enormous file but the other day I decided to have a clear-out, because the Kurds get this thick,' he said, holding his hands apart like an angler demonstrating the size of the one that got away, 'and the Sandinistas get this thick, and the whole thing becomes impossible. East Timor, too.'

'Yes, that's another one,' I said.

'Exactly, but anyway Castro said, "We lay claim to a world without ruthless blockades that cause the death of innocent men, women and children like silent atomic bombs" – I think that's very well put. Did you notice, he got a standing ovation, which is quite interesting, isn't it?'

'Yes. They also said it was the shortest speech he's ever made; a few minutes. I've heard him in Cuba and seven hours is just clearing his throat.'

'He's clearly a phenomenon,' said Pinter, laughing. 'Undoubtedly, he's ruthless to have hung onto power for all that time. But he has many, many virtues and finally he's a man of integrity. Of course, I deplore the attitude of the Cuban government to homosexuality and dissent.' Castro clearly had the support of the majority in Cuba, said Pinter. 'A few hundred people try to get out because they're starving, understandably.'

Having just seen *The Hothouse*, I was thinking about similarities between Pinter's Colonel Roote, who was the head of what appeared to be a sinister mental institution, and Fidel Castro. What they had in common included military trappings, a remoteness from the events around them, fits of temper, and self-proclaimed omniscience. But *The Hothouse* was written in 1958, a year before the Revolution. Pinter said, 'If *The Hothouse* had anything to do with Cuba, then it would have been to do with Batista. It's before Castro. When I wrote *One for the Road*, which deals with a torturer, people asked me if it was to do with Eastern Europe. But physical torture was very unusual there and rape was out of the question. But torture and rape were systematic throughout your Cuba, under Batista, and in Nicaragua.'

Despite Pinter's disclaimer, *The Hothouse* might be catalogued among a small but noteworthy body of work in which renowned British authors anticipated Cuban developments, albeit inadvertently. Graham Greene's *Our Man in Havana* foreshadowed the Cuban missile crisis. In Greene's text, Wormold, the eponymous agent, invented the spies who were supposedly working for him in order to draw money on their behalf, and mollify his – and their – paymasters in the British secret service. He needed the funds to keep his teenage daughter, Milly, in the style to which she threatened to become accustomed. But Wormold's characters took on a life of their own; in some cases, a death of their own, too. Perhaps he had unwittingly chosen names he'd seen in the newspapers. Perhaps Captain Segura of the Cuban secret police, having intercepted Wormold's cables to London, thought that he was reading about people already familiar to him now going under aliases, and seriously over-reacted. It was never fully explained in the book, and none the worse for that.

Greene has Wormold making up sightings of missiles – the sketches he forwarded to London were inspired by the vacuum cleaners he sold in his day job. The literary world was dumbfounded when real Russian projectiles arrived in Cuba within a year or two of the novel's publication. What Greene thought he had invented turned out to be true. *Our Man in Havana* was not quite the work of fiction it purported to be. I had the conceit – in more senses than one, no doubt – that some other aspect of what Greene imagined he had created could also have been real. The book was so redolent of Cuba that many obvious, intended parallels went without saying. What I was interested in doing was not confirming the historical fact of Batista's secret police, as it were, so much as trying to find the real Captain Segura. Or rather, the real Wormold.

In Habana Vieja, where much of Greene's novel is set, I bumped into an elderly, lame black man, like the limping figure who opens the book. He wouldn't have been old enough for the role when Greene was in the city, but he was no less of a seedy local character. 'That nigger', as Wormold's German crony, Dr Hasselbacher, calls Greene's black in the first line of the novel, ran a mucky playing-card racket. The black man I knew was similarly an accessory to vice, often to be found late at night near the bars and doorways where the prostitutes worked.

Wormold and Milly lived over his vacuum shop on Lamparilla in the old city. I discovered a house on that street where an old boy called Manolo had spent every one of his 68 years. He was there when Greene had visited Cuba, there too during the period just before the Revolution when *Our Man in Havana* is set. But Manolo couldn't remember a middle-aged Briton with a daughter. He couldn't remember a foreigner at all, nor a vacuum salesman. 'Only very wealthy people have vacuum cleaners in Cuba because we don't have carpets,' his wife pointed out. 'I've heard of Graham Greene but what I read is the Bible,' she said.

Julietta said that perhaps the novel was never published in Cuba. Greene noted in his autobiography, *Ways of Escape*, that it wasn't popular with the new revolutionary Cuban government. It was originally about the British secret service in wartime but Greene had relocated it to Cuba, sensing that its comic tone would be judged unacceptably light-hearted at home. It seems that the book provoked in Cuba just the kind of reaction Greene had feared. He wrote that the Cubans found it too glib, notwithstanding the presents he had made of knitwear to the former guerrillas when they were hiding out in the chilly Sierra Maestra mountains.

Wormold and Hasselbacher used to drink at a place called the Wonder Bar. Not far from Lamparilla, on the corner of Amagura, I came across a ruined joint called La Maravilla – the Wonder Bar, Wormold's old haunt. Augustina Rodriguez told me that it had opened in the thirties. La Maravilla had been popular with well-to-do types, politicians, she said. People came from far and wide for the steak mignon. Señora Rodriguez had seen me from her balcony. We talked in an evil-smelling corridor, eavesdropped upon by a man with hollow cheeks and Ancient Mariner trousers.

Señora Rodriguez couldn't recall a vacuum shop. The Ancient Mariner was consulted. The pair of them were old enough to have been around at the same time as a real-life Wormold, but none of them could place him. I was about to go when Señora Rodriguez said, 'I do remember someone. He was a foreigner, a widower. He had a young daughter. He used to live around here many years ago, in the fifties. I don't think he was British. I think he was from Poland.' A Pole living in Cuba – could he perhaps have been a spy? I hadn't identified *Our Man in Havana* but here perhaps was *Their* Man in Havana. It was a literary find of such inconsequence that I doubted whether there were more than half a dozen doctorates in it. Nonetheless, it chimed with Greene's book, I felt, that a man answering Wormold's description in several important respects – right sort of age, right domestic circumstances, right address – was going about his business when the writer was unsuspectingly making him up.

The staff of the Sevilla hotel appeared unaware that it featured in Greene's book. Perhaps Julietta was right and the novel hadn't appeared in the country. According to the plot, Britain's secret service chief for the Caribbean, Hawthorne, left the key to room 501 in a basin in a Gents for Wormold. Doubtful but impecunious, he picked up the fob and kept the bedroom rendezvous, having first shaken off the drunken Hasselbacher around the corridors of the hotel. When I asked if I could see *habitación* 501, the woman on the front desk told me that it was *ocupada*. She wouldn't even let me put my head around the door. I noticed that the key was missing from its pigeonhole behind her head, so perhaps it was literally *ocupada* at that precise moment. The woman had never been asked for a sight of 501 before, she said.

I had wanted to see the Gents where Hawthorne had recruited Wormold, and the place which corresponded most closely to the one in the book was the Gents at the Sevilla. Greene had set the action in the Gents at a bar called Sloppy Joe's, but I could find no trace of it. With the Wonder Bar, Wormold's other dive, also out of business, the Sevilla was the next best thing. It was, after all, the place where all the important 'i's were dotted and 't's crossed on his appointment. Nonetheless, fresh from being rebuffed at reception, I approached the Sevilla *baño* with little expectation of experiencing any of the atmosphere of the scene. There were two attendants by the open door. The *Caballeros*, as it was labelled, was done out in mock-marble. There was a battery of mid-calf urinals, in the Latin style.

Hawthorne, on hearing someone else enter the Gents, had bundled Wormold into a cubicle. The louvred doors of the Sevilla cubicles finished at least a foot off the ground, which was consistent with Wormold's facetious observation that his legs might have been recognisable. Paradoxically, however, I calculated that it was only the squatting patron who was afforded any privacy at all by a Sevilla stall. Who else had any need of it, you might well ask. The point was that anybody else using the Gents – availing himself of the upright vitreousware, for example, or checking his parting in a mirror – would have had no difficulty discerning the features of an individual who had just entered one of the cubicles, or was standing up on the point of leaving it. The cubicles were hopelessly compromised for undercover purposes. I was able to confirm this when, inspecting one in the interests of research, I was hailed by one of the lavatory attendants and found myself returning his gaze across the low stable-door of my water closet.

Was this a case of life imitating art, I wondered. In the same way that Wormold made up spies who corresponded uncannily to real people, had I, as it were, invoked this real-life sanitary encounter by half hoping for one? Or was the attendant the only Greene enthusiast on the hotel staff, hastening to make my visit complete with his own well-meaning recreation of the recruitment scene? Well, no, neither of these explanations held water. What the janitor was bent on doing was handing me the jealously guarded stock of toilet paper available for the dignity of guests. I accepted the absorbent wad with a sheepishness I hoped he put down to English diffidence, little suspecting that my embarrassment lay in the area of being discovered in a gentlemen's lavatory for purposes other than those intended by the manufacturers.

The only other chap in the *Caballeros* was a foreigner like myself, a European. He was wearing shorts. He was rinsing his hands under a tap which, I noted, had been far too sensitively plumbed to produce the kind of babbling noise which Hawthorne had trusted to mask his discussion with Wormold. Finding a place to hang the roll of toilet paper – on the low-lying WC handle, in the end – I barely noticed this fellow slipping into an adjacent cubicle. Indeed, I didn't tarry much longer in the bathroom. It was a poor substitute for the smallest room at Sloppy Joe's, I decided. The cubicles were far too vulnerable to counter-espionage for an operative of Hawthorne's experience, the waterworks far too dainty. And besides, I felt as though I had been rumbled, my own cover blown.

I returned the wad of paper to the attendant. His name was Alfonso del Toro Lopez. He had only been at the Sevilla for two years but clearly came with unimpeachable testimonials, having previously tended trough or waited WC at the Habana Libre. It was one of the little remarked boons of Cuba that it had kept on the cloakroom attendant, whose skills were so neglected elsewhere. The best-maintained washroom in the city belonged to an otherwise undistinguished restaurant, the Monseigneur, where the spaghetti arrived at the table already cut into manageable lengths, and diners were serenaded on a tuned-with-a-spoon baby grand. The *baño* curator set out his grooming wares and accessories on a kind of J-cloth. There was a choice of plastic combs, one large and one small; two polythene bags containing cashiered headache tablets; a bottle of cologne with what appeared to be a pipette applicator – the kind of thing for feeding milk to sickly calves – and a smaller, equally urine-hued, pot of hair oil. Beside all this, and scant recompense for it, was a saucer of let's-play-shop tourist coins.

For all that they shared the resourcefulness of this paragon, however, neither the Sevilla's Señor del Toro nor his older colleague, who sat twinkling up at me from a cane chair was familiar with *Our Man in Havana*. I was chinking some change into their own discreetly supplicatory crockery when a man I had never seen before, would never have picked out of a police line-up, walked smartly past us out of the *Caballeros*, and lost himself among a party of newly arrived Canadians. Neither attendant gave this elegantly dressed figure a glance. Here was a breed of men well versed in looking the other way, I saw. It went to show how shrewd Greene had been in setting a key scene of his cloak-and-dagger thriller in one of the rest-rooms of the Cuban capital. Only after applying the techniques of a fictional free-lance even greater than Greene's inspired amateur – I refer to Sherlock Holmes himself – did I decide that the only possible explanation for what I had just witnessed, fantastic though it was, was that the man in shorts who had been swilling his hands, and the man in trousers who had walked past me minutes later, were one and the same.

It was as if the very mock-marble furbishments, like those ancient tape-recorders, cave walls, had captured the intrigue of the novel in order to replay it for the benefit of doubting visitors like myself. I decided I had to know the secrets of room 501 while, it seemed, the hotel was in the mood to give up its mysteries, or collude in creating new ones. I took the elevator to the fifth floor, by now expecting to find that, like Wormold, I was sharing it with a half-cut German (not that that would be saying much in a hotel in the centre of Havana in season). In fact, I was alone. Turning left out of the lift, I was upon room 501 almost at once. It was just as Wormold's short journey had been, though he had covered the last few yards on the stairs. Had Greene paced out the landing, locating the room closest to the means of egress, making it easier for the vacuum salesman to give his friend the slip?

The door to 501 was closed. But 502 was open, the bed stripped, a chair upturned. There was a light on in the bathroom – the room was being made up. I knocked, went in, and started talking to the chambermaid. My story was that I was a guest of the Sevilla and wanted to see where my *amigos* in 501 had got to. The maid appeared to take this to mean that I had misplaced my key. We went to the door of 501. She tried her pass key and the door failed to budge and for a moment, I thought that it must be double-locked, as if the occupant had depressed the little nipple on the door handle, perhaps having decided to take a nap. How was I going to explain barging in? In the lift, I'd rehearsed that if anyone answered my knock at 501, I would simply apologise and say that I had got the wrong room. Trying to pass off the enlistment of hotel staff and a full set of master keys as absent-mindedness was another matter altogether. The door swung open. The room was dark, the curtains closed though it was the middle of the afternoon. Wormold, entering Hawthorne's rather grander 501 – something of a suite, it appeared – had found the bedroom door closed and briefly thought, 'Let sleeping dogs lie.' But I had surely disturbed the unsuspecting guest. He would be furious, the unfortunate chambermaid would get into trouble – and how did it look for me, after I'd been expressly denied sight of the room?

As my eyes adjusted to the gloom, and, more importantly, my ears detected no sounds of indignation coming from the bed, I realised that the room was unoccupied. I didn't have an attendant guest to worry about – though who knew when he might return? In any case, I had a fresh problem, in the shape of the maid. She had naturally expected me to thank her, recover 'my' key, and permit us to go our separate ways. Now she smelt a rat. I heard my alibi shift through several degrees – I appeared to be maintaining that I'd always fancied staying at the Sevilla (true, though not immediately relevant) and that I had wanted to look over a room before committing myself. 'You're not in this hotel?' she asked incredulously. 'No,' I said, recovering a limited poise, 'no, Habana Libre,' which is where I always claimed to be resident when in dubious circumstances. It was so big, and the staff so dilatory, that one might reside there undiscovered for weeks. Or *not* reside there undiscovered for weeks.

This scintilla of verisimilitude, or perhaps my recovering equilibrium, seemed to placate the maid, who raised no further objection as I made a whistlestop tour of the room where Hawthorne had explained Wormold's new role to him. Instead of the monogrammed silk pyjamas of the secret serviceman there was a tourist's drip-dry shirt. There were travellers' cheques rather than Hawthorne's code-book, Lamb's *Tales from Shakespeare*, and in the bathroom, male toiletries: a deodorant marketed squarely at blokes and a box of contraceptives. Room 501 was occupied by a single man, as it had been in Greene's novel. And as in *Our Man in Havana*, he appeared to have travelled to the city on a furtive and quixotic mission.

In the book, the character of a tearful American in a bar was called Harry Morgan. This was a crack at the expense of the man's-man hero of Hemingway's *To Have and Have Not* – unless Greene, like Wormold, had used the name forgetting that he had read it somewhere. Assuming it had been a tease, the last laugh belonged to Hemingway. In contrast to the ignorance of the Sevilla staff on the subject of Greene, the Cubans made a fuss of anywhere that Papa had hung his pelt-banded hat. Hemingway won the Nobel prize for a book inspired by his experiences of Cuba, *The Old Man and the Sea*. He left Cuba in 1960 – a year before his suicide – but his view of the Revolution continued to be debated. He hadn't sent the rebels winter woollies, as Greene had. But he was Cuba's most fêted settler, lauded by the regime like no other writer with the exception of José Martí, the warrior-versifier. (On the face of it, Martí was the very model of the two-fisted poetaster that Hemingway would have liked to be. Ironically, the strictly unofficial history of Cuba was that Martí was all fingers and thumbs in battle, and his fatal sortie against the Spanish had been tantamount to suicide.) You could pay homage to the author of *For Whom the Bell Tolls* in the room at the hotel Ambos Mundos where he had written it. You could visit the Vigia estate outside Havana where Hemingway had lived. There he had erected a tower, along the lines of the structures built at fire stations for simulating evacuations from tall buildings. The writer used to type in it, standing up at his keyboard. When I went to Vigia, the first thing I heard was the sound of typing – not Papa's ghost, but someone in one of the offices of the tourist bureau which administered the property. The house had been preserved as it was when Hemingway had left it. It was swept every Tuesday. Callers were not allowed across the threshold. You could only look through the open doors and windows. Papa's substantial groaning board was somehow diminished by the trophy animal heads lowering over it. There was the stamp he used for answering his mail – 'I don't write letters. Ernest Hemingway' – the 4,000 books, and an authentic pair of the writer's size 11s. Cabrera Infante told me about visiting Hemingway's house after the writer's death. 'I knew as soon as I walked in that Hemingway had never intended coming back,' he said. 'There were marks on the wall where his paintings had been. His butler, Rene, was very sentimental, always crying. I pointed at one set of marks on the wall and asked Rene which painting had hung there. It was *The Farm* by Miró. Hemingway bought it for $100 and took it with him everywhere. I knew then that Hemingway had never intended going back to Cuba.'

Arguably the most toe-curling feature of the Hemingway cult was the appropriation of the writer's name for a harbour frequented by corporate gin palaces. Through the drizzle at the Hemingway Marina in Havana, I made out a golden statue of a lioness in the bar of the *Lady Jann*, and a jet-ski in the stern. Scott, a New Zealander, told me that he skippered the *Lady Jann* on behalf of her owner, a French plutocrat whom he was unable to name on pain of collecting his cards. Scott wore a white T-shirt with the name of the ship over his breast, and shorts with a gold belt. The rest of the crew was similarly dressed in immaculate whites. The *Lady Jann* had been in port for five months. Her owner was taking some clients on a week's cruise to Cayo Largo the following morning, or at least that was the idea. 'Rubbish weather,' observed Scott with a seasoned expression. In the next berth along, the decks of another vessel were stacked like casino chips. There were highly polished wooden steps leading to her stern, where her jet-ski was housed. Like the one on the *Lady Jann*, it looked as though it had never been used.

In some access of conscience, the planners of the Hemingway Marina had made room for one or two lesser craft: fishing boats. I persuaded one of the fishermen, José Alvarez Lopez, to take me out, even though it was by now well after lunch, and the true disciple of *El Papa* properly craved greater sport than marlin in the afternoon. The lateness of the hour perhaps accounted for the high smell of the bait which José unwrapped from a copy of *Granma*, the revolutionary press having at least one function in common with the capitalist one. The newspaper was kept in an icebox with cans of Hatuey beer. José hooked the fillet onto nylon line coiled around an American-made Penn International 'Strike' reel. The reel was attached to a Fenwick Sea Hawk rod. The Sea Hawk and a spare were secured in rowlocks in the stern. Inhabiting Hemingway territory, however presumptuously, affected the way you saw things, the world condensed into a hobbyist's inventory.

José was 32, married with three girls and a boy. He had been fishing for ten years. He was talented enough – and trusted enough – to have taken part in fishing competitions off the coast of Mexico. He saw differences in water the way motorists did in road surfaces. A mile from the shore, he found a stretch with the camber of a motorway. He produced 37 knots out of the Volvo Penta engine, the boat pat-a-caking over the abraded surface, splash surging back across the bow. José said the marlin fed in water which was '*más corriente, más azul*', the fastest flowing, the most blue. You caught the fish with a trailing bait, he said. We were by now three miles out to sea. The water rolled as thickly as paint. In his book *Havana, Portrait of a City* (1953), G. Adolphe Roberts noted that tourists had once gained their first glimpse of Havana from the deck of a ship, steaming into port between the Morro and La Punta. In the 1990s, I had expected to be surprised at how sveltely modern the city looked. From the perspective of the dipping tropical horizon, I had imagined, the advantage would be with the tiered hotels along the Malecón. Havana would look like all waterfront cities did, once you were far enough away from them across the water: a trading post of white goods. Rain was cross-hatching the city, but even so my unexpected impression was that Havana was unspoilt. (A relative term, the eye held by the voluptuous dome of the Capitolio; but also by the Malecón – it was like looking at footage of a demolition site greatly slowed-down – and by the corroded radiator of the old Habana Libre on its knoll.) The greatest revelation was the

Russian embassy. On land, it was an ambitiously ugly column of cement, like a Mormon chapel. From the bay – and admittedly through a gauze of drizzle – it was an Easter Island statue.

While we waited for the rain to catch up with us, José and I sailed and trailed. We drank Hatuey. Flying fish bolted from the water like driven game. Suddenly, something seized the line and began paying the boat out along it. José slid off his seat and I took over the wheel. He decoupled the fishing rod from its rowlock and tucked the end of it into his belly. Whatever had snatched the line was taking it out to sea faster than I was taking the boat inshore. A mattress of vegetation slid over a wave into our path. I saw it too late and sent the boat into a wide, wallowing turn, almost pitching rod, line and skipper into the far from shark-free drink. At the first available opportunity, I looked over my shoulder to make sure that José was still with me. I found him winding in the line in a resigned sort of way, and saw that there was no strain on it. A barracuda had made off with the bait. This was the pattern of the afternoon: José and I fishing for marlin in good faith but failing to get this message across to the barracuda, who believed that what we were doing was laying on an irresistibly high-smelling finger buffet across Havana Sound.

The last survivor of Hemingway's court in Cuba was Gregorio Fuentes Betancourt. He had been the skipper of Hemingway's boat. Gregorio was 97. He took lunch every day at Las Terrazas, which was the restaurant where Hemingway used to dine with his fishermen cronies; or at least, it was a prototype of the dollar-friendly diner now trading under the same name. There was a mottled life-saver on a wall, and a view of the aquamarine bay of Cojimar, where Hemingway and the old salts had put to sea, and where children now swam. However, Las Terrazas was very much part of the tourist itinerary, and so was Gregorio. He would tell you stories of *El Papa* if you paid the barman to keep his toothglass topped up with whisky. ('You know, Hemingway only drank whisky, never rum.') He wore a checked shirt, blue slacks with a copy of *Granma* tucked in a pocket, and a metal watch bearing an image of a marlin. His eyes were *más azul*.

'I would take Hemingway far out to sea, so that he could write alone,' he told me. 'I used to tie his boat up here. He was an extraordinary man. He had a very humanitarian heart; I never met any other American with those feelings.'

'Have you read his books?'

'I don't need to read them because I was in them. But I have read *The Old Man and the Sea*. One day, we found a little boat and an old man. He was fishing. Hemingway said to me, "Why don't you go and see if he needs some help?" because he had a big fish to land. I said, "If you order me I will go," because Hemingway was the owner. When we got to the boat, the old man started saying bad things to us, like, "Go to Hell!" because he thought we wanted to take the fish from him. Later, Hemingway said, "Bring me some paper," and he wrote down what had happened. We went back to Cuba and he said he would go to the United States to write a book and make a movie.

He said, "The only thing I can't find is a title." I said to him, "Wait a minute, I'm going to tell you something," and after that Hemingway said, "We're going to call it *The Old Man and the Sea*." It was my idea.'

I said, 'Is there anything of you in the book?'

'Of course. I gave him the title.'

I asked Gregorio if he understood why Hemingway had killed himself. He said, 'In his will he left a letter for me – "to Gregorio". It said, "Don't be sorry. The boat is yours, take good care of it like you always did. If I shot myself it's because I'm sick and I know I won't survive the illness." ' Gregorio declined the bequest of the boat, unable to face putting to sea in her again. She was now on display at Vigia, next to the plot Hemingway had picked out as a cemetery for his pets.

'What have you done since he died?'

'I decided I wouldn't work again after he died.' Gregorio lived on his state pension. His meals and drinks at Las Terrazas were all found.

'Would you ever go back to sea?'

Gregorio rapped his knotty knuckle against the table. 'No. Not even for all the money in the world.' He took out a pipe. (His skin had the look of furniture over which tobacco ash had been tipped.) His great age seemed to demand the wondering question: what's the most important thing you've learnt in your long life?

He said, 'To know the world, and to know that everybody was born
into this world to be friends, to help each other. You're an Englishman
but you're a brother. That's what you have to know in this world.'

He asked for money ('for medicine'). The handshake which
acknowledged receipt was firm. Gregorio hobbled to the dining-room
where tourists from Mexico were having lobster and champagne. He
literally dined out on the Hemingway legend – the Old Man and the
Seafood – holiday-makers taking photographs of him while he ate.

12

A Certain Freedom

THE GRENADE WENT OFF as we were breasting the pampas. There was a bonfire of smoke, threatening to obscure the humid prairie of the Everglades laid out beneath us, and an incongruous whiff, like the smell of the stuff you dip mosquito nets in. We had successfully taken the high ground, or so we thought, and seized command of the field of sweet potatoes which stretched almost to the horizon. The Vietnam vet at my elbow reacted exactly as you would have expected a man of his experience to, and shimmied into the undergrowth. On the face of it, the explosion was a pretty substantial reverse for him. He had just been explaining how we were essentially bossing the entire situation. Now we were cut off from each other by a piece of ordnance which, you couldn't help noticing, had dropped right down our throats. On the other hand, as I heard him mutter, it was only a smoke grenade. And, when all was said and done, he had let the thing off himself. It was November 1995 and we were on weekend manoeuvres with Alpha 66, a volunteer commando dedicated to the overthrow of Fidel Castro, by means of violence if at all possible. A cursory examination of the group's form showed that there was nothing surprising about them shooting themselves in the foot – or grenading it, rather. Their record was: volunteers lost in missions against revolutionary Cuba: 105; Cubans for: nil. But in fact the Vietnam vet had known exactly what he was doing. He was putting the patrol to the test, just as we were within a few hundred metres of regaining base. I came through the stunt well enough to justify the award of an honorary sleeve patch worked with the Alpha 66 motto ('Death Before Slavery'), bolting through the grass before the smoke could disturb the idling alligators and baked snakes who lived there. I couldn't say the same for all of the unit. At least one of them, by day a plump hospital orderly, went to ground for long minutes, popping out of the flora apparently at random into the path of a Jeep full of bird hunters. The Vietnam vet bit his tongue. 'You can't push these guys as hard as you would in the service,' he told me. His time in the service had included tours of duty in Cambodia: 'We weren't supposed to be there but we were.' He was a sniping specialist, he said. 'You wake up at night in a lot of cold sweats. They say that you're too far away to see what happens, but if you recover quickly from the recoil of the weapon, you see the man hit and go down.'

His name was Carlos Iglesias. At my suggestion that he might be related to the swoon-making crooner of the same name, himself a resident of South Florida, Carlos said, 'I once heard him say that he had family in the same part of Spain that my people came from.' There was perhaps a familial likeness in Carlos's surprisingly bovine eyelashes.

Only a dozen men had turned up for the exercises. Alpha 66 claimed to have 15,000 men willing to bear arms but many of the volunteers in Dade County had to work weekends. Most of them, like Iglesias, were first or second generation Cubans 'in exile', though my patrol included a Puerto Rican who had come along, he said, because he supported the cause. Despite the closeness of the day, he insisted on wearing a woollen balaclava in case my snaps betrayed his identity to his employers in the mall security industry. Alpha 66 were widely thought to have been the inspiration for the eccentric guerrillas *Las Noches de Diciembre*, who frequent the Everglades in *Tourist Season*, one of the crime novels of *Miami Herald* columnist Carl Hiaasen. They were the best known, and best armed, of the exile groups which confronted the Cuban regime across the Florida Straits.

Alpha 66's camp, Rumbosur, (Pointing South), lay 40 minutes' drive out of Miami, beside an orange orchard at the end of a swamp turnpike. The real estate was rented from a sympathiser for a peppercorn dollar a month. There was a little clapboard house, with hurricane lamps and a couple of daybeds, and a room with a single dumbell in it – 'the gym'. Outside, a Cuban flag and weathered assault-course obstacles and motorboats made the camp look like a military base in Cuba itself. The group's slogan recalled the exhortatory maxim *Socialismo o muerte*, Socialism or death, which you saw in Cuba. Even the logo of Alpha 66 and other uncompromising exile groups, which depicted a launch cleaving surf (on its triumphal progress to Havana, presumably), brought to mind the Revolution's touching attachment to a gin palace called Granma, aboard which Castro and 80 others sailed to Cuba to initiate what became the *événements* of 1959.

One of the founders of Alpha 66, 76-year-old Andres Nasario Sargen, had driven me out to the camp in his small Ford. We had set out from Alpha 66's office on Flagler Street in the heart of Cuban Miami, accompanied by two of Nasario's fellow volunteers, including a man called Enrique Acosta who, ironically, sported a Che Guevara beard and beret. Nasario told me that he had been a comrade in arms of Castro in overthrowing the dictator, Batista. But he and some like-minded individuals hadn't appreciated the way things were working out under Fidel, and fled to the United States in the early sixties, where they were locked up for several months as illegal immigrants. Señor Nasario was short and leathery, like an old jockey. Clipping his nails over a copy of *American Rifleman* in the Rumbosur living quarters, he told me that there had been 66 Cubans at the first meeting of the organisation, hence its name. The 'Alpha' tag was intended to convey a sense of newness. The organisation depended for funds on donations from its sponsor-base of 40,000 supporters across the United States. Far from receiving backing from the federal government, overt or otherwise, they would be in trouble with the FBI if its agents caught them letting off live ammunition outside their compound, Nasario claimed. Despite yourself, you thought of ARP Warden Hodges of 'Dads' Army' turning his pump and bucket on the Walmington Home Guard. A boatload of Alpha 66 weapons had been confiscated at Florida's Sunshine Key by the coastguard, the FBI and Navy Seals. Nasario said, 'One guy who tried to start his own group was set up by the authorities. He was offered a heat-seeking missile for $15,000 to see if he would take the bait. He should have known there was something wrong: they're usually a quarter of a million bucks.'

Alpha 66 were not terrorists, Nasario insisted. '*No me gusta la guerra*,' I don't like war. He denied any connection with the blowing up of a *Cubana* airliner over Barbados in 1976, with which the cause of Alpha 66 has sometimes been linked. 'When anything happens, they blame us,' he explained sadly.

Having given up on the idea of another American-backed invasion after the Bay of Pigs, Alpha 66 was holding itself in readiness to support an uprising within Cuba. Nasario and the others talked about *clandestinas*, secret cells on the island. They had supplied contacts in their homeland with Alpha 66 pennants, which had defiantly if briefly flown under the noses of the authorities. A related organisation called 'The Sons of the Widows', which had the ring of Hiaasen's *Las Noches de Diciembre*, had carried out illegal bill-sticking of Alpha 66 posters in Cuba's Oriente province. There were groups of three or four individuals, taking trucks and equipment from the Cuban military and disabling them. Enrique Acosta, the Che-lookalike, said he had been part of a cell in Cuba. 'We used to go out after dark and burn down sugar cane,' he said. This recalled possibly apocryphal stories I'd heard from the days of the Revolution, of oil-soaked cats being set on fire and taking off through plantations, catching them alight. Alpha 66 confined its own military operations to occasional sorties against out-lying Cuban territory like Cayo Coco, where the Cuban coastguard apparently returned its fire in spades, and to shooting out beachfront windows at Varadero.

'Do you have a political platform?' I asked Nasario as tumblers of grape-flavoured soda arrived from the kitchenette, or mess.

'Sure,' he said. 'We believe people shouldn't work for more than six hours a day. We want free education for everyone. Each worker should have a good salary.' The fantastic agenda tripped off his tongue: it reminded me of the professed aims of the Cuban Revolution. Nasario went on, 'If Fidel leaves, and the military government transfers to a democratic government, and there's a free press, then Cuba is free.'

I asked Jesus Hoyos, one of two volunteers who lived at the compound, how many weapons the movement had. 'That's classified,' he said. He looked pleased to have had an opportunity of using the expression. Alpha 66 had Chinese AK47s, he said, and British-made firearms which normally retailed for $1,200 a piece, but which they picked up more cheaply from a sympathetic Cuban gunsmith. Their camouflage fatigues came from flea markets. 'One of our people works there.' Hoyos was 34, and had left Cuba as a boy.

'What do you do for women out here?' I asked him saltily.

'Well, we're not too far from the city. We drive in sometimes.'

'Do you like living out here? What do you eat?'

'We like Cuban food,' said Hoyos. He made me a present of eight sachets of Sazon Goya, a Cuban seasoning which had been prepared by a firm in New Jersey.

It was from Hoyos that I learned the statistics of Alpha 66's kill-rate. 'We have lost 105 people, either from here or within Cuba. We have no record of ever having hit anyone,' he said. Paradoxically, there was something winning about these figures, I felt.

Carlos Iglesias, who was approached to join the movement – with who knows what bashful hero-worship – on account of his specialist firearms knowledge, disembowelled the firing mechanism of a machine-gun on a bench. He was like a *babalao*, a priest of Cuban *Santería*, preparing a sacrifice for a *fiesta*. In the promiscuous discharging of their weapons by Alpha 66 cartridges flew like wood chips.

I suspect that I was at less risk from the itchy- but butter-fingered weekend warriors, as they were sometimes unflatteringly referred to in Florida, than I was from Miami's cabbies. I opted for taxis over a hire car on the calculation that I'd meet more Cubans that way. But also, to be frank, because I thought I'd avoid driving blindly into neighbour-hoods that I'd be well advised to steer clear of. Miami had a reputation as a graveyard of unwary out-of-towners. And not even the locals were safe. While I was visiting, the *Miami Herald* reported the trial of a man who had driven after a basketball team-mate and shot him dead for jostling him on court. To a considerable extent, my plan succeeded: I met more Cubans; and I avoided driving blindly into neighbourhoods that I'd be well advised to steer clear of. On the other hand, my cabbies didn't. Caleb, from Haiti, and his countryman Jean-Bertrand, my first two drivers, made unerringly for the shadows beneath the Miami River flyovers, where tumbleweeds of refuse blew. This trash was pathetic and unsettling: the unwanted contents of valises and grips and pocket-books, which were themselves often to be found discarded nearby. I know this because the unfazed Haitians toured these blocks at speeds which could only be considered breakneck by someone watching in the darkness with a length of rope cats-cradled expectantly around his fingers. To be fair to Caleb and Jean-Bertrand, they were on to something, since my hotel turned out to be situated in this district, though they were as surprised as I was when we found this out. It was in one of the neighbourhoods that I would have been well advised to steer clear of. In the days to come, cabbies who had not had the benefit of a Port-au-Prince upbringing would clunk their door-locks down as they approached my address on South River Drive. 'Why are you living in this dross?' one demanded. The reason was that I wanted to live where the Cubans of Miami lived, and this was the nearest place I could find to Little Havana. The hotel abutted a shabby waterfront, where pelicans in repose looked like folded umbrellas, and a hooter sounded when the bridge was raised, and children played till dusk in a park named after José Martí. The hotel was at the border of Little Havana and Downtown. Before you reached the Celebrity Cruises towerblock, or the offices of Breast Clinics of Miami, you drove down Eighth Street (Calle Ocho), where the old boys gnawed on cigars the size of French sticks in Domino Park. Before you took the bridge for South Beach and Liquid, the nightclub newly opened by Madonna's latest gal-pal, you passed the mom and pop businesses which harked back to a country unseen for 30 years: the Camaguey grocery store, the coin-washes and *cantinas* named after Havana streets.

Enrique Acosta of Alpha 66 took me to a house off Calle Ocho. He said that it was used as a hostel for Castro's former prisoners. Tomas

Mora, who was 61, told me he had been sentenced to eight years imprisonment. The charge against him was conspiring against the Revolution.

I said, 'True or false?'

Señor Mora raised his hands: a gesture of confession. He said, 'After I got out, I couldn't get permission to leave Cuba so I stole a boat. I was captured and spent another two years in jail.' Cubans in Miami had raised the money to pay for his ticket out.

Juan Sanchez Novillo trembled where he stood. He was 71. He had spent 27 years and four months in the prisons of revolutionary Cuba, he said. He didn't look at me when he was speaking. He didn't appear to be looking at anything at all. Señor Sanchez had served in the National Guard under Batista. His unit had intercepted Castro and his comrades as they were making for the Sierra Maestra mountains. 'I was tortured in a military prison on the Isle of Youth. They put electricity into my body. I only ate three times a week and the food wasn't good, it was bread and water.' Señor Sanchez's arm shook. His mouth hung slack when he wasn't talking and his trousers were soiled. After pressure from the exile community, the United States government had launched a campaign on his behalf. He said, 'I'm happy, I'm free. For this country I would give my life. I shit in Castro's mouth, because the people are going hungry.'

A painted gable end welcomed you to Little Havana on behalf of the Republic National Bank, the biggest Hispanic bank in the United States. Its guiding force was Luis Botifoll, aged 87. I barrelled over to see him at the bank in a cab driven by a Cuban. The cabbie was young and tubby and chewing gum. From my vantage point on the back seat, he could have passed for a much thinner man who was being pressed back into his seat by an inopportunely detonated airbag. The cab smelled faintly of sweat and, more pungently, of the grape soda I'd had a few days earlier out at Rumbosur: perhaps the cabbie was chomping grape-flavoured Chiclets, or perhaps the air-freshener on his dashboard was secreting essence of monosodium glutamate. My cabbie was a supporter of the Cuban groups who wanted nothing to do with Fidel: Alpha 66, and also the Cuban-American National Foundation, the most powerful Cuban lobby in the United States. It had been understood for years that the Foundation's figurehead, Jorges Mas Canosa, was Little Havana's choice for the next president of Cuba. 'I once did some driving for the Foundation,' the cabbie said. 'I never met, like, the senior guys, but I appreciate what they stand for.' He had left Cuba as a small boy. He told me that he hated the late-comers among the Cubans in Miami, the ones who had come over 'at the time of Mariel'. This was a view I heard many times in Florida, particularly from the lips of younger Cubans. The received wisdom was that President Carter, who agreed to a boatlift from Cuba in 1980 for humanitarian reasons, had been duped by Castro, who emptied his prisons and asylums onto the beach at Mariel where the evacuation took place. Inside and outside the exile population, the criminals and lunatics surreptitiously released into the community by Castro were blamed for a lot of Miami crime.

The cabbie supported Alpha 66, but did he actually go out on missions with them? 'No, actually I don't,' he said, a little sheepishly, 'I have, like, commitments.' We pulled into the forecourt of the bank. 'Hey, call me if you need a ride when you're through – okay?' he said, and handed me a card which listed his phone number and his call-sign, 'Top Gun'.

Luis Botifoll was styled as chairman emeritus of the bank he had built. The tableau he presented at his desk – a sober suit, reef-knot cufflinks cast in gold, owlish lenses – was very much that of the bank manager in his office, the only jarring note to British ears being piped muzak. Botifoll had arrived in the United States in 1960. 'I sent my family here before me. I was commuting from Cuba every weekend with my father but on one of those trips, when I went back to Havana, they took my passport.' Thanks to a connection in the passport office, who owed Botifoll a favour, he got his documents back. But the man warned him that they were now quits and that he'd be unable to do anything to help him in the future. 'I realised that if I didn't go like he said, I'd be in jail. I knew the Communists were taking over.'

I said, 'Castro didn't say he was a Communist, or rather a Socialist, until the Bay of Pigs in '61, did he?'

'Fidel didn't have to tell me that he was a Communist. I knew it.'

When Botifoll arrived in the United States, he wasn't sure that he'd settle in Miami. He had shared the view of many Cubans that the Revolution wouldn't last. But then he heard that the government had taken over his house in Vedado. To the accompaniment of a jazz-rock version of 'Greensleeves' on the bank PA, we roughed out a map of where his property was in relation to Hilda's. It was a couple of hundred yards away. Botifoll's country house was also requisitioned and lent out to foreign dignitaries. He said, 'After these things happened, I spent all my time working for the revolution *against* Castro. I was involved in organising the attempt on the Bay of Pigs.' A friend bought the Republic National Bank, which until then had been entirely American-owned. Botifoll became director of loans. 'This was about 1970. By then, Cubans had made up their minds to make a living here.'

'Were most of your clients Cuban?'

'*All* of our clients were Cuban.' Botifoll sat back and folded his arms. 'When I came here in the sixties, the WASP establishment ran everything. They discriminated against Blacks, Jews and the Spanish. I wanted to open the doors, so that other people could come in.'

Botifoll became chairman. The bank's net worth grew to $1 billion. Over the years, he had steered a lot of money Alpha 66's way, he told me. But then when I asked who else he had sponsored, Botifoll waved his hand and said, 'Everybody. From presidents down.' Everybody of a Republican stripe, that is. 'For the past 35 years, we have considered the Democratic Party very soft on Communism. Actually,' he said, leaning conspiratorially near, 'we agree with the Democrats on many social policies, but for us foreign policy is the key.'

'Did you know from the start that the Revolution was bad news?'

Botifoll smiled. 'I realised it was bad news but I didn't expect it to be so bad,' he said. He had that roll beneath his waistband that elderly men sometimes have, as though they had stuffed a bath-towel down their trousers.

From reading David Rieff's book about the Cubans of Miami, *The Exile*, I knew that the question of whether or not to talk to Castro – *el diálogo* – could be a hackle-raising one. But a reporter on *El Nuevo Herald*, the Spanish-language sister paper of the Miami daily, told me that people no longer foamed at the mouth at the idea. I asked Botifoll,

'Should you talk to the Cuban government?'

'If you want to talk to them in order to try to convince them to make changes and become democratic, you're wasting your time. Castro will never do that and he's said so. He's always tried to fool everybody but not in this respect.'

I said that I'd seen an opinion poll for a local television station which found that growing numbers of people in Miami considered themselves 'Cuban–Americans' rather than 'exiles'.

'For a simple reason: many of the ones who said they were exiles have died. If you take my family, my three daughters – all born in Cuba – consider themselves exiles. But only three of my grandchildren were born in Cuba; they don't know what Cuba is. And some of the people who came later, they haven't seen a Cuba which means anything good to them.'

I asked Botifoll the question that dominated discussion in Miami, at least among older Cubans. It was *el tema*, the theme: 'What will happen next in Cuba?'

'I see the possibility that the Cubans will start some sort of action against Castro. Why?' he asked himself, a rhetorical device much favoured by Cubans. 'Because now we have seen the emergence of the lawyers, the doctors, the economists, the newspapermen: the *Concilio Cubano*. It will be another voice inside Cuba. People here in Miami are trying to help. Well, this has never happened before. How far this reaction is going to go, I don't know.'

I asked Botifoll, 'Even after so many successful years in America, do you still regret leaving Cuba?'

'One thing you have to understand is the difference between the immigrant and the exile,' he said. 'The immigrant leaves his country for good because he's trying to live a better life. The exile expects to stay abroad for a while and then go back.'

He made me a present of his biography, *Luis J. Botifoll: An Exemplary Cuban*. It was published by the literary wing of the Cuban American National Foundation. The Foundation was set up in 1980, ostensibly to defend the good name of Cubans following a crimewave linked to some of the Mariel arrivals. This role was expanded to include rebutting Castro's propaganda, by beaming radio programmes at Cuba. The Foundation had stringers inside Cuba. They couldn't call the Foundation, but it could call them, at the homes of sympathisers. Their reports of people being improperly taken into detention and other abuses were recorded and replayed to Cuba. At the Foundation's studios in an industrial estate near Miami airport, a priest wearing a dog-collar was taping a kind of 'Thought for the Day'. More militant contributors reportedly broadcast in battledress. I met Ninoska Perez Castellon, who had a daily talk show. She was an attractive woman with a diamanté brooch in the shape of Cuba on the lapel of her suit. 'We tell people what happened in Eastern Europe, how other people have disposed of tyrants, why the mothers of the disappeared in Argentina were so effective,' said Señora Perez. 'We don't say "rise up", per se. It's hard for me to say that because I'm here and I'm not going to be the one that's going to be beaten up. However, I don't deny the fact that they have the right to do it.'

At the Foundation, there was a hurt perplexity over Europe's easy-going attitude to the Cuban regime. 'I remember when there was apartheid in South Africa, there was a lot of concern about that,' Perez said. 'There is apartheid in my country. You have to have dollars to buy anything but the people aren't paid in dollars.'

A poster at the studios showed El Malecón festooned with logos for fast-food outlets like Taco Bell and Wendy's. Was this a rare, unsentimental picture of what the Foundation saw ahead? No, this was a positive view, Perez assured me.

The artwork promoted a record by a Cuban singer, Willy Chirino. Chirino figured in *Next Year in Cuba*, an account by the writer Gustavo Perez Firmat of the warring polarities set up in him by his Cuban childhood, on the one hand, and his adult experiences in America on the other. A Friday-night cigar-smoker, Perez argued that it wasn't only in his tobacco habits that he was 'an occasional Cuban'. His memoir, the talked-about non-fiction title of the day in Miami, articulated an increasing if sometimes guilty drawing away by younger Cubans from their ancestral homeland. Surveys indicated that the citizens of Little Havana as a whole were more likely to visit Cuba after Castro's exit than they were to relocate there permanently. 'Next Year in Cuba' was no longer the cry of a people yearning to return home; it was more like vacation plans.

If the attitude of large numbers of the Cuban community in Miami towards Cuba was pragmatic, perhaps the tide was finally turning for Bernardo Benes. Disgraced and ostracised, he lived in well-appointed confinement in a condo in Miami Beach. At night, the moisture-slicked highway which led to his building brought to mind Norman Mailer's perspiring judgement on Miami real estate: 'Is it so dissimilar from covering your poor pubic hair with adhesive tape for fifty years?' he wrote.

Like Fidel, Benes had been a lawyer as a young man. Like him, he had participated in the revolutionary struggle: Batista's police had kept a file on him. But Benes left Cuba for Miami in the early sixties. He got a job in a bank, and rose to a position of financial and political leverage. Unusually, his allegiance had been with the Democrats rather than the Republicans. He was President Carter's choice to represent the Cubans in Florida, and he was courted by Fidel's aides during a holiday in Panama in 1977. The following year, Benes met Fidel himself in Havana and negotiated the release of thousands of political prisoners, the reunification of hundreds of Cuban families.

Even after dark, his balcony afforded a spectacular vantage of crashing surf. He drew on a cigar, which he had produced from his refrigerator. He was a large man with a flair for large language – right-wing Cuban émigrés had created 'a monstrosity of fear' within their community, he said; the investment denied to Cuba because of the United States embargo was 'a brutal amount of money'. What happened in 1978 'was the biggest opening-up of Cuban society in 37 years', said Benes. His efforts were not appreciated by his fellow Cubans in Miami; at least, not in public. On the contrary, he was vilified and received death threats. 'Until 1978, I was one of the most active members of Miami society. That year, I became a leper.' His crime had been to talk to the enemy. Benes was beyond the pale as far as many exiles were concerned. His business and family life suffered. But he was unrepentant. He said, 'The exile groups are a disaster. I hear a lot of people shouting but they're not offering solutions. These radio stations are a cancer. What the exiles say, and the more belligerent noises out of Washington, it's political masturbation.'

If Washington adhered to its policy of fortifying the embargo and repatriating Cuban boat people, it would be 30 years before there was any change in Cuba, Benes said. 'Let me tell you one thing that you probably have not heard,' he added. There was a theatrical pause, in the course of which Benes kicked off his shoes. 'The Democrats are going to start winning in Florida,' he went on. 'The Anglos are fed up with the White House appeasing the Cubans.'

The United States had turned back *los balseros* for 'sanitary' domestic reasons, Benes said. 'They don't understand that this is a very aggressive act against Cuba. America hasn't used diplomacy where Castro is concerned. The only decent solution is to move forward with Castro. One political prisoner is too many, but the repression in Cuba has been exaggerated. It's declined dramatically.'

The *Miami Herald* colour supplement had recently profiled Benes as 'the Schindler of Cuba'. Perhaps the efforts he had made in 1978 were due a reappraisal. He saw me to the lobby of his building, and shot the breeze with the doorman while we waited for my cab. 'The article in the magazine has had a very good reaction,' Benes told me. He sucked his cigar. 'I think I may be a free man again.'

When I'd first made plans to go to Florida, what I'd had in mind was looking at Cuba from a different perspective. I don't mean seeing the Havana of the late 1950s recreated on Miami's Calle Ocho, or at least, I don't *just* mean that. I was hoping that I might actually set eyes on a part of Cuba which was only visible from the United States. Guantánamo Bay was on Cuban soil. But it had been an American military base for most of the twentieth century. The United States presence was recognised by the signing of a lease in 1934, which gave Washington tenure of some 40 square kilometres of Cuba until the year 2033: not only did Uncle Sam have Fidel in his backyard but Fidel had Uncle Sam in *his* backyard too. In one of the quirkier anomalies of the American–Cuban relationship, those arch-foes of Communism in the Pentagon sent Castro a cheque for $4,085 every year, and every year Castro did his bit for the American tax-payer by refusing to bank it. Guantánamo, or Gitmo, was the size of a small town, with a residential population of 7,000. Secreted behind its defence systems were said to be all the attractions of Main Street USA: a shopping mall, a bowling alley, even a McDonalds. Guantánamo was a kind of bristling Camelot for hard-pressed Cubans. After the *balseros* crisis of August and September 1994, it had been overwhelmed by 30,000 migrants, as they were called. Some had made directly for the base. Others were taken there by the US coastguard after being picked up in the Florida Straits. They were put in camps and eventually relocated to the United States, after President Clinton agreed that 20,000 Cubans would be accepted by his country every year. If there was a spot you could point to as the real border between the odd Caribbean neighbours of Cuba and the United States then it was the boundary of the Guantánamo Bay camp. It was a closed border, for all but a handful of Cuban manual workers who walked through the Gitmo gates in the morning, and back through them at night. One writer described the perimeter of the camp as 'the Cactus Curtain'. To be strictly truthful, you couldn't view Guantánamo from Florida with the naked eye. For one thing, it was on the wrong side of the island, in Cuba's most easterly province. However, catching a plane from Florida was the only way of seeing the place – short of paddling or swimming there, as the migrants had done.

Before I went to Miami, I had spent nine months or so trying to get permission to visit Guantánamo. The trail wound back on itself to London, and the United States embassy on my own doorstep. There, I was politely but nixingly told that making all the arrangements for a trip to Gitmo would have to wait until after Christmas. By this time, I wasn't confident that this automatically meant Christmas *the same year*. I found myself thinking that getting into Gitmo was almost as difficult for me as it was for Cubans. At all events, I left for Florida resigned to the idea that I wouldn't be going anywhere near Guantánamo for the foreseeable future.

But in Miami's what's-on weekly, the *New Times*, I read that the Pentagon's Defense Reutilization and Marketing Service (DRMS) was taking out advertising space to promote what it called 'the best deal from Cuba since cigars'.

The article went on, 'The US Department of Defense sent out flyers to international purchasers of second-hand military equipment, announcing an unusual sale at an uncommon location: the Guantánamo Bay Naval Base. Among the items on the auction block are one ferry boat (original cost $750,000), 3,000 port-o-potties ($250 each), 2,452 folding cots ($90 each), between 300 and 500 general-purpose, medium-size canvas tents ($1,500 each), and an assortment of vehicles, including one trash-compactor truck, one wrecker, eight tractor trucks, fifteen four-wheel-drive utility-type trucks, and dozens of pickups.' A DRMS source was quoted as saying that the base command was anxious to remove the equipment, 'so we'll accept anything that's reasonable.'

Here, perhaps, was a way of going to Gitmo after all.

The DRMS was based somewhere in Middle America, according to its telephone voicemail message. At length, I told a woman called Victoria that I'd read the *New Times* article with interest. Would it be possible to visit the base, and cast an eye over the lots?

'OK, I'll need some details,' said Victoria. As she began to work through her checklist of questions, I wondered what I would tell her about what I did for a living. An admission that I was a journalist would surely earn me a referral to a press office, and – even in America, relative bastion of free information – another laborious cycle of wheedling for what would eventually turn out to be a shepherded tour, if I was lucky. As if she read my thoughts, Victoria said, 'Who do you represent, Stephen?'

This was too soon – I hadn't had time to think of anything yet. I might well have been on the brink of confessing 'Independent Television News' when Victoria went on, '– or are you representing yourself?'

This offered me a way out. After all, I wasn't actually on company business. And although I had a publisher, I wasn't strictly speaking an employee of the firm in question. To all intents and purposes, I was representing myself. If I said that, though, I risked exposure and embarrassment at any moment, not only for myself but for a reputable news organisation and a highly regarded publisher. I could gamble with their good names or I could make a clean breast of it. I knew at once what I had to do.

'I'm representing myself, Victoria,' I said.

'That's fine,' she said.

I was going to Gitmo as a second-hand arms-dealer.

Two airlines flew to Guantánamo, the dubious-sounding but no doubt unimpeachable Fandango Air and Air Sunshine. They both made round trips to the base out of Fort Lauderdale, which was half an hour's drive north of Miami. I gathered from Victoria that I was only entitled to an overnight pass for the base. The round trip cost $350. I bought my ticket at the Air Sunshine counter, and I paid cash. On the one hand, this was a deft counter-surveillance technique, to prevent an outwitted Pentagon from tracing me after I had penetrated Gitmo's security cordon. I also thought that peeling off a few large notes from a roll of greenbacks might lend credibility to my assumed, or implicit, role as a merchant of military cast-offs. The Air Sunshine supervisor glanced idly at the green tear-off strip in my passport. It was all that Miami immigration had left of my entry card when I'd arrived in the United States from Britain. I walked into a brilliant afternoon and across no more than a yard or two of airport apron to a twin-propeller jet.

Heading out over the Florida Straits, we skimmed the top of a weather system which might have been low cloud, or high mist. The woman in the seat opposite mine offered me cookies. Her name was Teresa and she worked for an aid organisation at Gitmo, attending to the welfare of the remaining Cuban migrants at the base. Our fellow passengers all worked at Guantánamo full-time, she said. The young woman behind me was a teacher who was giving the migrants English lessons; the man sitting behind Teresa was attached to the Justice Department, helping to process their applications to settle in the United States. 'What about you?' Teresa asked me.

I looked out of the window. I composed myself. 'Well, I saw this article in the paper,' I began. So long as I merely mentioned the auction, without actually claiming that I was a buyer, I haven't lied, I thought – not really.

Teresa drew me a map of the base. Here was the airport, and here was where you picked up the free bus to the commissary, and here was McDonalds – it was true about McDonalds, then – it was across the road from the soccer field. Teresa looked at me. 'I don't know if it's the maternal instinct in me but I'm worried about you,' she said. Well-meant as this was, it was the last thing I wanted to hear. Was this the effect that international purchasers of second-hand military equipment generally had on people? I didn't think so.

Fortunately, the marines who examined my papers at Guantánamo airport were less acute than Teresa. I didn't say anything, and nor did they, waving me off the runway towards an aircraft hangar as pastel pink as a house on the Malecón. A minibus was waiting to take the new arrivals to the ferry. The ferry was a 'small craft' in naval lingo, a gun-metal launch manned by ratings in hipster jeans. It crossed the bay from the airport on the leeward side to the main living quarters on the windward side. The spur of land facing the leeward jetty trailed its green tropical skirts in the water. The turkey vultures, and the sky of grey and plum and apricot, told you that you were back in Cuba.

The launch put in beside the exposed pipes and boilers of a desalination plant. A long single-storey building winking with fairy lights might have been a roughhouse bar. 'That's the office of the contractor,' Burgess corrected me. Burgess was a Jamaican who had served in Gitmo's fire service for six years. He was giving me a lift into town. He had overheard me asking for directions to the Navy Lodge. The DRMS had made a reservation for me at the base – it was reservation 24753, for what that was worth: the only thing Teresa had been able to make of it was that it might refer to a room at the lodge.

The road into town was metalled, intermittently lined by more single-storey buildings. They were offices and stores and bungalows. One section of kerbstone was being blancoed by men in camouflage fatigues. It might have been a punishment, a KP, like painting coal black.

Near the Navy Lodge was a hoarding of the sort you saw outside chapels and diners in the United States, spelling out chunks of the Old Testament, or special offers on seafood combos. Text could be assembled in its grooves, as if in the template of an outsize John Bull printing kit. The Gitmo hoarding, not altogether different in tone from a chapel one, said, 'Plan wisely your holiday episodes so a drinking incident doesn (sic) plan your life.' Inside the lodge, a broad-chested black sailor called Jim had been drafted as receptionist. He had no record of a reservation for me, but undertook to ring around the couple of other places at Gitmo where accommodation was sometimes available. He asked the base operator for assistance. Gitmo subscribers had numbers running into no more than four figures, as in the early days of mainland telephone communications. Jim was unable to shed any light on my phantom booking, however. Fortunately, there was one room left at the lodge itself. I would be very welcome to take it, said Jim. 'I'm very sorry, sir, but I regret the telephone in that room is not working at this time,' he warned. He poured me a complimentary cup of coffee from a simmering pot. One apparent spin-off of franchising hostelry work out to the military was the high degree of deference offered to guests. On the other hand, by the look of Jim, the arrangement would certainly have made you think twice about leaving without settling your bill. The wives and fiancées of servicemen stayed at the Navy Lodge while visiting their loved ones on the base: it was not the sort of hotel where people spent much time in the lobby. The only person I met was a marine who said he couldn't wait to leave Guantánamo. 'I don't like the people, sir, the Cubans.'

'But you don't see them.'

'On the border, sir. They're insulting of us. They make gestures from their watch-towers.'

By ticky night, I saw the sights of Gitmo. I walked past the soccer field, the softball quadrant and the horseshoe pits to a prefabricated hangar where servicemen were playing bingo. Instead of the hollering and high-fiving that you might have expected, the game had the atmosphere of an adult education class. The only sounds were the barely amplified voice of the caller and the noise of ballpoints connecting deliberately with card. It reminded me of a cigar factory I had visited in Havana, where the workers listened to plays or readings from *Granma* while they handled leaves which resembled relics of impossibly dainty mandarins' sandals. At the Marblehead Bowling Lanes, two alleys were occupied. Men with buzzsaw haircuts and immaculately pressed T-shirts sipped Diet Coke between balls. Monday night was men's night, I gathered from a noticeboard, but tonight, Thursday, was mixed. Two women were bowling. Another notice asked: 'Are you ready for some football? Come to the Clipper Club and watch Monday night football on the big screen. Non-alcoholic frozen fruit cocktails.' Another featured a cartoon of a trembling man who was naked apart from a *sombrero*. It was a recruiting poster for 'sexual assault survivor advocates'.

I had a drink in the marines' bar, the Lateral Hazard. Knots of shorn beefcake stood around pool tables – a slightly higher aggregate IQ and it could have passed for a gay bar. As it was, patrons sang along to country and western videos, and there was a certain amount of good-natured violence.

Morning found me beneath a pink-making Cuban sun, walking to McDonalds for the breakfast special. There was a line of men in fatigues at the counter. McDonalds was adjacent to the commissary, a mall for shoppers in battledress. There was a shop selling T-shirts which depicted Fidel Castro and a vulture above the slogan 'Birds of a Feather'. Outside the commissary was an early shipment of pine trees for Christmas.

I had told Jim at the Navy Lodge about the surplus sale, and he had arranged a taxi to run me up to see the lots. They were on display on a patch of sandy ground within sight of the border with revolutionary Cuba. The hulk of a ferry ('original cost $750,000') was decaying greyly. There were trucks and four-wheel-drive Jeeps and bulldozers and generators arranged higgledy-piggledy, the occasional crazed windshield and incongruous chalk marking among them, but otherwise they betrayed no clue as to why they had been deserted. They might have been the property of an invading army stopped in its tracks by the kind of bomb that withers flesh but leaves capital assets untouched. I couldn't see any tents or cots or porto-potties. A huge man with a bald pate was mopping his face with a handkerchief. He was wearing pumps, white socks and denim shorts. Nearby, a taller, cooler man was looking about with an appraising air. The huge man introduced himself. 'I'm Bill Edwards. I come from Carolina. I ain't saying I'm ugly but it's my own fault if my mirror breaks,' he said.

Bill gave me a brochure – 'Spanning the world to target the

market' was written on the cover – and invited me to look around. On an engine cowling, someone had scrawled 'Will not crank'. On another vehicle was a stencil of a locust. Many of the trucks were mustard-coloured; they were Gulf War surplus, redirected to Gitmo to be used in setting up and running refugee camps for Cubans. Bill Edwards caught up with me. 'I'm the meanest man who ever put on shoes,' he said. Bill had turned himself into a character.

I said, 'Really?'

Bill shook his head fondly. 'I found out long ago that I could get more done with a pleasant attitude than I could with a grouch. What do you think of my generators? I don't know if I'll get $2 for them, or $2,000. I haven't done a sale like this in eight years.'

I realised that Bill was steering me towards the machines. 'Do you need a cat?' he pondered mystifyingly. 'What would that be worth, now?'

I pulled a man-of-the-world face. 'It's difficult to say, Bill,' I told him. 'It depends on where you are.'

Bill seemed satisfied with my reply, or at least, he carried on the conversation. Or at least, he seemed to. What he said was, 'Six thousand dollars with a cone. Of course, it's not set in concrete. Maybe it could go as high as $13,000, in the business world. You know more about that than I do.' He slapped a generator with a broad palm. 'Now this beauty, she's going to go the full nine yards.'

Bill had been in the navy but now worked part-time for the DRMS. His wife was still an active servicewoman, he told me. 'The woman can understand me and I talk in my sleep, so I have to behave myself. She was raised with a 16-gauge shotgun: a bird ain't got a Chinaman's chance.'

I thanked Bill for his help. He told me that the closing date for bids was the following week. I said I would think it over. I had to go because the meter was still running on my taxi.

'Once you get to $50, you keep the car,' said Bill.

The taxi-driver, Donald Moore, a Jamaican, took me up to the perimeter fence. The road was open between sunrise and sunset. A sign read 'Danger: road within kill range of mines'. Stray deer often set the mines off, Donald told me. In the distance were spindly, wooden look-out posts where Cuban troops made insulting gestures towards the binoculars of blushing marines. Donald and I went to see the emptying refugee camps. They were fenced compounds of tents made out of wooden frames with a canvas covering. There were batteries of pay-phones. A dinghy set on its side, with oars protruding from it, was labelled *Liberty*: an installation dedicated to the exploits of the fugitive Cubans, though many of them had made their escape in much less substantial vessels. I asked Donald what it had been like at the height of the refugee crisis. The Americans had put tents up on the golf course, he said, and the soccer pitch had disappeared beneath canvas.

At the airstrip, my 24-hour pass having all but expired, I was congratulating myself on getting away with a trip to Gitmo when the pilot of the last aircraft out that night told me that he wouldn't take me. He had leafed through my passport on the runway and found no visa for the United States. Though it felt as though I had never left American soil, I would need a permit to negotiate immigration at Fort Lauderdale. I showed the pilot my green tear-off strip.

'It's not valid,' he said.

'But I got it at Miami.'

'Only the major carriers are allowed to take people into the States without a visa. We're not a major carrier.' There was a $3,000 fine – presumably for Air Sunshine, although not impossibly, for me.

I should have known. Getting into or out of Cuba was seldom straightforward. I thought of Carlo Gébler, concluding his book *Driving through Cuba* with an account of how his diaries were briefly impounded at José Martí airport. I remembered leaving the country in 1994 with dissident fiction in my bag, and a Ministry of Interior man tapping me on the shoulder in the limbo of the departure lounge: a technicality with my paperwork, as it turned out, but a pulse-troubling one for all that. I appeared to be stuck at Gitmo. With luck, I might get by for a while on an expired pass. I could perhaps take a room back at the Navy Lodge. But if I couldn't get off the base now, there was no reason for thinking that I would find it any easier at another time. Indeed, it was likely to be more difficult: my air ticket was not transferable. It was for this Air Sunshine flight, or nothing. I foresaw problems in raising the British Consulate in Miami on any of the four-digit telephone numbers available on the Gitmo switchboard, and I wasn't sure how sympathetic officials would be in any case. As for taking the US military into my confidence, could I be certain that they wouldn't become suspicious? I was here for the surplus sale, except that I was really a journalist: somewhere, no doubt, there was a record of the conversations I had had when I had been attempting to go legit to Gitmo. The more I considered my predicament, the more the doors of the camp brig yawned. The odds on my leaving Guantánamo for the United States having lengthened compared to those of the remaining Cubans, I was contemplating a Cuban solution, such as stowing away, when the pilot relented. 'If our people let you come, I suppose we had better take you back,' he said unhappily.

The tall, cool man I had seen at the auction site boarded the aircraft ahead of me. The plane was slightly larger than the one I had flown out on. It was full of middle-aged men with tough-looking skin.

In Florida, as I was walking across the runway, the tall, cool man let me know that he had spotted me inspecting the trucks and Jeeps. What was my line exactly, he wanted to know.

'I represent some people in London,' I said as enigmatically as I could. 'They're very interested in Cuba.'

'In London?' The look on the man's face suggested that he was reckoning the boggling cost of crating up four-wheel-drives and barging them across the Atlantic. Suddenly that look was succeeded by one of wonder. He said, 'Of course you guys aren't covered by the embargo, are you?'

I smiled noncommittally. I had the feeling my alibi was finally watertight. The tall man went on, 'So there would be nothing to stop you taking the vehicles round to Havana by sea. You could keep them there as long as you wanted ...' His voice tailed off wistfully. I fell out of step with him as we queued up at immigration but I noticed him talking to a man in a stetson. I had decided to be last in line. I was alone in the hall with an immigration official and the Air Sunshine pilot. The official flicked through my passport while the pilot paced the hall like an expectant father. When I was passed fit to enter the United

States, he shook my hand: Air Sunshine's $3,000 was safe.

The man in the stetson was waiting for me by the automatic doors. 'I hear you're an English fellow,' he said. He was a Texan, he said. He was in the salvage business. 'Now, you guys aren't covered by the embargo, are you? What exactly is your line?'

13

Christmas

IT WAS CHRISTMAS EVE in Havana and the fatted pig across the street was getting his. A black man who looked like he had once boxed kept the pig on the roof behind the Cabaret Las Vegas. Early on the morning of the 24th, there was a good deal of squealing coming from the roof. No country boy, the word I should have used to describe this squealing was incredulous. After several long minutes, it ceased; in the late afternoon, the man could be seen out on the roof again, gnawing a bone.

It was the coldest I had known Cuba. The temperature never fell below the middling teens centigrade during the day, but there was *mucho aire*, as the Cubans said, a lot of air. Hilda's front room had been redecorated while I'd been in Britain: there was a fresh coat of white paint, and a fan had been mounted in the ceiling. It would not be needed immediately. I put my *Santería* amulet in a saucer on the balcony; that was where I'd kept it when it was new, because of the sickly stench of blood and honey, and the window-ledge of the balcony had become its shrine. I would sometimes rattle the amulet on its dish in front of Hilda and shout '*Santería!*' or '*Changó!*', the name of one of the *orishas*, and we would laugh and pull faces at each other, half-fearful. In the evenings, she put a pan of water on for my bucket bath, except on days when there was no gas, shortages of this fuel compounding problems of electricity cuts and restricted water supply. The shortages reminded me of a film about an old lady who takes her dog to the pound in Havana because she can't afford to feed him. The warden confesses that he puts some of the dogs down because there are so many of them, but he can't do so today as there's no gas. The dogs are spared! 'What a wonderful country Cuba is!' chips in a passer-by.

Hilda and Nico complained that it was '*muy frio*'. He went around the apartment in his windcheater. He had acquired a well-thumbed photocopy of an English phrase book. It appeared to have been published in the United States in the fifties, and had a raffish tone. At mealtimes, Nico would practise: 'He's a swell guy'; 'Let me give you a tip'; 'Bunch of crooks'. He had finished at college but wasn't working, and on a day when he was feeling particularly chilly or at a loose end, he would go to the bedroom he shared with his mother and simply go to sleep. I would sometimes return to the *edificio* in the afternoon to find that they had both put themselves to bed. 'Time passes very slowly for me,' said Nico. Once or twice, it rained all day, drawing sparks from exposed electrical circuitry. The transformers across the street guttered like gas lamps.

The waters off the Malecón were darker and more violent than I had seen them before. They broke over the crumbling sea wall, not in the festive Christmas-tree shapes described in *Our Man in Havana*, but in avalanches of surf. Looking from the bottom of La Rampa, it was as though an entire stretch of the Malecón – further round the bay, towards Prado and the Morro castle – was overwhelmed by ridges and overhangs of white water. As far as you could make out, a breakaway plateau of the Atlantic was thundering into the lobby of the Hotel Deauville. The Malecón was closed for a time, or thought to be, or perhaps a certain length of it was; at any rate, only a handsomely remunerated taxi-driver would agree to point his Lada into the path of the shifting and treacherous escarpments of ocean. In the interludes when the sea was calm, the air on the Malecón was tangy with brine, and there were clods of green weed and chunks of sea wall on the road. At night, the ambient salt made the street lights hazy.

After dark, it was as quiet as a coup. The regime had been embarrassed by publicity surrounding the return of prostitution, a decadent scourge which the Revolution was hitherto credited with removing, and Ministry of Interior police had been posted outside every hotel and nightclub. It was difficult to believe that they were bent solely on saving the women of Havana from themselves. There seemed to be at least as many of them on duty as there were in the summer, when rioting was considered most likely. The officers in their peaked caps and denim fatigues, like a navy dressed in Pentagon seconds, made unlikely chaperones. Girls would hiss at you from doorways – the Havana come-hither – only to step back into the darkness at the report of a passion-killing hobnail. Going out in search of drink or music or company felt like breaking a curfew. The constabulary was walking the streets of Centro and Vedado, two-by-two. On Calle 25, a light left on in a mechanic's workshop projected the outsize shadow of a slowly revolving ventilator fan onto a wall. A Chevrolet with its lights off rumbled across the street at one junction. At another, two men muttering to each other under their breath went in the opposite direction. Rounding a corner onto Infanta, you stepped directly into the path of a police foot patrol. Havana's finest doubtfully returned compliments of the season.

I arranged to meet a girl after she finished work. 'Not in the bar; wait for me outside in the street,' she said. In the rainy doorway, with the barman peeping out at me through a blind, I felt like a fugitive. The 'love police' had handcuffed two *extranjeros* and their female companions in the old city that morning. But there was still a full house at the Palacio de la Salsa in the Hotel Riviera, South American businessmen of dubious renown keeping up the old mobster associations of the place. And the most beautiful prostitutes in the city danced to up-to-the-minute international hits at the Havana Club in Miramar. They were far too tall to go by the abusive Cuban epithet *jiniteras*, the jockeys. The aloofness of the girls and the modishness of the music wouldn't have been out of place in a Western capital.

At less discreet places like La Pampa, or Bulerias near the Habana

Libre, where the pimps asked you if you required '*una chica por tu habitación*', a girl for your room, it was easy to imagine a disturbance getting out of hand, the police over-reacting, casualties prompting wider unrest. I kept turning over in my head the old saw that trouble comes not when people are desperate but when some of them aren't quite so desperate anymore. Resentment is supposed to breed in such circumstances. Ministers were announcing that more than 200,000 Cubans had gone into business for themselves. In Havana, every other backroom seemed to have been converted into a *paladar*; every other private car had a strip of card saying 'Taxi' behind the windscreen.

Christmas being the time of year when people call on family and friends, I had a visit from Julietta and her unsmiling new boyfriend. Julietta was now working for one of the state tourism agencies – her dream had come true. She had heard about an opening through a friend and she was now a guide, escorting holiday-makers around Havana or out to Varadero. Her boyfriend was a guide too. He asked whether I had noticed that everyone talked now. He said, 'They are not frightened by what they say anymore,' before going on to deliver himself of some critical remarks about Spanish entrepreneurs who were telling the Cubans how to run their hotels. It struck me that what this serious-looking man was saying was right. More than the revamped airport and the fleet of tourist coaches, more than the culture of self-employment and dollar legalisation, what was truly different about Cuba compared to my first visit more than five years earlier was that people on the street weren't frightened by what they said. They had caught up with the divinings of Western embassy officials who had been saying for 18 months that the Cuban government was so preoccupied with solving the crisis of post-Communism that there was simply not enough time or energy to go around suppressing speech. An old woman I vaguely knew in Centro stopped me and said that Fidel was '*como un erizo*,' like a hedgehog. It wasn't clear whether this was a reference to his bristling defensiveness or just a broad piece of abuse at *El Comandante*'s expense, but it scarcely mattered. It was as if there was a new phrase book now. Were the measures of freedom that Cubans enjoyed enough to save the Revolution? Or was it going to be on my watch that the authors of those only slightly apocryphal works

Castro's Last Gasp and *Sugar Caned: Why Fidel Must Fall* would at last have satisfaction?

I'd wanted to spend Christmas in Havana because I thought it would be the last word in those unlikely Yuletides we read about in the northern hemisphere every December, culminating in plum puddings on Bondi beach. In the event, Hilda, Nico and I didn't quite rise to sand-gritted turkey. Instead, there was *pollo frito* on the sunny porch of La Exquisita paladar in Vedado for Christmas dinner. It didn't tarry on the palate in the same way as the meal I had in the town of Viñales over Christmastide, a dish that my Cuban friends envied me and I found impossible to forget. Viñales is in the westerly tobacco-growing province of Pinar del Rio, but from the hills which overlooked it, the town was English pastoral: a steeple, a market square and, encircling these, cow-cropped meadow. You knew you were in the Cuban countryside by the ubiquitous turkey vultures, the palms, the thatched barns where crops were stored. A private restaurant, Casa Dagoberte, was on the main street. There were no Christmas decorations, but the fairy lights and twinkling baubles of other premises were more than outshone by a gilded cocktail bar with bottles of highly coloured spirits in wicker holsters, and a carpet, hung as a tapestry, in which Arabian horsemen were rescuing a princess by improbably starry night. By the standards of what was to follow, the dinner I had at Casa Dagoberte on my first night in town was unremarkable: frog's legs, not yet cooked, presented at the table for approval with a sommelier's solicitousness; monkfish from the lake; a strolling guitarist and the ballad of Che Guevara; mine host, a brawny man sentimental with drink, calling the town whores in to partner me in a *salsa*; and making his daughter cry – a ten-year-old in her mother's heels and best hat, dismissed when the opening notes of *Bésame*, 'Kiss Me', eluded her.

At the end of the evening, Señor Dagoberte led me through his house – past a metal stand, like a shrine, where water dripped through purifying limestone; through the *al fresco* kitchens, where pork rind blistered in a fatty pan – to the yard, where a hen's feathers glimmered in a wire cage. Even by the dim light cast by the ovens, it was possible to make out something darker in the cage with the bird. A cigarette-lighter flared, and for a moment, there was the sight of rippling fur, the blond quill-tips of a soft brown pelt. There was the glimpse of a dully gleaming eye, a tail like a cosh, and a rattle of wire as the creature shrank from the flame. None of the victims of Saki's suavely deadly rodent, Sredni Vashtar, felt their neck-hair prickle more disquietingly than I did at the rear of Casa Dagoberte. A cook put his hands inside the darkened cage, there was the sound of something sinewy struggling, and then the proprietor was exclaiming '*Jutia! Jutia!*' and into the kitchens came an animal as big as a dog, hanging by its thick, smooth tail. The cook put one hand around the neck of the creature, so that I thought he was going to kill it. Instead, he held it out to me, its belly uppermost, its whiskery upper lip drawn back in fear, exposing two front teeth. I thought of the amulet that Kiki had given me: each of the animal's teeth was as long as the lozenge of ivory – a nugget of rhinoceros's horn? An elephant's nail-clipping? – that Kiki had fastened to my *Santería* familiar. The beast of Casa Dagoberte was what guidebook writers had had in mind when they had written of a fabled delicacy of Pinar del Rio for which visitors scanned restaurant menus in vain. If only they had found their way to the kitchens behind the main street. We went through the polite little rite of the frog's legs all over again, only this time with a *Jutia Conga*: Chef wanted to know how sir liked his giant rat.

I was to have it next day, for Sunday lunch. In the morning, I wandered the aisles of the *tienda* in my hotel, distractedly wondering what went with rat. I decided that they would know at Casa Dagoberte, and would keep a bottle of whatever it was on the gilded bar. *Chez* Dagoberte, there was no sign of the owner. You imagined him sleeping off the effects of whatever tiresome behaviour he had been inflicting on his family until the small hours of the morning. However, his wife, recommending rice and a salad with my *jutia*, spoke loyally of an appointment in Pinar. She said I should drink rum, and produced a brown and potent 1992. I stood drinking on the verandah while I waited for my food. There were wooden display cabinets containing lollipops and a pizza which had been folded in half. Men were working in the bakery next door with their shirts off. A man who spoke good English said he knew where he could lay his hands on cheap *especial* petrol. When I returned to my table, I found a dish of tomatoes and what looked like a kebab. The cut of rat I had been served resembled pork, and the flesh was just coming away from the bone. Though it was darker than pork – it was the colour of the dark meat on a Christmas turkey – I was able to establish, after no more than a further two double measures of rum, that the texture and even the taste were pork-like. I ate more than the minimum required by common manners, but rather less than a healthy Cuban would have done: perhaps it was the after-taste of urine. However, I have found that my fear of rats has dwindled since I ate one.

The man with the petrol lost only as much time as it takes to cock a disbelieving eyebrow before accepting my offer of *jutia*. After lunch, I went out to the kitchens to present my compliments to the chef. In the dirt was a coulis of blood, and in the chicken-wire cage, the hen and a second giant rat. Now that they had sold one to me, a kitchen-hand explained, his boss would be able to place an order for another when the hunter returned to Viñales. This wily and expert man would go back to the forests with his dogs. I paid no more for lunch than I would have done for a pail of fried chicken in London. But it was as though I had dined on the exquisite eggs of a practically extinct, Alpine-nesting bird, or on truffles which only grew on what was presently a mined and disputed border, rather than on the flesh of a flea-loud rodent. On the road out of Viñales, I was passed by Dagoberte, who was riding home on a motorcycle with every show of sobriety.

I wanted to be in Cuba at Christmas because I was intrigued by travel agents' reports that December and January were the most popular months for the island, despite or perhaps because of the fact that the closest visitors would get to a white Christmas would be a slushy *daiquiri*. Tourists who spent Yuletide in the Caribbean presumably fancied the idea of getting away from European winter. And it was reasonable to assume that at least some of them were hardcore Christmas-haters; or at the very least, that they were ill-disposed to the tinselly trappings of the holidays back home. If so, then Cuba was perfect for them. In what was almost literally a pantomime of hard-heartedness, Fidel had cancelled Christmas. (The idea of ignoring

Christ's birth was such a byword for misanthropy that Hollywood had recently written it into a script to emphasise what a bad sort the Sheriff of Nottingham was.) I could never understand why Castro's critics in Washington and Miami hadn't made more of this. There was good knocking copy in the irony that the man whose beard was almost as well known as St Nick's was the Scrooge of the Caribbean. Perhaps he was aware of this danger. In an interview in 1985, he fondly recalled his childhood Christmases. 'Christmas Eve was a wonderful thing, because it meant fifteen days of vacation – and not just fifteen days of vacation, but fifteen days of a festive atmosphere and treats: cookies, candy, and nougat.' Cuban children wrote their begging letters not to Santa Claus but the Three Wise Men. The future guerrilla and revolutionary asked them for cars, trains and movie cameras, but received toy trumpets on three consecutive Noels. 'I should have become a musician,' he joked. It all begged the question of why he had vetoed Christmas, the negligence of the Magi notwithstanding.

In one sense, the most obvious impact of his decision was that 25 December was not a public holiday for Cubans. In London, I had complacently anticipated writing: 'It was just like any other day in Havana, business as usual, which was to say, *no* business – people going off to their non-jobs; shops open at their accustomed hour, ready to sell nothing to their penniless customers.' It was true that at one or two of the barren official *tiendas,* assistants sat unconsidered at their counters like Bob Cratchit. But otherwise the above would have been an injustice to Cuban ingenuity. On Christmas morning, a truck laden with boxes of food pulled up outside Hilda's and began unloading at the *bodega,* where they had decorated a small, false fir. After a walk down Calle Neptuno, I found myself speculating where else in the Christian world I could buy freshly breaded chicken croquettes on Christmas Day; where else the speeches of Fidel Castro, that last-minute present for a difficult relation; or a short back and sides – and so reasonable, literally a snip at less than a dollar. There might have been little that you actually wanted on display – you looked in vain for a mince pie, a robin redbreast, a paper hat – but there were plenty of Cubans who appeared to be enjoying the *paseo.* The *camellos* had roared past the *edificio* first thing, as on any other day, taking people to work, and schoolchildren wore their pillarbox or mustard tunics, but it seemed as though leisurely shopping, or window-shopping, was indulged by managers and teachers alike on *La Navidad*.

A sensitive issue about the de-recognition of Christmas in Cuba was what it meant for Christians, and, in a less immediate way, for all their fellow Cubans. Going to church had never been illegal in revolutionary Cuba, but for a time it had been very difficult. Another reason for being in the country in late December was mass on Christmas Eve. Walking onto Infanta at night and seeing the Carmen statue lit up; Hilda telling me that this was the most *tranquilo* time of year; birds – or were they bats? – skittering around inside the cupola of the church: this was the Cock Mass. The title suggested a dawning, a renewal, but also spoke of the country's mingled African and Spanish past. We arrived at the church early, by 11 o'clock, and it was soon clear why. It was packed. There were smartly-turned-out ladies of a certain age, courting couples, men in their best suits. A black man of about 45 was asleep at the end of our pew. In front of the monstrous sideboard of an altar was a Christmas tree – unlike the pines at the Gitmo Bay commissary, this one wasn't real, but it was decked out with all the trimmings, including flashing lights. Homemade wreaths decorated the columns. People took a turn around the mezzanine of the Franciscan seminary next door, apparently in the forlorn hope of a seat becoming free by the time they returned to the church. The Cubans were *queueing* for mass. For people so accustomed to standing in line, an hour's wait for God was not out of the way.

Why were all these people here, I wondered. Did they all believe? Midnight mass on Christmas Eve always draws a crowd, I remembered, even in Britain. It remained a free, or more or less free show in a country of poverty. But a Hollywood blockbuster was screening on Cuban television, an entirely cost-free alternative attraction. Hilda, Nico and I had left it in the first reel, having sat through a Brazilian soap opera, our makeshift Cuban family gathered in front of the television set on Christmas Eve.

The choir entered singing a carol. The priest brought up the rear, with a doll of Jesus. There was the camphor smell of the censer. The priest, standing at the altar, was momentarily blinded by a cloud of incense.

Carmen was the closest thing I had to a regular place of worship. It was my nearest church, and the one Hilda attended. I liked the way the congregation yodelled the 'glorias', and the statue of a mischievous infant on the giant sideboard who was dangling an *escapulario*, a kind of holy sash, as if he was toying with dropping it. He might have been a *niño* holding a scarf of his mother's over a Havana balcony. There was a frieze on the ceiling depicting a black man in the prow of a rowing boat which was beaching beneath palm trees. It was a scene from the works of the patron saint of Cuba, the black virgin of El Cobre. She was said to have appeared during a storm and guided the sailors safely to land. At El Cobre, which was near Santiago de Cuba, a vast, white, marble tabernacle honoured the virgin in a cool chapel on a hill. The virgin herself was no bigger than Tonka, the plastic Red Indian whom Kiki had recovered off Mariel. But there were eloquent testimonials to her powers in a kind of holy Lost & Found elsewhere in the chapel: discarded wheelchairs and redundant prosthetics. Outside, a gaggle of touts sold pyrites – fool's gold – and crude, pleasing carvings of the altar.

The first time I had been to a service at the Carmen church, it was in the summer with Julietta, and the priest had circulated among the congregation followed by a white-haired man in a *guayabera* who held a pail of holy water. The priest dipped what looked like an ice-cream scoop in the pail and swatted the congregation with it, as though to cool them. A lame woman, her mouth hanging slack, shuffled to the end of her pew to be sure of a dousing. Sitting on a chair by a side door was the sickly-looking friar who had once asked me for vitamins. The priest, a short man in spectacles, told the congregation that they should be humble before God. 'I'm poor, I need you, everything I have is given by you,' he urged them to tell God. 'Finally, everybody has to have in mind that everything – salvation, everything – depends on the will of God.'

The congregation sang a hymn to the tune of 'Fol-de-ray'. When they said 'Our Father', everyone spread their arms. Two women – one black, one white – linked their fingers. The black man in front of me had a prayerbook in his outstretched hand. It appeared to be bound in mother-of-pearl and had gilt-edged pages. It looked as out of place as a cigarette-case.

The queue for communion was another kind of bread line in rationed Cuba. There were two rows leading down the aisle. The priest attended to the line on my right. The old boy who carried the pail of holy water for him stood by with a kidney-shaped tray, apparently in case of spillages. The malnourished friar dispensed wafers to my queue. No more than half of the congregation went forward to receive the host: the others hadn't been to confession, you supposed, though it crossed your mind that, in the 'special period', perhaps there weren't even enough wafers for everyone to have one once a week.

It was my turn. The friar slid a wafer from his pot between his fingers. His sideman moved forward with the kidney-shaped platter, like a dental nurse. I opened my mouth, and hoped that I didn't favour the friar with the odours of rum and tobacco which I suspected still clung to me after a visit to the Cabaret Las Vegas the night before. The dental nurse analogy didn't turn out to be very wide of the mark, because the exercise of receiving the host on my tongue, and its taste, put me in mind of having my tongue palpated with a spatula. The wafer tasted of wood. Thin as it was, it sat bulkily on the tongue, like a penny: it was about the same circumference as an old British 1d. I followed the example of others, and walked off to the left, behind the columns, where I slipped the wafer out of my mouth. It was now folded in half, like the little plugs of blotting paper I used to carry around in a pencil-case at school because of leaky cartridge pens. It wasn't that the wafer was unpalatable, or that I feared gagging on its fibrous coat, though there was something in both those concerns. The reason I removed it was that I had begun to wonder – having found it tough-going on the gullet – whether I had got it all wrong, and the wafer, in straitened Cuba, was only figurative; that you popped it on your tongue and then slipped it into your pocket or purse, for discreet disposal later.

Julietta had seen me remove the woody disc from my lips, and now told me (in her increasingly authoritarian style – why couldn't she be as firm with the people I was trying to interview?) that I must eat it. So I slipped it back into my mouth and did. The wafer melted almost at once, and though its taste didn't improve, it did at least slip easily enough down my throat.

In the mezzanine of the seminary, I found the priest at the doorway to a room where parishioners were sitting on stiff, upright chairs, awaiting his attention. I wanted to discuss the irony of the Revolution filling the churches. But when I asked if we might talk, he said, '*Ocupado*'. He had receding grey hair, treated with oil to keep it neat. He wore an open-neck shirt beneath which a singlet was discernible. His name was Father Teodoro Becerril. I persevered and suggested that the churches were popular in Cuba.

'Yes, you can see it,' said Father Becerril.

'Why?'

'People always came to church, before and now.'

'But you're noticing more now?'

The priest said, 'When there was repression, people came. Now more people come because the repression is over. But some of them used to have problems with work and the ones that came then were the ones who had less fear.'

I said, 'Are people coming because their needs are greater in the special period?'

'*Pregunta politica*,' said Father Becerril with a foxy smile; a political question.

I said, 'Is it hard to be a priest in Cuba?'

'I'm a priest by the grace of God. It's a vocation. But it's easier to be a priest here than in England. It's always easier to be a priest where life is not so comfortable.' I thought of something Almeida of the Press Centre had told me. He claimed that a lascivious priest once cried from a Havana pulpit: 'The men with the men, and the women with me,' excusing his own dubious conduct. If you believed Almeida, there were comforts of a sort for the Cuban clergy.

I talked to Hilda about going to church. Yes, she had always gone, she said.

'*Antes?*' Before?

'You weren't supposed to, you were afraid, and you thought that you were being watched, but you came,' said Hilda.

*

A large woman in a yellow skirt, Maria Robles, told me that she had gone to prison for trying to keep her local church open. It was not long after Castro had come to power. Castro had had the Spanish Franciscans thrown out, said Señora Robles, the men who now offici-ated at Carmen. In her former parish, at Camagüey in central Cuba, soldiers closed the church. She didn't seem to care whether other people heard our conversation or not, but Hilda thought that for the woman's sake we should talk away from Carmen.

On a noisy Neptuno, I said, 'Did the soldiers nail up the church?'

'No, they only locked the door. I persuaded a soldier to go and find the key. He didn't agree with sealing the church.' The soldier didn't get into trouble but Señora Robles did. She led the local children back into the church. She said, 'I was given warnings that I might be sent away. I said, "I'm from Camagüey and I will be buried in Camagüey and I will never go." I was 18, very stubborn.'

Maria Robles and 21 other parishioners were accused of being counter-revolutionary. 'I was represented by a lawyer at the trial. He said, "This woman is a Christian. She might not be in favour of the Revolution but she's not against it. What she was doing was only for the church."' Señora Robles and the others were convicted. She spent two and a half years in prison, 'with marginals: prostitutes and petty criminals.'

I wondered whether the experience had shaken her faith. But in her almost recklessly unshaken tones, Señora Robles said, 'Look, I never married. Why? Because I have always worked for the church. That is my answer.'

The closing of churches marked the nadir in Castro's relations with Christians. In his most lengthy statement on religion, an inter-view with a Brazilian priest, Frei Betto, conducted in the mid-eighties, *El Comandante* explicitly denied that a single church door had been shut. But senior figures in the Catholic church told me that this, among other things attributed to Castro in *Fidel & Religion*, was an untruth. Castro told his interlocutor that Catholicism was the religion of Cuba's old, Spanish, slave-owning elite; perhaps this helps to explain why Christmas was removed from the Cuban calendar: it wasn't regarded as a festival of the people. Castro added that there were no churches in the Cuban countryside. But that was only true in the sense that he had authorised their closure, I was told. Ninety per cent of churches in the sugar-growing areas, such as Señora Robles', were sealed. Hospital chapels were also closed. Priests were expelled and the clerical population of Cuba reduced from 800 in early 1961 to fewer than 200 six months later. Similarly, a community of 2,500 nuns became one of 200. Catholic schools with 100,000 children on their rolls were closed. 'The church was disactivated,' was how a senior clergyman recalled the process.

Fidel said that the well-to-do had used their church in an attempt to obstruct the Revolution. The priesthood was accused of disseminating black propaganda against the new order from the pulpit. 'The priests said that Fidel and the others ate babies,' Julietta once told me in scandalised tones.

One high-ranking cleric conceded that some 'vivid' things might have been said. 'You have to divide the history of Cuba into before and after the Revolution,' he said. 'Whatever you have heard, the church was uncomfortable at the time of Batista. Don't forget that the church participated in the Revolution. As Fidel himself acknowledges, they had a priest with them in the Sierra Maestra. But the bishops were very disappointed to find that there was a Communist state after the triumph of the Revolution.'

I was so surprised to hear this cant phrase – 'the triumph of the Revolution' – from the lips of a priest that I checked I had heard him correctly.

'That's what I'm telling you,' he said. 'The church was happy in 1959.'

Amado Hart, Cuba's long-serving Minister of Culture, claimed in a preface to *Fidel & Religion* that Castro's encounter with the Brazilian was amazing. 'If we stick strictly to the definition given in the diction-ary, we might say that those who study this talk in depth will find "an extremely outstanding or unusual event, thing, or accomplishment" – that is, a *miracle*.' The italics are those of the Cuban state. In fact, the priest's toadying sallies – 'questions' is hardly the word – elicited typically baroque monologues. The interview at least cleared up that Freudian theories wouldn't do to explain the harrying of the priests: the boy Castro seems to have enjoyed being educated by the Christian brothers and the Jesuits. And the book put on record that *El Jefe* was comfortable with 'co-existence' between church and state, if nothing more. Cuba's Catholic leaders, for their part, told me that the book had had a positive effect, by breaking a taboo about the church which had existed for 20 years.

An interview with Jaime Ortega, the man created Cardinal of Cuba in 1994, was almost as rare as an audience with Fidel. He was, after all, the second most important man in the country – his elevation in Rome had seen to that. There hadn't been a cardinal in Cuba for 30 years. It was assumed that the position had been in abeyance as a mark of the Vatican's displeasure over the expulsion of the priests. The fact that a notably itchy-footed Pope, John Paul II, had never fitted Cuba into his itinerary, was also taken as a snub to the regime. To Frei Betto, Fidel claimed that the Pope had been in a dither over visiting Cuba in 1979, on his way back from a bishops' conference elsewhere in Latin America. The Pontiff, or his advisers, couldn't decide whether to accept Castro's offer of a stay in Havana, and risk offending Cuban exiles in Miami, or go to Miami and disappoint Catholics in Cuba. 'Frankly, I didn't like it when on that occasion the Pope didn't even make a modest stopover in our country,' Fidel added. According to senior church figures in Cuba, however, no such invitation from the Cuban government was ever received. In 1996, it was reported that Cuba's Vice-Minister for Foreign Relations had visited the Vatican to discuss a possible papal visit.

When I heard that Ortega would see me, church leaders were saying that things stood pretty much where they were at the time of Betto's book. 'Co-existence' remained the order of the day. There had been important concessions. Attending mass was no longer a bar to worldly preferment. On my first day back in Cuba for Christmas, a woman called Maria Christina, my then handler at the *Centro de Prensa*, told me that church-going was no longer an impediment to membership of the party.

I sat in an ante-room of the Cardinal's residence in Habana Vieja. On the shelves beside leather-bound religious texts was a wooden chicken which could apparently forecast the weather: its base was bafflingly calibrated for sunshine, humidity, storms. At length I was admitted into the presence of a balding man in gilt-framed spectacles. He was wearing a crucifix on a chain made of surprisingly large links. But for this and his ecclesiastical double-breasted, he might have passed for a dentist, but one of the genial sort whom you almost looked forward to visiting. When he laughed, he sounded like Alistair Sim.

The role of the church in Cuba was the same as it was anywhere else, the Cardinal said. There was its prayer mission, its charitable mission, and then there was *la misión profética*. 'The first two are more easily accepted by the state in Cuba.'

'Why does the state have a problem with the prophesying role of the church?'

The Cardinal put his palm to his forehead in a gesture of concentration. 'It's not only the state. When the Pope talks, some people in the street who have their own problems disagree with what he says.'

'But specifically with regard to the state?'

Cardinal Ortega said that a statement by the Cuban church in 1993 entitled 'Love Endures All', about the country's 'special period', was 'angrily rejected' by the government. 'They wrote many articles in the newspapers for a month after it came out.' The Cuban bishops had suggested dialogue between all Cuban nationals, including those who lived abroad; they had appeared to criticise Cuba's economic and political systems. The Cardinal said, 'What's the place of the church inside the monolith? The problem here is not one of atheism or anti-clericalism or hatred of God. It's a political problem, and it comes from the philosophical conception of the state.'

'Have *you* decided what the place of the church is inside the monolith?'

'This concept remains difficult,' he said. 'The government wants a strong state because they think it's the best way to protect the country in a time of crisis. But the people want something else. They're trying to be independent of the state, in commerce, work, other forms of liberty.'

'And you're on the side of the people?'

'Oh sure, and not only with theories about the best way forward for the political system. We also have a vision about the human being – that's the problem. This vision of mankind comes from the Gospel and claims respect for the dignity of the person. We want to help the people. We can't solve the problems of the people but we can understand them.'

The Cardinal told me that he thought the Cuban regime was conservative; more conservative than China's. 'But I believe the history of the world and the global economy will push the government to make changes.'

I asked Cardinal Ortega for his opinion of Castro. 'If you ask Fidel Castro about me, he would say, "I prefer not to answer that question." I say the same.' Journalists in Miami had asked him the same question when he went there, he said. He fixed the doily on the arm of his chair.

'Do you consider the Cubans in Miami part of your flock?'

'The church always considers that the pasture of the priest is the place where he lives. However, I regard the refugees as a matter of special pastoral attention. The Cubans living abroad have a strong relationship with the Cubans here. They're joined by blood. We are all Cubans. When the Pope made me Cardinal, Cuban Catholics all over the world said, "He's our Cardinal." I consider that that is the case.'

I asked Ortega if he didn't feel he was walking on eggshells in Havana.

'You can't lose your balance,' he admitted. 'We're meeting a daily, historical reality with a global vision. The world is changing faster than before. On the other hand, faith can be counted in centuries.'

'The changes you anticipate here – will they be peaceful?'

'I believe so, yes,' said the Cardinal. 'The peace that comes from quiet, not the peace that comes from the heart of a happy man.'

14

Fidel Castro: An Unauthorised Interview

THE UNAUTHORISED BIOGRAPHY is a familiar literary genre. Jealous of his independence, the author has little or no contact with his subject. Either that or the boot is on the other foot and the author is crabbed and thwarted, forbidden to quote from the much-loved verse, denied access to the campus stacks and the first wife, unavailed of the journals, the desk blotter, the fridge-door *aide-mémoire*. In a word, he must lurk in the bushes and hope to jump out on J.D. Salinger. In the style of an unauthorised biography, what follows is an unauthorised interview. Its subject is Fidel Castro. It was done without Fidel's prior knowledge, without his consent, very nearly without his participation. Very nearly, but not quite. I leave it to the reader to decide whether I have been independent or a crabbed and thwarted lurker.

The *authorised* interview with Fidel Castro proceeded within well-defined parameters. It was a rare phenomenon, but that encouraged a minute recording of every detail, the more substantial encounters subsequently published in book form – by an Australian house, for no clear reason – and a pattern emerging. Be he ever so distinguished, the interviewer (and it usually was a he) might make one or more visit to Cuba without striking lucky. The Brazilian priest Frei Betto, who eventually interviewed Castro in 1985, had several wasted journeys. 'On one of those trips, I drew up a draft for the interview and the book but got no reply,' he wrote. Fidel's prospective interlocutor was allowed to cool his heels in Havana for days, or even weeks. The priest appears to have come close to cracking under the strain. 'I stayed at home, waiting for his office to phone me. Nobody called, and the day dragged slowly by, weighing on the harsh agony of my silent anxiety.' At last, there would be the ringing of the telephone late at night, the augury of an even more ungodly limousine ride, to fortified catacombs beneath the Plaza de la Revolución. Fidel, in his olive warrior weeds, would invariably be waving off a charabanc of Latin American VIPs. Interviewer and subject would repair to Fidel's office where there would be a certain amount of tittle-tattle: the view from the window of the statue of José Martí (which appeared, in the right light, to be a work of scrimshaw from a single, mighty whalebone); the portrait above Fidel's escritoire of his late *compañero* Camilo Cienfuegos, the casualty of a mysterious air crash; Fidel's love of, and talent for cooking. ('The best thing is not to boil either shrimp or lobster,' *El Comandante* instructed Father Betto, 'because boiling water reduces the substance and the taste and toughens the flesh.') A certain amount of tittle-tattle, but never enough. The unauthorised interviewer was tantalised by moments like the following one, also from Betto's *Fidel & Religion*: 'Fidel put his cup of tea down on the saucer and said, "Latin America borrowed devalued dollars and now has to repay its debt with dollars that are worth more." ' Not a bad quote on debt, but I mean to say: Fidel's cup and saucer! Was it too much to hope that, blooming with rust in the vaults of the Museum of the Revolution, were Che's fish kettle and the cruet of the Sierra Maestra? The unauthorised interviewer had the instinct of the medium and the bloodhound that you could tell a lot about people from the personal effects they left lying around. All of Ceauşescu's vanity had been in the mock-onyx coat-hanger I had taken away from his hunting-lodge.

All too soon, the authorised interviewer had moved on. He was rehearsing exactly how tough he had been on Fidel. To his unembarrassable manuscript, he recalled with what hard-nosed professionalism he had set aside their years of intimacy – those nights, he seemed to imply, when no bottle of Havana Club was safe from the pair of them; those not-to-be-repeated heart-to-hearts when manly tears were close. This muscle-flexing turned out to be the warm-up for a sucker-punch, however, and this set the tone for what was to follow. Tomas Borge, the former Sandinista Minister of the Interior in Nicaragua, who was granted an interview in 1992, limbered up with the words, 'This time, I was approaching him as a journalist, with the role of stirring him up.' Borge was as good as his word. His opening question would have stirred up a lesser man than *El Comandante* to the point of calling for the sick-bag of state: 'You know something about this impressive flood of light that surrounds you, Fidel, and you accept it, aware that it belongs to history more than to any human being in this period of history. What do you feel, now that your immortality is assured?'

The note of sycophancy, of the interviewer blowing Fidel's trumpet, was a recurring one. Even the Italian journalist, Gianni Mali, one of the more robust of Fidel's approved interrogators, remarked a propos of Castro's record on human rights, 'The problem … must touch the Cuban leader deeply; he is affected by ideological rigor, reasons of state and concerns as a humanist and intellectual.' Well, up to a point, as Amnesty International, *Index on Censorship* and others might rejoin. As for the good father, he wrote, 'I was swept by a wave of fraternal admiration for Fidel and offered up a silent prayer of thanks to the Almighty Father.'

The authorised interviews went on for hours, often over successive nights, and there was always an opportunity for Fidel to say, or to have it said on his behalf, that he had a punishing schedule. Perhaps this was intended to explain the longeurs over slotting the interviews. Reading the transcripts, it was possible to build up a picture of *El Jefe*'s day. He rose early, to all the newspapers and a ticker-tape parade of wire service copy. To Borge, Fidel disclosed the existence of a character named Chomy, the keeper of the revolutionary in-tray. At the time of the interview, Chomy was absent for some unexplained reason, and Fidel was breaking in a new man. 'Well, now it isn't

Chomy; it's another comrade. Now I have to give him a few lessons – let's put it that way – about my reading habits and my ideas about the quantities of papers I should be given every day. The new man, simply because he is new, is increasing the number of papers. I've noted an increase recently; every day, there are hundreds of them.' It could almost be Bertie Wooster, complaining that one of Jeeves' stand-ins had been salvering an improving *Times* to his bedside between the covers of the racing press.

Fidel worked through a slate of meetings and public appearances, which were noticeable for the charge conducted through the crowd by his presence. At the same time, there were exchanges between leader and hoi polloi which were almost Greek in their unabashedness. The other striking features of the daily round were Fidel's omnivorous interest and breadth of knowledge. On the question of his learning, he tried to have it both ways with Frei Betto. He admitted that as the son of a wealthy man, he had been to the best schools in the country. But later in the same discussion, he claimed that he was self-taught in many subjects. 'Somehow I managed to understand them. I developed a capacity to unravel the mysteries of physics, geometry, mathematics, botany, and chemistry with textbooks alone. I usually got excellent grades.'

Fidel's self-pedagogy was one of the themes of an introduction which Gabriel García Márquez contributed to Mani's book, *An Encounter with Fidel*. The Colombian novelist said that no-one knew where the Cuban leader found the time to be so well informed, nor what tricks he used. One secret was the reading light in the rear seat of his official car, and his habitual trunkful of reading matter. All the same, Fidel would often pick up a book in 'the pre-dawn hours', it seemed, and offer his closely argued critique of it over the breakfast chafing-dishes. García Márquez's essay cemented Fidel's reputation as an indestructible polymath, breaking off from his roster of nocturnal meetings with eggheads and laureates to freshen up with a few laps of the pool.

On this evidence, there was almost something supernatural about him. You were nearly persuaded to give houseroom to beachcombings from the wider shores of plausibility. Take the theory of Castro's double. Castro described himself as an 'Olympic champion' at surviving assassination attempts. The better-documented bids on his life began in about March 1961, with a plot to poison his food. It was one of the less outlandish explanations of President Kennedy's death that Castro had had a hand in it, in revenge for American attacks against him (which reminds you of what the more outlandish explanations were like). As Gore Vidal has observed, conspiracy fanciers and spook-confidants have nourished the idea of the two Oswalds: the hypothesis that Kennedy's killer, the pro-Cuban Lee Harvey Oswald, had had a double. This alter ego was a crackshot, the theory went. He had done the deed. But it was the other Oswald, the one known to history – the Castro-loving but, it emerged, butter-fingered one – who got the blame.

Perhaps it was worth considering that there had been more than one Fidel too. What if a Mickey Finn had done for him after all, and a lookalike, or even a succession of stand-ins, had been taking his place all those years? For all that we saw of Castro at close quarters, the Cubans could have achieved such a *coup de théâtre* with a line-up, an ID parade, of stockily built men capable of carrying off the necessary accessories: the facial hair, the smokes. Until he quit the weed, Castro's signature cigar and beard were the most internationally recognisable combination of tobacco and barbering since Groucho Marx. (The American secret service acknowledged this; that we do know. Some of their attempts on Castro's life underlined how import-ant his props were to his image. Agents hatched a scheme to make his whiskers fall out, and even targeted him with an exploding stogie. Perhaps they were hoping to expose a clean-shaven imposter, blinking disbelievingly as the smoke cleared at the blackened banana-skin of a butt between his fingers.)

If anyone was in a position to know the truth, it was Gabriel García Márquez. He was more than Fidel's authorised interviewer. He was court scribe, with the run of any number of grace-and-favour beach houses, or so his less-favoured Cuban contemporaries liked to say. His photograph hung in the bar at the Nacional Hotel. The writer Antón Arrufat told me that García Márquez's writ ran as far as offering notes on the text printed on Cuban spaghetti packets. In time, however, the relationship between author and President cooled. Some critics even claimed to see Castro's likeness in the doddering, out-of-touch Simon Bolivar of García Márquez's *The General in his Labyrinth*. The liberator of Latin America was one of Fidel's acknowledged heroes. For the unauthorised interviewer, though, what was instructive about García Márquez's insight were his comments about those who would insinuate themselves into *El Comandante*'s presence. 'Everyone who goes to Cuba hopes to have the chance to see him in whatever circumstance, although there are many who dream of a private interview, especially the foreign journalists, who never consider their work finished until they can carry away the trophy of an interview with him,' wrote the author, not without *de haut en bas*. 'There is always a journalist waiting in an Havana hotel, after having appealed to all kinds of sponsors to see him. Some wait for months.'

This carried the whiff of truth. I had tried for an interview through the Cuban embassy in London. I had tried at the Press Centre in Havana. Nothing ever came of my visits to its premises on La Rampa, but this dismal record was on no account to be spoken of. My minders appeared from their backroom to break the bad news that there was no reply to my request. We pretended that I had not heard it all the day before, and that I wouldn't be hearing it again tomorrow. Would it be less painful, I used to wonder, if one of them would only wink at me when reporting that Fidel's office had failed to respond? In Tomas Borges' interview with Castro, the President had compared Borges favourably to 'an enemy journalist'. Was I an enemy journalist? Broadly, my feeling was that the Revolution had been a good thing, but Cubans were in need of change. One of my Press Centre helpers once let slip the perhaps unsurprising intelligence that there was a file on me.

'A file?' I said, delighted.

'It's all good,' said the woman.

I took my interview bid to the top, to Alfredo, the head of the Press Centre: at least he was licensed to speak his mind. Unfortunately, my interview with Fidel wasn't on it. In the presence of two of his female colleagues, Alfredo said, 'You like Cuban women?'

Picking up the unmistakable locker-room tone in the question, I said, 'Sure. They're one of Cuba's greatest attractions.'

'Which part of the Cuban woman do you like best?'

'I suppose I should say the brain,' I offered. 'You?'

'The ass,' he said, and sucked his teeth.

'Right. But about this interview, Alfredo …'

Alfredo had passed my request on personally, he said. He said there was a 'ghost situation': officials simply melted away, like phantoms, when you tried to contact them.

I went to see a journalist who was resident in Havana. He had been filing stories from the city for years. Like Señor de Armas of the London embassy, he thought that there was a possibility of seeing Fidel – he would put the odds no higher – if I could get hold of an invitation to one of the diplomatic cocktail parties which *El Comandante* occasionally attended. A likely one was coming up. The French were holding a reception for 14 July, Bastille Day. It was a hot ticket; it was acknowledged that the French did these things well. Through the railings of the French embassy, a gendarme accepted my accreditation and told me to wait. He opened a gate, and began doughtily to listen to the complaints of a string of people who, I now realised, had been waiting beneath various trees for this very opportunity. I felt pity for le flic. A man in a mauve shirt and thinning grey hair slipped out of the gates – an obvious diplomat. I said, 'Excuse me, sir, do you speak English?'

'No, I don't,' he said. I told him that I was a journalist. But what did I want? After I had told him, he said, 'It's not possible. We cannot accept every journalist. Only those who are living here. Are you?'

'Yes,' I heard myself say. 'I have an apartment.'

'Call me tomorrow. I am the First Counsellor.' He climbed into the rear of a diplomatic car.

When I finally got through to the legate the next afternoon – Hilda having listened to the tone of the phone when I tried in the morning and scornfully said '*Ocupado*' – the First Counsellor regretted that he had bad news. 'I've been speaking to the Ambassador. He has decided to keep the original guest list.' He said that the domiciled hacks were being asked in their capacity as 'friends of the embassy'.

I said, 'That's very disappointing. I was hoping to meet everybody, as I'm new in town.'

'I'm disappointed for you,' said the First Counsellor blandly. 'Maybe next year.'

Next year? 'Tell me, Counsellor, has the *Comandante*'s office indicated whether he will be attending?'

'Who knows in Cuba? We won't know until he arrives. They take great trouble over security.'

I wondered whether the regime's concern really was with the security of the *maximum jefe* – and if so, where they thought the threat might lie at a diplomatic cocktail party – or whether Castro's careful rationing of himself hadn't been one of his greatest strengths. I said, 'Is the reception at night or during the day?'

It was at night. I told Julietta that I might go and stand outside the embassy and wait for him. She said, 'Do you really think they will let you stand in the street?' I knew when she thought one of my ideas was stupid because she asked me a question about it prefixed with 'Do you really think …?' It occurred to me that Castro probably wouldn't get out of his limo until well within the French compound.

Notwithstanding the *Santería* amulet provided by Kiki, all ways seemed closed to me. Gabriel García Márquez's knowing observations rang in my head: 'There is always a journalist waiting … having appealed to all kinds of sponsors to see him.' The lack of response from Fidel's office reminded me of the eloquent silence of Cubans in polling stations, the people Nestor had told me about, those who took a ballot paper and put nothing on it. After the abortive Moncada raid, the incarcerated Fidel had composed his prison jottings in a solution of lime juice which had the properties of invisible ink. My request for an interview with him might as well have been written in lime juice.

For a time, it looked as though the only Castro interview I was going to get was with Fidel's sister. Juanita Castro owned a chemist's shop in Miami. I had asked a contact at the *Miami Herald* if Fidel had any surviving relatives among the overseas community, and my source told me about Juanita. She was a somewhat reclusive woman in her sixties, who didn't care to be reminded of her past in Cuba. I called her.

Reluctantly, she agreed to see me. 'You are from England?' she asked, or double-checked, over the telephone. Perhaps this was in my favour.

I rode the bus for block after block out of downtown Miami before reaching the anonymous strip where ivory soap was advertised for 99 cents in the window of Juanita Castro's chemist's shop. I asked for Señora Castro behind the drug counter. A well-turned-out woman in a grey suit appeared from a back office and showed me into it. She was wearing brown shoes and she smelled of toilet water. I'm not sure I would have guessed a family connection if I hadn't known who Señora Castro was. She said, 'We are sisters and brothers and have some things in common: the eyes perhaps. Some people say I look more like Raul than Fidel.'

She had left Cuba in 1965, after her mother's funeral. 'Our father had died in October 1956, the year in which Fidel went to the Sierra Maestra.' Juanita Castro said she had had no contact with her brother since she left. She had written a letter to him, which had been published, on the occasion of a visit he made to Spain. He had not replied.

'Why did you leave Cuba?'

'Because I was against the regime. It was to the contrary of what had been promised to the Cuban people. I thought that with the arrival of the Revolution, everything would change for the best: social justice, education, the same opportunities for everybody; all these ideas. I was very proud and I worked side by side with Fidel, worked very hard for our objective, which was supposed to be real democracy. "The Switzerland of America" – this is the expression that he used in 1959: freedom for everybody, no more exile.'

We were sitting by the cassette deck which programmed the muzak for the shop. Juanita was the fifth of seven children, she said, Fidel was the third. 'The one I was close to when we were growing up was Raul.'

I mentioned the rumour I had heard since I first visited Cuba, that Raul was gay.

'No, this is not true', she insisted. 'The private lives of Communist leaders are always a mystery. A woman called Celia Sanchez was close to Fidel but they weren't married. He's married now to a lady from Santa Clara.'

I wondered how Juanita Castro had been received when she arrived in Miami. She said, 'At the very beginning, I had problems, particularly from the *Batistanos*. They didn't want to see me in the United States. But most people have been really nice with me, they respect me.' Fidel's sister lived quietly, she said. Her business had been successful and she had bought a home in Kendall, a prosperous neighbourhood in the south-west of Miami. Sometimes she went to Mexico, to see another Castro sibling, another sister.

'Do you hope to go back to Cuba?'

'I can't tell you right now. I don't want to say yes, I don't want to say no. It will be very sad for me if I do. You know, I'm not the only Cuban in a situation like this, a divided family. The only difference is because of the relationship between me and the Cuban government. This situation is one of the tremendous tragedies we are living with today.'

Juanita Castro, who had been part of the revolutionary struggle in Cuba, had also figured in the counter-revolutionary backlash, orchestrated from Miami. She felt 'deep respect' for the Cuban-American Foundation. 'I don't belong to any group in particular but I have travelled a lot; I've been involved very strongly in order to see my country free.'

'What about *el diálogo*? Is it worthwhile talking to Fidel?'

'Fidel does what he wants. He was like that as a boy: he liked to impose his decisions. He hasn't changed at all. It's very difficult to make any negotiation with that kind of personality. It's a shame. Perhaps he wants to remain leader until he dies. He wants to have power in his hands. He's making economic changes in order to survive but political changes are not possible with him. There's no evolution, like in other Communist countries. What happened in Eastern Europe will never happen in Cuba. I feel sad about that.'

'Do you foresee a violent end for Fidel and Raul?'

'I'm worried that that could be the end: tragedy, violence. Not only for them but for many innocent people. You know, I still love them both like a sister. I would like them to leave power and for Cuba to go through a pacific transition.'

Juanita Castro said that she didn't sleep very much. 'I don't dream too much. I worry about my brothers. I worry about my country. The two feelings go together.'

'Do you think you'll ever see your brothers again?'

'Who knows?' She folded her hands in her lap. Did Juanita Castro believe that history would absolve Fidel? I was thinking of the speech he made at his trial after the raid on the Moncada Barracks in 1953.

'I would like to think that history would absolve him at the end of his life, but if he continues to go on the way that he's going, I don't know how.' The cassette deck was playing 'Guantanamera'. 'I'm not a happy person. It's impossible to be happy looking at everything. I have happy moments but it's difficult to be a happy person.'

'After so many years in Miami, do you still feel Cuban?'

'I'm a Cuban-American, an American citizen. I'm half and half,' said Fidel's sister. 'I love Miami. I think this country has been very generous to the Cuban people.'

'Would you like to be buried in Cuba?'

'What's the difference? I'll be dead anyway. There's no difference. The only difference is that here we have sand. In Cuba, we have soil.'

In Havana, I continued to hope for an audience with Juanita's brother. I tried bribery. I had a new contact at the Press Centre, and once when we were talking about our respective plans for the day, she said she would be celebrating her mother's birthday. Except that celebrating was hardly the word. 'We cannot afford to go out,' the woman told me, 'I cannot afford to buy her a gift.'

I said, 'I hope you won't be offended if I make a small contribution towards a gift for your mother.' This could go either way, I thought: my money will be accepted – it might even grease a few wheels – or else I'll be publicly upbraided, at the very least, and might even have my hard-won visa revoked. The Press Centre woman smiled at me and thanked me for my $10. I wasn't to be upbraided. On the other hand, long after I had parted company with the $10 bill, there was no sign of the interview either.

At Christmas, I wrote Castro a card. I said I hoped that he hadn't forgotten our interview: *El Comandante, Felice Navidad! Yo espero que usted no olivides nuestra entrevista. Soy periodista inglés y yo escribo un libro sobre Cuba. Recuerdos, Stephen Smith.* (Commandant, Happy Christmas! I hope you have not forgotten our interview. I am a journalist and I am writing a book about Cuba. Regards, Stephen Smith.) I got Hilda to okay my Christmas message and then I took it round to the Press Centre, which like every other official building, was open on 25 December. You could say that a Christmas card for Castro was a stunt, one not calculated to incline the world's last surviving Marxist to my project. I thought that it was worth trying. And I supposed I liked the idea of him opening my envelope (with a service blade, do you suppose? Of course: his mail would be opened by someone else, perhaps the faithful Chomy) and of my card, a carefully selected London scene, taking its place on an otherwise threadbare mantelpiece, joining a few perfunctory greetings from ambassadors, heads of joint ventures, would-be investors.

In the end it was Roberto, the CDR boss, the man who knew everyone, who pointed me in the right direction. At Julietta's apartment one evening, I was explaining the difficulties I was having over the interview. Roberto said, 'This man may be able to help you,' and he wrote the name 'Jesus Montane' and a telephone number on a scrap of paper. The name was familiar. Frei Betto recounted that one of the meetings he had with Fidel prior to their interview was attended by a Jesus Montane Oropesa, 'a member of the Central Committee and one of Fidel's oldest comrades in the July 26th Movement's struggle against the Batista dictatorship'. Roberto's contacts went to the very top, it seemed. Roberto added, 'If this man cannot help you, maybe you could see Fidel in the municipal elections. He always votes at the same electoral college, in Vedado.'

I dialled Montane's number. He wasn't there. He was out of town. I left messages but my calls were never returned. It was a ghost situation. I was down to my last chance: the municipal elections. They would be held on the ninth. I remembered that nine was the number I had backed in guinea-pig roulette – unsuccessfully. There was a crumb of comfort in García Márquez's essay about Fidel: 'It is not unusual for some lucky journalist to ask him a casual question in the course of a public appearance and for the dialogue to end in an interview.'

On the morning of the elections, my alarm went off at five thirty. The polling stations opened at seven o'clock and I wanted to be in position in good time. I thought it might be an idea to shave. I didn't want to prejudice my chances of talking to Fidel with five o'clock shadow.

The cabbie pulled up at the address Roberto had given me, but it seemed a little deserted – not like the polling station we had passed on La Rampa, where elderly people were queueing outside the still-closed booths. At first sight, this was a show of devotion to the Revolution. I remembered that it was among the old of Romania that the myth of Ceauşescu had died hardest: they had actually been better off under him. Journalists to whom I mentioned the elderly voters were sceptical: there were material incentives to voting early, they thought. How could you begin to predict the future of Cuba when you felt as though you were guessing the present?

When I got out of the cab, it became clear that there was a substantial presence of police and other security forces, if not of the electorate. Soldiers were fastening their boots in the back of a minibus. I was taken up a sidestreet by two men who were wearing *guayabera* shirts and trailing a puppy. This was a sniffer dog called, unless my ears deceived me, Lassie. I was being submitted to what one of the men euphemistically described as a technical check. We stopped at an anonymously ruined Spanish *casa*. The pink doors of the garage blended in with the rest of the house, but on closer inspection they were newer, disproportionately thick, possibly fortified. The doors opened and there was a man holding a torch. He shone it into my rucksack, felt around inside it, and told me to leave it with him.

On the stoop of the *casa* was a motorcycle and sidecar combination. A photographer was enjoying an early-morning cigarette, using the sidecar as an ashtray. The foreign press had begun to arrive in cars with plates beginning 'PEXT', for *Prensa Extranjera*. A Cuban television truck looked like the kind of thing in which a third-rate rock band might tour the students' union circuit. I met a German photographer who had been in Havana for two years. I said that I supposed the thing was to be a member of the resident press. 'Is it?' said the German languidly. He told me that he waited to get invited to events, with a phone call from the authorities. The photographers were given permission to go to Fidel's electoral college and take some pictures of last-minute preparations. I retrieved my camera from my rucksack and took a group shot of the press – something for which I was rebuked by the chief press handler, a man in a grey *guayabera* and slacks. He made me return my camera to the garage. It was important not to interrupt the technical check, he said.

The view among the reporters was that we took our cue, in terms of whether or not we dare ask Fidel a question, from the doyen of the Havana press pack, a plump Cuban greeted by colleagues as 'Poppy' or 'Pappy'. He looked like J.B. Priestley. The plan was that if *he* asked the *maximum jefe* anything, it would be all right for the rest of us to do the same.

'What happens in ver?' It was Tom, the television producer I'd met in the Press Centre, asking about the man with the torch in the garage. Tom brought me up to date with his news. He was enjoying himself hugely in Cuba. But he was worried that he might not be allowed to take his Cuban cameraman to film Castro voting, as the cameraman didn't have press accreditation. Tom and Pascal Fletcher, a resident correspondent, stood chatting, arms folded. Pascal described the 'rush of paranoia' that attended media events in Havana. He said he now took more of a back seat, acting – he searched for the word – independently. But you could tell by the way he said it that he wasn't free of the paranoia entirely. Perhaps it was a necessary part of being a journalist in a place like Cuba.

A soldier of the *Ministerio del Interior* passed me on the *casa*'s garden steps. An old boy in a purple shirt came to look at the drains. He raised a manhole cover, looked in doubtfully, and left. An abandoned cigarette butt started a small fire in a flower-bed. Pascal said that he was going to leave unless something happened by ten o'clock. He had a half-written piece on the stocks and was thinking about deadlines in Europe.

Just before nine o'clock, we were allowed to collect our equipment from the garage, file down the street behind the security men, and reassemble in the small, dusty playground of a school. There was a bust of the ubiquitous José Martí. Some of us – myself included – got excited, thinking that this was where Fidel would be putting his cross. But it was only a getting-to-know-you session with the two candidates, one of whom Fidel and his fellow electors in this part of Havana would be elevating to municipal office. Tom made a joke about a 'bitterly fought campaign'. Of the two contenders, one was an old stiff, with the look of a Sicilian mayor. The other was younger, olive-skinned, wearing jeans. We learnt that the first 35 electors through the doors of Fidel's college would receive a certificate, attesting to the proud record of the Cubans in carrying on voting without surrendering their dreams for the 35 years of the Revolution. By eight forty-five am, we were told by a press aide, a total of 541 voters had exercised their franchise in this typical Havana college, which had an electoral roll of 1,662. Pascal said that even some of the Cuban press were planning to pick up the result of the elections the following day, so predictable – or, if you prefer, well organised – were they.

After 40 minutes, we were walked a block or so to Calle 10. The ground floor of an apartment building had been turned into electoral college 266 for the day. A girl in the top apartment was reading a comic on her balcony. I noticed the bristling moustaches of a security man on the roof of the building. There were uniformed guards on the street, and obvious heavies and spoilers in plain clothes. The pavement was decked with flags. The media retreated into the dwindling shade of a lime tree. We sweltered. People coveted my small bottle of mineral water and, after a time, my bush hat. There was no sign of the President. I thought of a line of Gabriel García Márquez. Castro's arrival, he said, 'was as unpredictable as the rain'. A guard embraced a woman passer-by. I thought that it was hard to imagine that happening in Ceaușescu's Romania. There were perhaps 300 onlookers. I suggested to the German photographer that they appeared to be there of their own volition.

'Do they?' he said.

At eleven o'clock, the Cuban press was allowed to enter the electoral college. As they crocodiled up the steps in the harsh sunlight, I found that instead of envying them, I was almost ashamed to watch them. They were almost like collaborators, or prisoners.

There was still no sign of Castro. I talked to the doyen of Cuban reporting, Poppy or Pappy, whose real name was Victorio Copa. He had clocked up 30 years of covering the Revolution, first with the domestic agency, *Prensa Latina*, and now with a German outfit. I asked Copa's advice – would he be asking a question? Did Fidel generally come over to the reporters, and if not, was it done to yell? Copa shrugged.

I said, 'I suppose you have interviewed Fidel many times.'

'I've asked Fidel maybe two or three questions,' he said.

A press aide summoned five members of the foreign media to join the Cubans inside the college. The people he selected were all photographers and cameramen. The chosen included a Mexican television cameraman, another from Reuters, and the German photographer. There were to be no 'writing journalists'. Pascal was in the thick of complaints over this decision, but the press handler was unmoved. Pascal and others staged a walkout. I didn't realise that they were going until they had gone. When I did realise, I admired their principled stand, while secretly gladdened that my coast was slightly clearer.

At eleven thirty, five hours after the early-risers among the press, Fidel arrived. At first you heard a cheer – half-delight, it seemed, half a kind of *cave*! There was a round of applause, no bigger than the one that might greet a minor royal at a garden-party. My plan was to photograph Castro as he entered the polling station and hope to catch him with a question as he left. I had written a letter requesting a formal interview, an authorised interview, and I planned to hand this to him or one of his entourage. He was wearing olive fatigues and a peaked cap. The beard was wintrier, less tropically exuberant, than in his old pictures. He walked erectly, the gait that athletes and stout men have in common. He passed along the line of onlookers: a word here, a pat for that childish head. I was taking pictures. Castro peeled off smoothly but unambiguously before getting anywhere near the depleted ranks of the international press. As he took the steps up to the college, grasping a hand, I was put in mind of Father Christmas – it must have been the whiskers. I have a memory of the broad back of him, the webbing belt, a slight bagginess about the tunic jacket. I won't pretend an immunity to his charisma; is it just the shock of famous people at last in the flesh? Fidel disappeared into the apartment building. His presence behind the shutters was given away by a flickering strip-light effect produced by flashbulbs. There was the faint, faraway tone of a PA system. He had begun to talk.

Outside, I was learning my lines. Knowing that I'd be lucky to get a single question in, and with a view to the long term, I thought I'd better try to elicit an answer that might be of interest months ahead, even if Castro had finally departed the scene by then. So, recalling his famous courtroom speech, I had decided to ask: 'Do you still believe that history will absolve you?' A patsy, you might say, but then I couldn't see Fidel stopping to answer a question about human rights abuses. I had checked my translation of the question with Julietta and now I was muttering under my breath: *Crée usted que la historia aún lo absolvá?* The press handler who had quarrelled with Pascal called out more cameramen and photographers to go into the *edificio*. On the kerb, in the ranks of the unselected, I found myself gallingly fighting off children who were trying to push in. The sun was directly overhead. I pulled my sleeves down and my collar up. I decided to stick with the sunhat – it ought to make me unmissable, I thought, assuming that Fidel came within hailing distance. There was a metallic taste in my mouth. I worried that I wouldn't be able to muster enough spit to get my question out: *Crée usted que la historia aún lo absolvá?* I felt, as I always do on these occasions, like an assassin. It's partly the looks the security guards give you; you know that they're thinking, 'Well, he *could* be an assassin.' A few feet in front of me, a man with a crewcut regarded me warily. He was suspicious when I produced an envelope from the breast pocket of my shirt. He wasn't to know that it was my letter to Fidel; it could have been poison or even a bomb, a letter-bomb, for all he knew. And Fidel had had one of the most *attempted* lives in modern times. I thought of the CIA's exploding cigar, its depilating device, and the display in the museum at Trinidad, a lint indicating the path that an assailant's bazooka shell would have taken had something about *El Comandante* not stayed his trigger-finger. It wasn't that I wanted to take his life, any more than I had homicidal fantasies about any of the (one or two) world leaders I had been a grenade's throw from in the past. It was a kind of vertigo, a what-if state of mind.

The photographers and cameramen who'd been allowed inside the college came out – not, according to the Reuters man, because they'd been thrown out, as I assumed; no, they'd simply had enough. Would the rest of us now get a look-in? With most of the foreign press having walked off, I fancied my chances. The press aides came to the door, deliberated with each other, looked at me across the road's width, while I suffered an agony of titillation. I made faces at them, pointed at the doorway behind them. They raised wait-and-see palms.

I found myself reckoning the odds on outflanking the security and reaching the hall – surely it would be too undignified for the Cubans to manhandle me out while the cameras were rolling? But then I remembered that they were Cuban cameras, they could be doctored. In point of fact, it wouldn't be necessary to doctor them. It would be understood that certain things were not to be shown, or even recorded. Besides, though I thought I might steal a march on the three bodyguards nearest me – the one with the crewcut now had a perfectly trimmed moustache of perspiration on his upper lip – I couldn't see me beating the two at the foot of the steps. Then I wondered what would happen if Fidel objected to my question. I seemed to nurse violent thoughts concerning him of which I'd previously had no intimation. I imagined him, brow blackening, making contact with a surprisingly sinewy right, scattering my teeth among the low-hanging branches of the lime tree. There was nothing in the question that warranted such a reaction: perhaps I just liked the idea of the stir that the punch would create. (I must have been serious about this because I whiled away long minutes wondering how to get good dental work in Cuba.) Papers nailed to the noticeboard, naming the candidates, were listless in the close noon. The flags didn't stir. A security man leant against a palm tree, as surly as a waiter. A schoolgirl, in her red tunic even on a weekend, chalked the Cuban flag onto the road. The cellular phone of the Reuters cameraman, on my right, seemed constantly busy. But his calls were the only noise, apart from the muffled speech within the *edificio*. Fidel was still talking. He was so prolix that an occasion which another world leader might have turned into a photo opportunity was for him a portraitist's opportunity, a sitting. He was talking about the unrest at the time of the *balseros* crisis, which he said had been put down without bloodshed – by which he presumably meant without firearms since it was common knowledge that heads had been cracked and bones broken.

I swotted my question. What if I fluffed it? Dare I consult the page in my dampening notebook where I had it written down, or would referring to this prompt cost me Fidel's attention? When I *did* look at my notebook, I found that I was blinded when I looked up again. In the polling booth, some of the dignitaries at the back were fidgeting. A woman in high heels rocked on a step. Two men muttered to each other. The sky was swimming-pool blue. I whispered my lines. I worried about ruining a sequence for the Reuters cameraman, who was going to be at my shoulder when I bellowed my question – I supposed I *would* have to bellow it. I was afraid I would be drowned out by the crowd; that Castro had already taken a decision to ignore the foreign press.

At last I could see his back. As Fidel turned and stepped into the sunlight, I had the sense of someone behind me, to my right, orchestrating the applause. The schoolchildren struck up with 'Fidel! Fidel!' as though they had learnt the chant by rote. Castro paused on the top step. There was a comradely hand on the shoulder of a middle-aged woman in an orange blouse. He came down the steps, went to his right, my left. I watched him like a target. There were two or three olive-uniformed men by him, and others in *guayabera* shirts. His expression suggested that he bore a welcome, familial responsibility for the crowd. I rehearsed again: *Crée usted que la historia aún lo absolvá.* I stepped off the kerb, to get a better angle, but security men pushed me back. I had the impression of people restraining me, though it may only have been onlookers craning for a view. There was a point I had fixed on Fidel's progress around the crowd that was my sweet spot: it was as he reached this point that I would have to shout my question if I was to stand any chance of getting it in before he passed out of earshot. When he reached his mark, I opened my mouth but the question didn't come out. Instead I said, '*Comandante!*' It was satisfyingly loud but there was no reaction from Castro, not even the fixed look that politicians favour when they're ignoring something.

He was still in my sights, but still moving. And still the question wouldn't come. '*Soy periodista inglés,*' I said. At last, Castro's eyes made contact with mine and I said, '*Crée usted que la historia aún lo absolvá?*' (Do you still believe that history will absolve you?)

He stopped. He came to a complete halt in front of me, a fraction to my right. He stared at my sunhat, as he was bound to do. He said, '*Ahora más que antes, porqué en ese momento no habíamos efectuado aún cinco por ciento de lo que hemos acontecido ahora.*' (Now more than before, because at that moment we hadn't done even five per cent of what we've done now.)

He looked at my hat again. He said, '*A quién representa usted?*' (Who do you represent?)

I said, 'ITN. *Pero escribo un libro sobre Cuba.*' (I'm writing a book about Cuba.)

He put his hand on my shoulder. '*Muy bien,*' he said. He cocked an arm, making a fist. He winked. His aides surrounded him like pilot fish. He might be *El Jefe* but they were gently steering him away. I had to give him my letter. I handed it to him. That is, I moved the hand which had the letter in it: a thicket of highly trained arms pinioned mine to my side. I said, 'It's okay! It's a letter, it's a letter!' It wasn't as if it was explosive! I didn't know the Spanish for explosive – it's *explosivo* – so I cried, 'It's not explosive!' – with hindsight, an incautious thing to cry without having first established how well Fidel Castro's bodyguards understood English. Fortunately one of them said, '*Carta, carta*', and I watched Castro take the letter and slip it into the pocket of his tunic. Now he offered me his hand. We shook. He went. No-one else had asked him anything. I followed him as he rounded a corner into a sealed-off section of street where a black Mercedes was waiting.

My letter to Fidel introduced me and minuted my interview requests. It acknowledged the fullness of his schedule and requested – as an absolute last resort – that he answer half a dozen questions in writing. How important is tourism to Cuba? I began hard-hittingly. Wasn't there a contradiction between the principles of the Revolution and opening Cuba to foreign companies? What memories did he have of Graham Greene, who had kept a painting that Fidel had given him until his death? What sacrifices had Fidel made for the Revolution? Many observers had criticised human rights in Cuba – what was his response? I had heard many Cubans describe their country as the land of miracles – what did Fidel say?

After he had been driven out of sight, one of his team – a stay-behind man rather than an advance man – told me, 'Fidel has the letter. You will be contacted through the Press Centre.' Pascal rang me that night. He had heard that a man in a green hat had spoken to *the* man in the green hat. It was a coup. 'So you're the man who spoke to the great leader. It doesn't happen very often, I can tell you,' he said. Pascal wanted to know what Castro had told me. I said, 'I don't think it will make for you.' It was a coup but it wasn't a scoop.

As Fidel's back-up man had predicted, the Press Centre contacted me. It was Almeida, wanting my CV. A bit of a nerve, I thought: I had spoken to Fidel himself – no thanks to the Press Centre – and here they were, belatedly wishing to satisfy themselves about my qualifications. Or perhaps my résumé had been requested by an officious clerk at a ministry where I had an appointment. So I asked Almeida, 'Who wants my CV?' and he said, 'You can guess.'

The document I submitted was an entirely authentic record of my career, but nostril-pricklingly airbrushed. I included not only my verifiable interviews with 'world leaders' (Iliescu, the President of Romania, and the Prime Minister of Ireland) but also my near misses and close calls, retouched and enhanced: the time I cried out inaudibly to Jacques Chirac from the bottom of an Elysées media scrum was, I implied, a tête-à-tête of almost mortifying candour.

Despite this, no military driver called up to Hilda's balcony for me. Her telephone went on failing to ring late at night. I thought of what García Márquez wrote about Fidel: 'It is not unusual for some lucky journalist to ask him a casual question in the course of a public appearance and for the dialogue to end in an interview.' At most I had a soundbite, and that from a trencherman among public speakers.

But anything more would have been an *authorised* interview. Elizardo Sanchez, the Cuban human rights campaigner, had told me that Castro was incapable of listening. I remembered a story I'd heard from a newspaper editor in Miami: in a quiet moment at an international summit, a senior European politician had personally appealed to Fidel for change. The Cuban leader had heard him out and then told him how much he admired the politician's tie-pin. After the journalist Isabel Hilton tracked down General Stroessner of Paraguay, she had been asked by a friend – 'a man who knows as much about Latin American dictators as anybody' – whether Stroessner had said much. 'No,' she said. 'They never do,' said her friend.

Fidel Castro spoke at prodigious length to his official interviewers, but he didn't say much: the authorised interviews were all the same. An unauthorised interview – or, if you want to be really picky, a *non*-interview – said everything that Fidel spent nights dictating to an approved scribe, a friendly journalist – 'I regret nothing.' And I had space left over to record Cuba's eloquent silence on the subject.

Postscript

SHUFFLE THE DECK of the morning post as I might, I never turned up an airmail envelope from Fidel. There was not so much as a postcard from his bunker in Havana. It saddened me to think that our correspondence was closed. Surely he hadn't mislaid my Christmas greeting and the note I had handed him? Perhaps they were preserved with the other paperwork on my file, or pressed like leaves in an in-tray. I wondered whether the trusty Chomy had ever cleared his throat at his master's elbow and raised the question of giving me an interview. It would be flattering to think that Fidel, running an eye down my questions, had decided to spare himself the ordeal of a grilling by me, not fancying his chances with an 'enemy journalist'. But it may be that my handwritten CV wasn't sufficiently gilt-edged for him. At least I could console myself with the thought that Fidel *had* read everything I had sent him, assuming Gabriel García Márquez was right on the question of his old friend's habits. He should be reading this too, come to that, other things being equal.

I hadn't wanted to leave Havana. I cancelled my flight home and I rang work and told them I was going to be late. I wanted to sit on at 25 y O with a tarry thimble of coffee and a Popular. I liked the idea of becoming an English maroon. Sometimes tourists who had taken a wrong turn out of the Hotel Vedado or St John's walked past the *edificio*. I used to hope that they would catch sight of me on Hilda's balcony, the *Santería* amulet glimmering in the saucer by my side, and take back word of the figure they had decried in Havana's heart of darkness – *Oh the languor, the languor!* My press accreditation had run out. In a sense, as I would hope to have shown by now, this made no difference to me whatsoever. And to be fair to the Press Centre, they didn't make an issue of it, as they might once have done. There was no threat of expulsion or demand for a renewal fee. Instead, the official to whom I had once given $10 as a birthday present for her mother made a sweet formal speech of farewell, in English and Spanish: 'Thank you for your gesture of support to my mother and your interest in interviewing *El Comandante*,' she said. 'Have a safe trip and a very successful year.' I had been dismissed. I was only half-Cuban, after all.

A dark-skinned tout on La Rampa claimed to have met me at the Habana Libre, where I hadn't stayed for at least 18 months. 'You buy me one beer. You tell me you buy me two more but you disappear,' he said accusingly. I laughed at him and said, 'I'm going now.' 'I don't think I can sell you anything,' he said, laughing himself.

Hilda asked me, 'When are you coming back?' There would always be a room for me, even in the new house, if there was a new house. '*Mi casa es tu casa,*' she said, the familiar expression of ready Cuban hospitality suddenly sounding personal. Julietta said she would come with me to the airport; there would be a tourist bus she could pick up back into the city. We went in Ramon's car. I threatened that I would only pay him if his driving had improved. Julietta held my arm. 'Oh, Stephen,' she said: from the tone of her voice, you would have assumed that I had done something wrong. At some point, I referred to her boyfriend and she shooed away the mention of his name. At the airport bar, she said that she was not very intimate with him. 'We have much more confidence with each other,' she told me.

I made jokes, or at any rate attempted to, about going back to England, moving out of London, and I saw that she was crying. She had both hands over her mouth. A fellow Havanatur guide came over to speak to her about something: the moment passed. Then Julietta and I reminisced about some of the places we'd seen: the Motel Las Rosas, the love hotel – 'Don't let my father find out!'; the motel in Trinidad with adjoining cabins. She said, 'My door was locked,' and it was a moment before I realised that she was mimicking me.

'Well, I wanted you to feel safe,' I said.

'I always did. You were always talking about your girlfriend.'

'And you talked about Erik the Viking.'

'Did I? I suppose I did.' Now Julietta's thoughts were of her new boyfriend, the unsmiling man. He told me that Julietta was what the Cubans called 'good wood'; she had the makings of a fitting woman for him. 'This is man to man,' he advised me, looking for my reaction. He wanted the two of them to live together. Julietta said, 'We'll see,' but I had the impression that she liked the *idea* of moving in with someone, of leaving home, as much as anything else.

Cuba receded tantalisingly beyond the Caribbean horizon again, making only occasional appearances in the foreign pages: the size of the sugar harvest; the row over the Helms–Burton sanctions. I now thought that Cuba's remoteness was as it should be – for the prototype of *Treasure Island*, for an earthly version of paradise. Perhaps I was secretly hoping that I could keep Cuba to myself: Cuba didn't *seem* remote to me. A statue of the Madonna in the garden of an old nunnery in the village where I now lived in the north of England, brought to mind Our Lady of Charity of El Cobre: beside each of the Madonna's feet was a horn like a spur, a device I recalled from likenesses of Cuba's patron saint. When my fellow journalists were staking out the rear door of a soccer training ground, hoping for a glimpse of an expensive South American star who had signed for a British club, I ran into him shivering in a sheepskin coat inside the front door, and we spent the time I should have devoted to getting my scoop in conversation in Spanish about Cuba. Hosepipe bans and water conservation campaigns which lingered into a damp British winter made me smile when I thought of the oil drum in Hilda's bathroom.

Havana's resident correspondents, the lucky few who were welcome at the French embassy on Bastille Day, sometimes filed stories on subjects like the liveliness of Cuban slang. (How rich it was! A *posada*, a love hotel, was 'a place to rest'; two cashiered Ladas, lashed together, a Creole limo). 'To resolve', reported one piece of agency copy, was a catch-all verb, meaning 'to obtain some rare or complicated item or service by any means possible'. Running a taxi or a private restaurant to make a few dollars; dodging the draft of military employment and finding a job in tourism instead; living on gifts of pork and rum by interceding with *Orula* – resolving was what life was all about in Cuba. Cubans were born with a stamp on their backside, they liked to say: this brandmark read 'We don't have' or 'It's finished' or 'Who's the last?' – the typical remark of a *habanero* resignedly joining a queue. 'To resolve' meant squaring the circle of life in 'the most beautiful land that human eyes have ever seen' at the time of the special period. It meant living in the country of corks, the land of miracles. You had wanted to make sense of Cuba – a way of understanding the paradox of the Caribbean Nirvana which accommodated the last bastion of Communism – and *resolving* turned out to be the answer as well as the problem.

El Comandante might have forgotten to write but I did receive letters from Havana, I spoke to friends by telephone. They were busy resolving. Nico was still without a job but somehow had a little money. His mother felt the gypsy itch to move on from 25 y O. Nestor continued to supplement his meagre legal fees by driving a cab. Kiki's business was thriving. Julietta's father loyally sifted soil samples eight hours a day for the good of the Revolution; her married sister was due to give birth to her first child. Julietta herself escorted European visitors – 'Frenchies and Belgies', she called them – to Tropicana and Varadero. She was still seeing the unsmiling man, although she had turned down his proposition that the pair of them move in together.